Galaxy S5

the missing manual®

The book that should have been in the box

Preston Gralla

O'REILLY®

Beijing | Cambridge | Farnham | Köln | Sebastopol | Tokyo

Galaxy S5: The Missing Manual
By Preston Gralla

Published by O'Reilly Media, Inc., 1005 Gravenstein Highway North, Sebastopol, CA 95472.

O'Reilly books may be purchased for educational, business, or sales promotional use. Online editions are also available for most titles (*safari.oreilly.com*). For more information, contact our corporate/institutional sales department: 800.998.9938 or *corporate@oreilly.com*.

July 2014:   First Edition.

Revision History for the First Edition:

    2014-07-08   First release

See *http://www.oreilly.com/catalog/errata.csp?isbn=0636920033806* for release details.

ISBN: 978-1-4919-0453-4
[LSI]

Contents

The Missing Credits . . . . **ix**

Introduction . . . . **xv**

PART I   **The Basics**

CHAPTER 1

The Guided Tour **5**

Power/Lock Button 5

Headset Jack 8

About the Screen 8

Status Bar Icons 10

The Three Keys 12

Multipurpose Jack and Charger 15

Ringer Volume 17

Microphone 17

Battery 17

SIM Card 18

MicroSD Card 19

Camera 20

Water-Resistant Case 20

Samsung and Google Accounts 21

Home Screen 22

Easy Mode and Standard Mode 27

Customizing the Home Screen and Panes 27

The Magic of the S5's Gestures 36

Using Multi Window 38

CHAPTER 2

Typing, Texting, and Searching **41**

Using the Samsung Keyboard 42

The Magic of the Microphone Key 48

Copying and Pasting Text 51

Text Messaging 53

Searching Your Galaxy S5 63

Voice Search 65

CHAPTER 3

Phone Calls **69**

Placing a Phone Call 69
Dialing a Call 71
Managing Contacts 77
Designating Favorites 83
Answering Calls 84
Conference Calling 86
Voicemail 88
Call Waiting 89
Call Forwarding 90
Caller ID 91
Bluetooth Earpieces 91

PART II   **The Built-In Features**

CHAPTER 4

Music **97**

Where to Get Music 98
Using the Music App 98
Playing Your Music 102
Creating Playlists 107
Google Music Cloud Player App 111

CHAPTER 5

Camera, Photos, and Video **115**

Opening the Gallery 115
Tagging Faces in Photos 122
More Photo Options 123
Working with Multiple Photos 126
Videos in the Gallery 127
Taking Still Photos 129
Using the Onscreen Controls 131
Using Different Modes 133
Taking Video 135
Playing S5 Video on Your TV 136
Using Your S5 as a Universal Remote 137

CHAPTER 6

Maps and Navigation **141**
Google Maps. 141
Finding Businesses and Contacts 152
Getting Directions 155
Turn-by-Turn Navigation 157

CHAPTER 7

Calendar **161**
Using the Calendar 161
Calendar and Geolocation 172
Working with Multiple Calendars 172
More Calendar Options 174
Google Calendar on the Web 176

PART III   **The Galaxy S5 Online**

CHAPTER 8

Getting Online: WiFi, 3G/4G, and Mobile Hotspots **183**
How the Galaxy S5 Gets Online 183
Connecting via WiFi 184
Configuring Wi-Fi Direct 196
Wi-Fi Calling. 196
Airplane Mode 198

CHAPTER 9

The Web **201**
The Galaxy S5's Browser 201
Basic Navigation and Managing Windows 204
Navigating a Web Page 204
Web Pages Designed for Mobile Phones 206
The Address Bar 208
Bookmarks 209
The History List 214
Tapping Links 215
Saving Online Images 217
Selecting and Copying Text 221
Online Privacy and Security 222

CHAPTER 10

Email and Gmail 227

Understanding Email on the Galaxy S5 227
Setting Up Gmail 228
Reading Mail in Gmail 229
Replying and Forwarding in Gmail 235
Understanding Gmail's Organization 235
Managing Incoming Mail in Gmail 236
Writing Messages in Gmail 240
Working with Labels and Search 242
Searching Gmail 244
Setting Up Email Accounts 245
Reading Mail 248
Managing Mail 254
Creating and Sending Mail 255
Using Web-Based Mail Programs 257

CHAPTER 11

Facebook, Twitter, Google+, Chat, and Videochat 259

Facebook 259
Twitter 267
Google+ 271
Chat and Videochat with Google Hangouts 274
Chat and Videochat with ChatON 280

CHAPTER 12

Downloading and Using Apps 283

Apps and Multitasking 284
Where to Get Apps 286
Using Google's Play Store 288
Downloading from the Web 294
Updating Apps 297
Troubleshooting Apps 302
Thirteen Great Apps 303

PART IV Advanced Features

CHAPTER 13

Transferring Music, Videos, Pictures, and Other Files, and Using Group Play. **319**
Transferring Files by Using Your PC. 321
Transferring Files by Using Your Mac. 323
Using the Galaxy S5 My Files App. 324
Sharing Files by NFC and Beaming 328
Quick Connect 329
Checking Space on Your Galaxy S5. 330
Using Group Play. 331

CHAPTER 14

Taking the Galaxy S5 to Work. **335**
Virtual Private Networking (VPN) 337
Using Polaris Office 343
Using Google Docs 344

CHAPTER 15

My Magazine, Google Now, and Voice Search and Control. **349**
Using My Magazine 350
Using Google Now. 352
Using the Magic of Voice Search and Voice Control 357

CHAPTER 16

Settings. **365**
Quick Settings. 365
Network Connections 366
Connect and Share 371
Sound and Display. 372
Personalization 378
Motion 381
User and Backup. 382
System 384
Applications 393

PART V   **Appendixes**

APPENDIX A

Setup and Signup **403**
Choosing a Plan 403
Making Account Changes on the Web. 404
Upgrading to the Newest Software 404

APPENDIX B

Accessories. **407**
Useful Accessories. 407
Places to Shop 408

APPENDIX C

Troubleshooting and Maintenance. **411**
Make Sure Your Software Is Up to Date 411
Fixing a Frozen Phone 412
Correcting Email Settings. 412
Troubleshooting the SD Card 413
Resetting the Galaxy S5. 414
Warranty and Repair 415
Where to Go for Help. 415

Index **418**

The Missing Credits

About the Author

Preston Gralla is the author of more than 40 books that have been translated into 20 languages, including *Galaxy S4 The Missing Manual, Windows 8 Hacks, NOOK HD: The Missing Manual, Galaxy Tab: The Missing Manual, The Big Book of Windows Hacks, How the Internet Works,* and *How Wireless Works.* He is a contributing editor to *Computerworld,* a blogger for ITWorld, and was a founding editor and then editorial director of *PC/Computing,* executive editor for CNet/ZDNet, and the founding managing editor of *PC Week.*

He has written about technology for many national newspapers and magazines, including *USA Today,* the *Los Angeles Times, The Dallas Morning News* (for whom he wrote a technology column), *PC World,* and numerous others. As a widely recognized technology expert, he has made many television and radio appearances, including on CBS's *The Early Show,* MSNBC, ABC *World News Now,* and National Public Radio. Under his editorship, *PC/Computing* was a finalist for General Excellence in the National Magazine Awards. He has also won the "Best Feature in a Computing Publication" award from the Computer Press Association.

Gralla is also the recipient of a Fiction Fellowship from the Massachusetts Cultural Council. He lives in Cambridge, Massachusetts, with his wife (his two children have flown the coop). He welcomes feedback about his books by email at *preston@gralla.com.*

About the Creative Team

Nan Barber (editor) has worked with the Missing Manual series since its inception—long enough to remember booting up her computer from a floppy disk. Email: *nanbarber@oreilly.com*.

Kara Ebrahim (production editor) lives, works, and plays in Cambridge, MA. She loves graphic design and all things outdoors. Email: *kebrahim@oreilly.com*.

Yvonne Mills (technical reviewer) is a writer, blogger, and gadget-addicted she-geek, equally comfortable in the corporate world as she is blogging from within a fort made out of her extensive tablet collection. Follow her musings at *www.acerbicblonde.com*.

Julie Van Keuren (proofreader) quit her newspaper job in 2006 to move to Montana and live the freelancing dream. She and her husband (who is living the novel-writing dream) have two hungry teenage sons. Email: *little_media@yahoo.com*.

Ron Strauss (indexer) specializes in the indexing of information technology publications of all kinds. Ron is also an accomplished classical violist and lives in Northern California with his wife and fellow indexer, Annie, and his miniature pinscher, Kanga. Email: *rstrauss@mchsi.com*.

Acknowledgements

Many thanks go to my editor, Nan Barber, who not only patiently shepherded this book through the lengthy writing and publishing process, but also provided valuable feedback and sharpened my prose. Thanks also go to Brian Sawyer for making the introduction that ultimately led to this book.

I'd also like to thank all the other folks at O'Reilly who worked on this book, especially Kara Ebrahim, Yvonne Mills, Julie Van Keuren, and Ron Strauss.

—Preston Gralla

The Missing Manual Series

MISSING MANUALS ARE WITTY, superbly written guides to computer products that don't come with printed manuals (which is just about all of them). Each book features a handcrafted index and cross-references to specific pages (not just chapters). Recent and upcoming titles include:

Access 2010: The Missing Manual by Matthew MacDonald

Access 2013: The Missing Manual by Matthew MacDonald

Adobe Edge Animate: The Missing Manual by Chris Grover

Buying a Home: The Missing Manual by Nancy Conner

Creating a Website: The Missing Manual, Third Edition by Matthew MacDonald

CSS3: The Missing Manual, Third Edition by David Sawyer McFarland

David Pogue's Digital Photography: The Missing Manual by David Pogue

Dreamweaver CS6: The Missing Manual by David Sawyer McFarland

Dreamweaver CC: The Missing Manual by David Sawyer McFarland and Chris Grover

Excel 2010: The Missing Manual by Matthew MacDonald

Excel 2013: The Missing Manual by Matthew MacDonald

Facebook: The Missing Manual, Third Edition by E. A. Vander Veer

FileMaker Pro 12: The Missing Manual by Susan Prosser and Stuart Gripman

FileMaker Pro 13: The Missing Manual by Susan Prosser and Stuart Gripman

Flash CS6: The Missing Manual by Chris Grover

Galaxy Tab: The Missing Manual by Preston Gralla

Galaxy S4: The Missing Manual by Preston Gralla

Google+: The Missing Manual by Kevin Purdy

HTML5: The Missing Manual, Second Edition by Matthew MacDonald

iMovie '11 & iDVD: The Missing Manual by David Pogue and Aaron Miller

iPad: The Missing Manual, Sixth Edition by J.D. Biersdorfer

iPhone: The Missing Manual, Seventh Edition by David Pogue

iPhone App Development: The Missing Manual by Craig Hockenberry

iPhoto '11: The Missing Manual by David Pogue and Lesa Snider

iPod: The Missing Manual, Eleventh Edition by J.D. Biersdorfer and David Pogue

JavaScript & jQuery: The Missing Manual, Third Edition by David Sawyer McFarland

Kindle Fire HD: The Missing Manual by Peter Meyers

Living Green: The Missing Manual by Nancy Conner

Mac OS X Lion: The Missing Manual by David Pogue

Microsoft Project 2010: The Missing Manual by Bonnie Biafore

Microsoft Project 2013: The Missing Manual by Bonnie Biafore

Motorola Xoom: The Missing Manual by Preston Gralla

NOOK HD: The Missing Manual by Preston Gralla

Office 2010: The Missing Manual by Nancy Conner and Matthew MacDonald

Office 2011 for Macintosh: The Missing Manual by Chris Grover

Office 2013: The Missing Manual by Nancy Conner and Matthew MacDonald

OS X Mountain Lion: The Missing Manual by David Pogue

OS X Mavericks: The Missing Manual by David Pogue

Personal Investing: The Missing Manual by Bonnie Biafore

Photoshop CS6: The Missing Manual by Lesa Snider

Photoshop CC: The Missing Manual by Lesa Snider

Photoshop Elements 12: The Missing Manual by Barbara Brundage

PHP & MySQL: The Missing Manual, Second Edition by Brett McLaughlin

QuickBooks 2013: The Missing Manual by Bonnie Biafore

QuickBooks 2014: The Missing Manual by Bonnie Biafore

Switching to the Mac: The Missing Manual, Mountain Lion Edition by David Pogue

Switching to the Mac: The Missing Manual, Mavericks Edition by David Pogue

Windows 7: The Missing Manual by David Pogue

Windows 8: The Missing Manual by David Pogue

WordPress: The Missing Manual, Second Edition by Matthew MacDonald

Your Body: The Missing Manual by Matthew MacDonald

Your Brain: The Missing Manual by Matthew MacDonald

Your Money: The Missing Manual by J.D. Roth

For a full list of all Missing Manuals in print, go to *www.missingmanuals.com/library.html.*

Introduction

WHAT GIVES YOU HIGH-SPEED Internet access, runs the hottest games and apps, lets you take high-resolution photos and HD videos, gives you immediate access to your favorite social networks, handles any email you can throw at it, and keeps you in touch by phone, text, and video chat?

It's the Samsung Galaxy S5—the smartphone with a big 5.1-inch screen that you can control with a wave of your hand.

The Galaxy S5 brings together superb hardware from Samsung with Google's powerful, flexible Android operating system. Many people consider the Galaxy S5 to be the best smartphone on the planet. If you're holding this book in your hands, you're probably among them—or soon will be.

This book will help you get the most out of your Galaxy S5, and there's a lot you can get out of it. Whether you're just looking to get started or want to dig deep into the phone's capabilities, this book has got you covered.

About the Samsung Galaxy S5

WHAT MAKES THE GALAXY S5 so great starts with its hardware. Samsung gave it a 5.1-inch, high-resolution screen; a 16-megapixel camera for high-res photos and video; and a front-facing 2-megapixel camera for video calling and video chat. Its brain is a superfast 2.5 GHz four-core processor. For keeping you connected, the Galaxy S5 has antennas for Bluetooth, WiFi, and GPS.

NOTE This book was written based on the T-Mobile version of the Samsung Galaxy S5. Versions from other carriers may have minor variations in what you see onscreen.

It has access to speedy 3G and 4G networks, which let you talk, text, and surf the Web almost anywhere in the U.S. (anywhere important, anyway).

Google contributed its Android operating system, with seamless access to YouTube, Google Talk, and other Google services. The worldwide developer community has created hundreds of thousands of apps in the Google Play store (with more coming every day).

Put it all together, and you can do just about anything. You can get turn-by-turn directions, check weather and traffic, and identify landmarks. You can work with word processing and spreadsheet files and manage your email and calendar. You can take pictures and share them on Facebook, or shoot videos and upload them to YouTube. You can even turn the Galaxy S5 into a WiFi hotspot for getting up to five computers online.

Oh, and it's also a darn good phone with great sound quality and all the calling features you could ask for.

You could figure out how to make the most of all these features on your own, but by that time there'd be a whole other generation of smartphones to learn. This book will put you on the fast track to all the Galaxy S5's magic.

What's New in the S5

ITS PREDECESSOR THE SAMSUNG Galaxy S4 was a very popular and powerful smartphone. But the Samsung Galaxy S5 is nothing short of remarkable. It introduces countless new features, all of which are useful, and some of which seem more akin to magic than anything else. Here are some of the highlights:

- **Fingerprint scanner.** Want to make sure only you can use your Samsung Galaxy S5? It's now got a fingerprint scanner so you can unlock your phone by having it check your fingerprints.

- **Heart rate sensor.** Put your finger over this sensor and it'll check your heart rate.

- **Faster downloads.** The S5's new Download Booster lets you create a big pipe out of your data and 4G or 3G networks for faster downloads.

- **Water resistant.** Worried about dropping your S5 into a puddle of water or having it rained on? Worry no more. It's now water resistant. No, it won't keep water out if you're way underwater scuba diving, but in normal everyday use it's got you covered.

- **New TouchWiz.** The software that Samsung layers over Android has changed. It's now simpler and less cluttered.

The Samsung Galaxy S5 Family

As this book was being written, there was only one version of the Galaxy S5 available. But by the time you read this, there may be more members of the family. Rumors are that Samsung will release a phone called the Galaxy S5 Prime with a faster processor, more RAM, and a higher-resolution screen than the original. Also said to be in the works is a Samsung Galaxy S5 Google Play Edition, which would have the same or similar hardware as the original S5, but somewhat different software. The Google Play Edition would have a pure version of Google's Android operating system on it—the KitKat version (Android version 4.4, for those of you who are keeping track). The original S5 also has KitKat under the hood, but layered on top of it is Samsung's TouchWiz interface, which contributes many additional features. And there may also be a Mini version with a smaller screen and less powerful processor than the original.

The software on the Galaxy S5 Mini and Prime would likely be the same as the software on the original version. This book will help you learn about all the TouchWiz Galaxy S5 models, but it doesn't cover the pure-KitKat Google Play Edition.

About This Book

THERE'S AN ENTIRE WORLD to explore in the Samsung Galaxy S5, and the little leaflet that comes in the box doesn't begin to give you all the help, advice, and guidance you need. So this book is the manual that should have accompanied the Galaxy S5.

The brain running the Galaxy S5 is a piece of software from Google called Android. Samsung then tweaked Android to operate seamlessly with Samsung's TouchWiz interface. Both Google and Samsung regularly issue updates that improve the way the Galaxy S5 works. So there's a chance that since this book was written, there have been some changes to the Galaxy S5. To help keep yourself up to date about them, head to this book's Errata/Changes page at *http://tinyurl.com/gS5-mm*.

About the Outline

GALAXY S5: THE MISSING Manual is divided into six parts, each of which has several chapters:

- **Part I.** Covers everything you need to know about using the Galaxy S5 as a phone, as well as how to type on it, send text messages, and use all the phone features. So you'll get a guided tour of the S5, learn how to dial calls, manage your contacts, use caller ID and similar features, make conference calls, and more, including fancy phone tricks like Visual Voicemail. You'll even learn how to control your phone without using your hands.

- **Part II.** Gives you the rundown on using the Galaxy S5 for taking pictures, recording videos, viewing pictures, playing videos, and playing and managing your music. You'll also learn all the new Google Maps features, how to navigate using GPS, and how to find any location in the world. There's also the Calendar app, which you can synchronize with your Google or Outlook calendar.

- **Part III.** Tells you everything you need to know about the Galaxy S5's remarkable online talents. You'll find out how to get online either over your service provider's network or a WiFi hotspot, see how you can turn your Galaxy S5 into a portable WiFi hotspot, master email, browse the Web, and download and use countless apps from the Google Play store.

- **Part IV.** Covers a wide variety of advanced subjects, including how to sync and transfer files between the Galaxy S5 and your PC or Mac, how to use the Galaxy S5 at your workplace, and how to control the Galaxy S5 by talking to it. You'll also find a comprehensive listing of the Galaxy S5's settings.

- **Part V.** Has three reference chapters. Appendix A shows you how to activate your Galaxy S5. Appendix B shows what kind of accessories you can get for your Galaxy S5, such as cases, chargers, and screen protectors. Appendix C offers plenty of help troubleshooting issues with the phone's operation.

About→These→Arrows

IN THIS BOOK AND in the entire Missing Manual series, you'll find instructions like this one: Tap Settings→Call Settings→"Voicemail settings." That's a shorthand way of giving longer instructions like this: "Tap the Settings button. From the screen that opens, tap Call Settings. And from the screen that opens after that, tap 'Voicemail settings.'"

It's also used to simplify instructions you'll need to follow on your PC or Mac, like File→Print.

About the Online Resources

AS THE OWNER OF a Missing Manual, you've got more than just a book to read. Online, you'll find example files so you can get some hands-on experience, as well as tips, articles, and maybe even a video or two. You can also communicate with the Missing Manual team and tell us what you love (or hate) about the book. Head over to *www.missingmanuals.com*, or go directly to one of the following sections.

Missing CD

So you don't wear down your fingers typing long web addresses, the Missing CD page offers a list of clickable links to the websites mentioned in this book. Go to *www.missingmanuals.com/cds/gS5tmm* to see them all neatly listed in one place.

Registration

If you register this book at *www.oreilly.com*, you'll be eligible for special offers—like discounts on future editions of *Galaxy S5: The Missing Manual*. Registering takes only a few clicks. To get started, type *http://oreilly.com/register* into your browser to hop directly to the Registration page.

Feedback

Got questions? Need more information? Fancy yourself a book reviewer? On our Feedback page, you can get expert answers to questions that come to you while reading, share your thoughts on this Missing Manual, and find groups for folks who share your interest in the Samsung Galaxy S5. To have your say, go to *www.missingmanuals.com/feedback*.

Errata

In an effort to keep this book as up to date and accurate as possible, each time we print more copies, we'll make any confirmed corrections you've suggested. We also note such changes on the book's website, so you can mark important corrections into your own copy of the book, if you like. Go to *http://tinyurl.com/gS5-mm* to report an error and to view existing corrections.

Safari® Books Online

SAFARI® BOOKS ONLINE IS an on-demand digital library that lets you easily search over 7,500 technology and creative reference books and videos to find the answers you need quickly.

With a subscription, you can read any page and watch any video from our library online. Read books on your cellphone and mobile devices. Access new titles before they're available for print, and get exclusive access to manuscripts in development and post feedback for the authors. Copy and paste code samples, organize your favorites, download chapters, bookmark key sections, create notes, print out pages, and benefit from tons of other time-saving features.

O'Reilly Media has uploaded this book to the Safari Books Online service. To have full digital access to this book and others on similar topics from O'Reilly and other publishers, sign up for free at *http://my.safaribooksonline.com*.

The Basics

CHAPTER 1:

The Guided Tour

CHAPTER 2:

Typing, Texting, and Searching

CHAPTER 3:

Phone Calls

You'll learn to:
- Lock and unlock the screen
- Add apps and widgets and change wallpaper
- Use Easy mode
- Replace the battery
- Control the S5 by touch and with the magic of gestures

The Guided Tour

THE SAMSUNG GALAXY S5—a svelte, elegant phone—is an enticing gadget, and the first time you hold it in your hands, you'll immediately want to put it through its paces: calling friends, browsing the Web, checking your email, and more. As you'll see in the rest of this book, it can do some remarkable things that make you feel as if the phone has superpowers.

To help you unlock all those powers, though, you need a solid understanding of how the Galaxy S5 works and familiarity with all its different parts. You'll want to know where all its buttons, keys, and ports are located, for example—not to mention how to get to your Home screen and panes, and use some of the device's amazing new features, like its ability to let you navigate by merely moving your eyes.

Power/Lock Button

THREE-QUARTERS OF THE WAY up on the right side of the Galaxy S5, you'll find a small, rectangular silver button. It may be only a single button, but it's a hardworking one, and it performs multiple functions. Press it with your S5 turned off, and the phone springs to life. Press and release it when your S5 is turned on and active, and it puts the phone into Standby mode. If your S5 is turned on, press and hold it to show a screen that lets you do the following:

- **Power off.** Turns off the S5's power.

- **Airplane mode.** In Airplane mode, all wireless communications are switched off, but you can still use the phone's apps and other features. Tap this option to enter Airplane mode. If you're already in Airplane mode, tap again to get out. As the name suggests, Airplane mode is what the cabin crew wants you to turn on while in the air.

- **Restart.** Turns off your S5 and restarts it.

- **Mute.** Turns off all sounds.

- **Emergency mode.** Tap this to use an emergency feature designed to have the S5 automatically alert people—by text message—if you need emergency assistance. It also sends your location information. You need to enable Emergency mode before you can use it.

- **Vibrate.** Turns off vibration. If vibration is turned off, you can turn it back on here.

- **Sound.** If your phone is muted, tap here to turn the sound back on.

> **TIP** The Power/Lock button also performs a useful trick that people near you will appreciate—it shuts off your ringer when you receive a call. Press it once when you get a call, and your ringer turns off. You'll be able to see who's calling, without the ring, and decide whether to answer the call or ignore it. If you ignore the call, it gets sent to voicemail.

Locking the Screen

When you put the Galaxy S5 on Standby using the Power/Lock button, the screen stops responding to touch. It blacks out, indicating that the screen is *locked*. Always lock the screen before putting the Galaxy S5 in your pocket or bag to avoid accidental screen taps and potentially embarrassing unintended phone calls. In fact, every time you leave the phone untouched for a certain amount of time—as little as 15 seconds to as much as 10 minutes (page 374)—the screen automatically locks itself.

While the screen is locked, the Galaxy S5 still operates behind the scenes, checking email and Facebook on schedule. You can still get phone calls and text messages, and even listen to music while the screen is locked.

When you again want to use the Galaxy S5, you'll need to unlock it. Press the Power/Lock button or the Home key. Then put your fingertip on the screen and slide it to the right or left. Your Galaxy S5 is now ready to do your bidding. You'll get notifications about missed calls, text messages, and so on. If you've set up a PIN on your phone so that only someone with a password can use it, you'll have to type in the PIN before you can use your phone. (See page 376 for details on how to set up a PIN.)

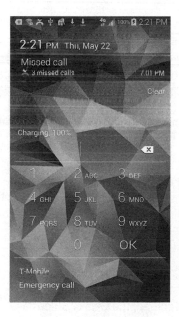

Headset Jack

AT THE TOP OF the Galaxy S5, you'll find a 3.5-millimeter headset jack. Notice that it's a head*set* jack, not just a garden-variety head*phone* jack. It doesn't just let you listen; it accepts incoming sound as well. That's so you can plug a headset (like an earbud headset) into it and use it for making phone calls.

Of course, it's also a headphone jack, so you can plug in headphones or even external speakers and enjoy the phone as a music machine, since it also offers full stereo.

About the Screen

THE SCREEN IS WHERE you and the Galaxy S5 do most of your communicating with each other. Compare the Galaxy S5's screen to that of almost any other phone, and you'll immediately notice how roomy it is—5.1 inches, measured diagonally (technically, that's 1920 × 1080 pixels). It's got extremely high resolution (432 pixels per inch, for the techie crowd). When you turn it sideways, it switches to a widescreen TV and movie format.

But there's a lot going on behind that pretty display.

Built-in Sensors

Underneath its flat black screen, the Galaxy S5 has a whole bunch of sensors that perform a lot of its magic:

- **Proximity sensor.** Have you ever noticed that when you're talking on your S5, the screen often goes blank? That's thanks to the proximity sensor. It senses when your face is close to it during a phone call and automatically turns off and blanks the touch screen as you keep talking. It does this to save power, and so you don't accidentally touch the screen while talking and perform some unwanted task.

- **Ambient light sensor.** Senses the light level and adjusts your screen's brightness as a way to save battery power. So in bright light, it makes the screen brighter and easier to see; in dim light, it makes the screen dimmer, since bright light is not needed.

- **Accelerometer.** As its name implies, this sensor measures acceleration and motion. The Galaxy S5 uses the accelerometer to sense the orientation of the screen and turn it to either landscape or portrait mode. But clever app makers use it for other things as well, such as automatic collision notification, which detects when you're in an accident and then automatically makes a call for assistance for you. There's even an app that works with the phone's magnetometer to detect potholes as you drive and create a log about their locations, which you can then email to your local department of public works. (It's called Pothole Agent. Search for it on Google Play, as described on page 289.)

- **Magnetometer.** Measures the strength and direction of the earth's magnetic field. It's used for compass apps and can also work with the accelerometer.

- **Gyroscope.** This motion detector is used for a host of features. For example, the S5 uses the gyroscope in concert with the accelerometer to interpret motion gestures you make and let you operate the phone by waving your hands.

- **Barometer.** Measures the current atmospheric pressure and altitude. The most obvious use is for weather-related apps. But it's got a lot of other uses as well. For example, when you use an app that measures the number of calories you burn, that app takes the barometric pressure and altitude into account, because you burn a different number of calories based on those readings.

- **Gesture.** This sensor uses infrared light to sense your gestures so that you can control the S5 without touching it. Yes, you read that right. You can control it by waving and other gestures thanks to this sensor. And as you'll see later in this chapter, you can even control scrolling by moving your eyes. (You'll learn all about these tricks later in this chapter on page 36.)

- **Fingerprint.** Yes, the S5 has a fingerprint sensor. Why? So you can unlock your screen using your fingerprints. (To see how, turn to page 376.)

- **Heart Rate.** On the back of the S5 near the top of the screen, just below the camera lens, you'll find a heart rate sensor. To use it, turn to page 305.

- **Hall.** This sensor recognizes when the phone's cover is closed or open.

Status Bar Icons

THE GALAXY S5 MAKES sure to keep you updated with information about its current status and any news, updates, and information it thinks is important. It does so by displaying a variety of icons in the status bar at the top of the screen. The status bar is divided into two parts. On the right side, you'll find icons that inform you about the current state of the Galaxy S5, such as signal strength, 3G or 4G connection status, the time of day, and so on. At left is the Notification area, which alerts you when you have email or voice messages waiting, when an event on your calendar is about to occur, and more.

NOTE Many applications have their own icons that notify you about news, information, and updates. These always appear on the left side of the status bar. You'll see alert icons from Gmail, Facebook, and others.

Here are the most common icons you'll come across:

- **Cell signal.** ▦ The more bars you see, the stronger the signal. The stronger the signal, the clearer the call and the lower the likelihood that you'll lose a connection. If you have no connection at all, then instead of this signal, you'll see the much-hated warning: (No service).

NOTE When you see a notification on the left side of the status bar, drag down the Notification panel to see more details. You can also act upon the notification by tapping its icon after you drag it down—like checking your email or running an app that you've just downloaded. There's also a Clear button that makes all notifications go away.

- **Roaming.** ▦ If you're outside your carrier's service area and connected via another network, you'll see the Roaming icon. Keep in mind that typically you're charged for making calls or using data when you're roaming, so when you see this icon, be careful what you do on your Galaxy S5—maybe it's not the time to download 30 songs and a half-hour TV show.

- **3G/4G.** ▦ This one appears when you're connected via 3G or 4G high-speed broadband service, which should be most of the time. It means that download and upload speeds are fast.

Status Bar

- **Bluetooth connection.** ❸ This icon indicates that you've turned on Bluetooth, for making a connection to a headset or some other device.

- **Mobile hotspot.** 📶 Your Galaxy S5 can serve as a mobile hotspot, providing Internet service to up to five computers, smartphones, or other devices via WiFi. See page 193 for details. When you turn the phone into a mobile hotspot, this icon appears.

- **Airplane mode.** ✈ When you use Airplane mode, you turn off WiFi and cellular communications. You can still keep using your phone's apps, but it doesn't interfere with navigation equipment.

- **Downloading.** ❶ When you're downloading an app or media file, you'll see this icon.

- **New email message.** 📧 You've got mail! See page 248 for more about reading new email.

- **GPS.** 📍 Your GPS radio is turned on.

- **Upcoming event.** 📅 Now you'll never forget your anniversary—or your dentist appointment. The Galaxy S5 alerts you via this icon when you've got an event about to happen.

- **Voicemail message.** 📟 You've got mail—voicemail, that is. (See page 88 to learn how to check your voicemail.)

- **Missed call.** 📞 Someone called you, and you didn't answer. You see this icon appear even if the person left no voicemail.

- **Vibrate.** 📳 This symbol indicates that you've set your Galaxy S5 to vibrate when you get a call.

- **TTY symbol.** 📠 You've turned on Teletypewriter mode, a special mode that lets the Galaxy S5 communicate with a teletypewriter. That's a machine that deaf people use to conduct phone calls by reading and typing text.

- **Alarm.** ⏰ Who needs an alarm clock when you've got your Galaxy S5? This icon indicates that the alarm is on. You can even set multiple alarms.

- **Time.** 11:03 AM Shows you what time it is. Say goodbye to your watch.

- **Battery.** ▣ Get to know this icon—it shows you how much battery life you've got left. When the battery is charging, you see a battery-filling animation and a tiny lightning bolt.

- **Connected to VPN.** ▣ If you use your Galaxy S5 to connect to your company network via virtual private networking (VPN), this icon shows when your connection is active. You can check your work email and do anything else your company lets VPNers do. (If you're interested in getting VPN access, you'll need your IT department's help, as described in Chapter 14.)

- **Disconnected from VPN.** You were on the VPN, and now you're off.

- **USB connection.** ⚇ You'll connect your phone to your computer via a USB cable for a variety of reasons, including copying and syncing files (Chapter 13). Here's the icon you'll see when you make the connection.

- **SD card is full.** ▣ This icon appears when your SD card (page 19) has run out of space. It's time to get a bigger or newer one, or start deleting files.

- **Smart scroll.** ▣ This icon appears when you're using the S5's amazing Smart scroll feature, which lets you scroll through pages by moving your eyes. To turn it on, tap the Settings app on the Apps screen and select Accessibility→"Dexterity and interaction" and turn the Smart scroll setting to on.

The Three Keys

MOST OF THE TIME you use your Galaxy S5, you'll be tapping virtual buttons on the keyboard. But down at the bottom of the Galaxy S5, there are three keys: one fat, white physical one in the middle, and two virtual ones (touch keys) that light up only when you touch them. From left to right, here's what they do.

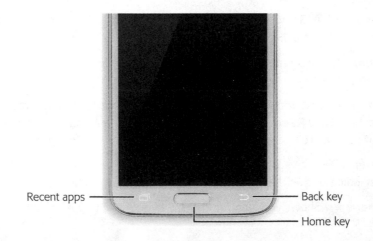

Recent apps ——— ——— Back key

——— Home key

TIP Don't like the elusive behavior of the touch keys? You can make them visible all the time by changing the setting. See page 375.

Recent Apps

Tap this button and you'll see a list of the apps that you've most recently run, including currently running ones. Scroll up and down through them, and then tap the one you want to jump to.

Look toward the bottom of the screen at the two icons—the pie icon on the left, and the icon with an X on it (End All) on the right. Tap the pie icon and you'll see a list of all the currently active apps. Up at the top of the screen, you'll see how much total RAM you have on your S5 and how much you're currently using. That way you can see whether you're running out of memory, and if you are, shut down an app or two. To shut down an app, tap the End button to its right. To kill them all, tap "End all."

TIP What if you want a faster way to kill all of your currently running apps? On the Recent Apps screen, tap the icon with the X on it down toward the bottom. Boom—they're gone!

Home Key

Repeat after me, Dorothy: There's no place like home, there's no place like home... Wherever you are on the Galaxy S5, press the Home key and you'll come back to the familiar Home screen. You won't even need to tap your ruby slippers together. But there's more the Home key can do as well. Hold it down, and you'll launch an app called Google Now, which is a kind of personal assistant that gives you all kinds of advice, such as what route to take home from work to avoid traffic. See page 352 for details.

Back Key

Wherever you are, tap this key, and you go to where you just were. The Back key works in apps as well as in menus. So when you're browsing the Web, for example, it acts as your Back button. Pressing the Back key also makes a displayed keyboard or menu disappear.

Hey, Wait! Where's the Menu Key?

On previous Galaxy S series phones, there used to be a menu key where the Recent Apps button is now. Tapping it opened up a context-sensitive menu that gave you a number of options for whatever app you were using. No more; it's gone to smartphone heaven. However, that doesn't mean there's no way to get to the menus when you're in an app. Almost every app you run has a Menu button. Just tap it to get to a menu of popular commands. It's always on the upper right of the screen, and it looks like three small squares on top of one another. On page 237, you can see it in action in the Email app. Also, a long press on the Recent key will also bring up the menu in some apps.

Multipurpose Jack and Charger

FOR TRANSFERRING FILES AND syncing music and movies between your computer and the Galaxy S5, there's a multipurpose jack at the bottom of the phone. It normally has a small silver cover, so to get to the jack, flick it open. The multipurpose jack is composed of two small ports—a micro-USB port on the right and a smaller one to its left. The S5 comes with a special cable that connects to both ports on one end and plugs into a USB port on the other end.

You can use that special cable with your S5, or just use a normal USB cable with a micro-USB connection.

If you're simply looking to connect your S5 to a PC or Mac to transfer files, you can get by with just a normal USB cable with one end for a micro-USB port. Just plug the cable into your S5 and the other end to a USB port on a PC or Mac, as described on page 319. However, you don't have to buy a USB cable if you don't have one—you can do the same thing with the S5's own special cable.

So what's the point of having a multipurpose port rather than a normal USB one? With the multipurpose port and cable, you can charge your phone more quickly. Plug the multipurpose cable into the port, and then plug the other end into the USB charger that comes with the S5, and your phone gets charged even faster.

If you use power-hungry features like video and GPS, you may have to charge the S5 every night. If you stick to mostly phone calls and text messages, you may be able to get by with charging only two or three times a week.

TIP You can use the Galaxy S5 while it's charging, unless the battery has run down completely. In that case, it'll need to build up a charge before you can turn it on.

This port does one more thing as well. The S5 may be small enough to fit in the palm of your hand, but it's still a big-time entertainment machine. That's because it's HDMI (High-Definition Multimedia Interface) capable. With it, you can view videos and photos taken on your Galaxy S5 right on your computer or TV screen—as long as they also have HDMI ports. Plug one end of the cable into your Galaxy S5, the other into your PC or TV, and you're ready to go. What does that have to do with the USB port? Plenty: You can buy a special attachment to connect your phone to an HDMI device. See page 136 for details.

When you connect your Galaxy S5 to a PC for the first time, your PC may not recognize it. That's because your PC may need special drivers (small pieces of software) to communicate with the Galaxy S5. Windows will try its mightiest to find the drivers, but there's a chance it won't be able to locate them. If it doesn't, you can go over to the Samsung help website (*www.samsung.com/us/support/*) and search for *Samsung Galaxy S5 drivers.* Then download the drivers and follow the instructions for installing them.

Ringer Volume

IS YOUR RINGER TOO loud? Too soft? Get it just right by using this long silver key on the S5's upper left. Press the top part to make the volume louder and the bottom one to make it softer. When you press, a ringer volume app pops up on your screen, showing you how much louder or softer you're making the ring.

Microphone

THAT TINY LITTLE HOLE at the bottom of the Galaxy S5 is the microphone. Yes, it's small, but it does the job very nicely.

Battery

THE GALAXY S5 HAS a battery cover. Yes, that's right, an actual battery cover—you can remove the battery and replace it with a new one, unlike some other cellphones. To remove the battery, flip the S5 over, put your finger underneath the small plastic slot on the upper left, and pull off the battery cover. You'll see the battery, which you can easily remove by putting your finger into the slot at the bottom and gently pulling up. Don't pull it hard or yank it.

Before removing the battery, make sure to turn the Galaxy S5's power off via the Power/Lock key.

To replace the battery, simply put it back into place and then replace the battery cover. Now turn the phone back on.

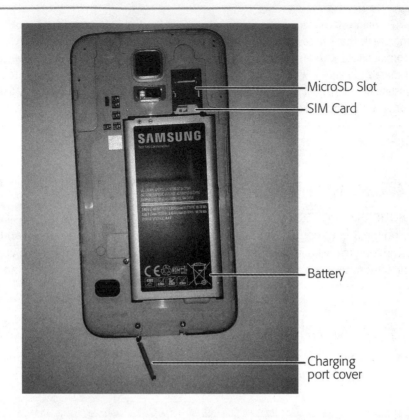

MicroSD Slot
SIM Card
Battery
Charging
port cover

SIM Card

DEPENDING ON YOUR CARRIER, you may need a SIM card to use your phone.
If so, you'll get the SIM card when you buy the phone. The carrier may put it in
for you, or you may need to do it yourself. It's located above the battery, and
you'll have to remove the battery to get to it. When you insert it, make sure the
gold-colored contacts face down.

WARNING Don't put a microSD memory card into the slot for the SIM card—it's easy
to confuse them. If you do that accidentally, don't force it back out. Contact Samsung and
ask how you can get it to a Samsung Service Center.

Maximizing Your Battery Charge

The Galaxy S5, despite its large screen and considerable capabilities, can go a reasonably long time on one battery charge. But if you use a lot of power-sucking features, you may not even be able to get through one whole day without having to recharge. In addition to turning off the screen or putting it into Standby mode when you're not using it, there's a lot you can do to make your battery last:

- **Be smart about email fetching**. The more often the Galaxy S5 checks email, the faster the battery runs down. Either check email manually only when you need to or increase the interval at which the phone checks. Launch the Email app, press the Menu key, and then select Settings and tap the name of your email account. Tap "Sync schedule"→"Set sync schedule." You can choose from intervals between 15 minutes and 12 hours, or manually.

- **Use "Power saving mode**." Power saving mode turns your Galaxy S5 into a power-sipper. To do it, from the Home screen, tap the Settings button, select Settings→"My device" and then turn on "Power saving mode."

- **Turn off antennas you're not using**. If you're not using a Bluetooth headset and don't need WiFi or GPS services at the moment, by all means turn them off. They use up tons of power. Pull down the Notification panel, and you'll find widgets for turning off (and back on) WiFi, GPS, and Bluetooth. Putting the Galaxy S5 into Airplane mode turns off all these settings at once, as well as turning off the radio that connects you to the cellular network. Find the Airplane mode widget by sliding the widgets to the left.

- **Watch out for power-sapping apps**. Some, such as 3D games, can use serious amounts of juice. If, after installing an app, you notice your battery running low quickly, consider deleting it, or running it only when necessary.

MicroSD Card

ATOP THE SIM CARD, you'll find a small slot for the microSD card. It's about the size of a fingernail—and much smaller than the normal SD memory cards used in cameras. Your Galaxy S5 may not have come with an SD card, so you may have to buy one. The S5 can use any SD cards that store up to 128 GB of data. Place the card in the slot with the arrow facing in. You'll hear a click when it's in place. After that, replace the battery cover.

After you install the card and turn on the phone, you'll see a notification that the S5 is preparing the microSD card for your use. When it's done, go to the Home screen, tap the Apps icon at lower right, and then tap Settings→Storage. You'll find a new group of settings under "SD card," listing information like how much total space is on the SD card and how much space remains. (If that information doesn't appear, it means that your SD card hasn't been formatted properly. There's a simple solution: tap "Mount SD card." If your phone doesn't recognize it after that, then tap "Format SD card." That should do the trick.)

> **WARNING** If you've got a microSD card in your phone and you've stored files on it, make sure not to tap "Format SD card." When you do that, you erase all the data stored on it.

If you want to replace the SD card—for example, if you have a 16 GB card and want to replace it with one that has more capacity—it's easy. Return to the Storage settings and tap "Unmount SD card" in the SD card section.

When you've done that, turn off the phone's power and remove the battery cover. You can then slide out the microSD card. Then insert a new microSD card and follow the instructions in this section for telling your Galaxy S5 to recognize it.

Camera

YOUR SAMSUNG GALAXY S5 includes not one but two cameras, both capable of taking videos as well as photos. The camera on the back, which is the one you'll normally use for taking photos and videos, has a whopping 16-megapixel resolution. The camera that faces you is for video calling and video chat, although you'll probably take your share of selfies as well. It's got a 2-megapixel resolution. Don't look for a physical camera button for taking photos; instead, you tap an onscreen button (page 129).

Water-Resistant Case

THE S5'S EXTERIOR LOOKS like just any other smartphone's, although maybe a little snazzier. But its beauty is more than just skin deep. Its case is water-resistant and dust-resistant. That means it's less likely to go on the fritz if you splash it when you're washing your hands, or even if you drop it into a lake, pond, or some more unpleasant watery environment.

Keep in mind, though, that it's not water*proof*. So you can't use it for taking photos when scuba diving, for example. To avoid water damage, keep the following in mind:

- **Don't put it in water more than a meter deep** or submerge it in any water for more than 30 minutes.

- **Make sure that the case is tightly closed** after you open it to access the battery, SIM card, or microSD card. Also, make sure that the multipurpose jack's cover is closed tightly as well.

- **Don't expose the S5** to soapy water, salt water, or ionized water.

- **If you drop the S5, or if it receives an impact of some sort,** make sure the cases and covers are still tightly sealed.

Samsung and Google Accounts

TO ENJOY ALL THE services your Galaxy S5 is capable of delivering, you need to have a Google account, and possibly a Samsung account as well. On your smartphone, an *account* is a central location for managing all the services you can get. The Google one is absolutely necessary, but you may want to set up a Samsung one as well. This section tells you what you need to know about each.

Google Account

In order to use your S5, you need a Google account. That's because the S5's underlying software is made by Google and uses many Google services, such as Maps, Gmail, and more. If you already have a Google account—if you've ever used Gmail, for example—great! You can use that account and all the information and settings you've stored in it. Or you can create a new Google account when you sign into your S5 for the first time and start fresh.

When you first start your phone, it prompts you to walk through logging into your account or setting up a new one. After that, if you want to make changes, you can head to one central location. At the Home screen, tap the Apps icon, and then choose Settings→Accounts→Google.

Samsung Account

If you'd like to use additional Samsung services, you can also set up a Samsung account. Otherwise, you don't need it. Depending on your carrier, you may be prompted to create a Samsung account or to log into an existing one when you first set up your phone, right after you log into or create a Google account. But if not, you can create one afterward. At the Home screen, tap the Apps icon, choose Settings→Accounts→Add Account, and follow the prompts. To change settings, at the Home screen, tap the Apps icon and then choose Settings→Accounts→Samsung Account.

Home Screen

WELCOME TO YOUR NEW home, the Galaxy S5 Home screen. Get to it by pressing the Home key no matter where you are.

NOTE What you see on the Home screen and panes may differ somewhat from what you see here. Cellphone carriers often customize them, put their own apps on them, and sometimes even change them over time.

The screen is chock-full of useful stuff, populated by the following:

- **Status bar.** As detailed on page 10, this bar displays the status of many phone features and a variety of notifications in the notification area, like when you've got email waiting for you.

- **Notification area.** The Notification area takes up the left side of the Status bar, and it's where you'll get most of your messages from your phone and apps.

- **App icons.** The Home screen has a number of icons on it, for checking email (right on the icon, you see how many new messages you've got), for using the camera, and one, called Play Store, to let you search for and download new apps—tens of thousands of them, many of them free. As you'll see later in this section, you can add or delete icons from the Home screen.

- **Dock.** Just below the app icons is a row of five icons. They sit in an area called the *Dock*, and they're different from the app icons. Like the app icons, you can move or delete them—except for the Apps icon. As you'll see in a little bit, there are other screens you can move to, called *panes* or *panels*, but the icons in the Dock stay in place no matter which pane you visit. (The app icons change according to what pane you're on.) The Phone icon launches the Phone app; the Contacts icon shows you your contacts; the Messages icon lets you send and receive text messages (it shows how many messages you've got waiting); the Internet icon launches your web browser; and the Apps icon reveals a whole new screen called the Apps screen, filled with apps, apps, and more apps.

- **Pane indicator.** Just above the Dock you'll see six small icons, the most noticeable of which is an icon of a house—the Home screen. To its left is an icon of two horizontal lines. That launches My Magazine, a nifty Samsung app for reading articles from the Web (page 350). To the right of the Home icon are four rectangles, each of which represents a different panel. The brightest rectangle indicates which pane you're currently viewing. To jump to any pane, tap its button (or slide your finger across the screen).

Above the icons you'll find widgets—a text input box for searching Google, a weather widget that shows you the current weather, and, above that, the date and the time.

Notification and Quick Settings Panel

Drag down the Status bar, and you'll display the Notification and Quick Settings panel. It displays all of your notification messages and also gives you access to changing the S5's most common settings, such as for WiFi, Bluetooth, sound, and so on. The quick settings are at the top of the screen; just tap the icon of the one you want to use. There are more than you see there—swipe to access them. If you prefer, tap the icon all the way on the right, and you'll see a neat grid of many settings. To get access to all of your settings, tap the gear icon at the top of the screen. For details on all of the Galaxy S5's settings, see Chapter 16.

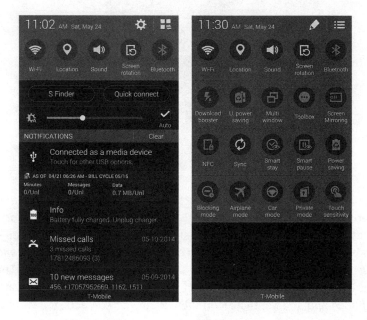

Tap any notification and you'll see more details about it, such as information about missed calls, Facebook notifications, and files you've downloaded.

Apps Screen

Tap the Apps icon, and up pops the Apps screen, which includes all the Galaxy S5's preinstalled applications, plus any apps that you've installed. There's more than can fit on one screen, so swipe your finger to the right to get to another screenful. You can also tap one of the square icons at the bottom of the screen to move from screen to screen. Tap any icon to run the app.

TIP If you get bored swiping through the Apps screens to find the one you want, you can make it easier for yourself. Press the Menu icon and select "View as," and you can rearrange the app icons in alphabetical order, or create a custom arrangement. (Select Custom and press the menu key again to see your options.)

The Panes

What you see on the four panes to the right of the Home screen varies according to your carrier—and what Samsung put there before you bought the phone. You may well see things onscreen that aren't covered in this section.

In general, though, you'll find apps and widgets that perform plenty of common and not-so-common things, like checking your calendar and weather, seeing what your friends are up to on Facebook and other social networking sites, playing music and videos, and more.

To get to another pane, slide your finger to the left or right on the Home screen, and you move from the Home screen to one of the panes. What's on the pane changes—you'll generally see a mix of app icons and widgets. If you don't like what you see on any pane, don't worry; as you'll see on page 27, you can fiddle with it to your heart's content. (The Dock, however, remains the same no matter where you go.) The pane indicator has changed—a different button now shines brighter, to show you which pane you're on.

The Software Behind the Galaxy S5

I hear a lot of names for the Galaxy S5's software—TouchWiz, KitKat, Android. Well, which is it?

The short answer: All of the above.

Here's the long answer:

The Galaxy S5 is powered by an operating system from Google called Android, as are many other phones. The Android operating system is constantly getting updated, and those updates are automatically sent to your phone when they're available. So what you see on your S5 may vary slightly from what you see onscreen here, depending on the version of Android you have on your phone. At this writing, the Galaxy S5 comes with Android version 4.4.2, nicknamed KitKat.

Also, it's common for the manufacturer to tweak the phone's interface, sometimes in significant ways. Samsung adds its own TouchWiz interface, which makes many changes to Android. So when you compare the Galaxy S5 to other Android phones, you'll notice differences.

There's still another reason why your Galaxy S5 may differ from what you see in this book. This book happens to be written based on the Samsung Galaxy S5 sold for T-Mobile phones, so it may differ slightly from what you see on phones from other carriers.

Easy Mode and Standard Mode

WHEN IT COMES TO the basic layout of your Home screen, you've got two choices: Standard mode and Easy mode. In Standard mode, you see the normal Home screen layout described so far in this chapter, with all its widgets and apps. But maybe you don't want to see all those widgets and apps. Maybe you want something simpler, with big, easy-to-see icons and a big font. In that case, you want Easy mode. On the Home screen, tap the Apps icon, and then select Settings→"Easy mode." On the screen that appears, choose "Easy mode" to switch to it. If you want, you can also select which apps you want to appear on your Home screen and panes. Out of the box, you see them all. To switch back to the normal Home screen, tap the Apps icon and select Settings→"Standard mode."

Customizing the Home Screen and Panes

HERE'S ONE OF THE many nice things about the Galaxy S5—it's easy to put your personal mark on it. Wish there were different apps on the Home screen? No problem; you can easily add them. Want to change the location of apps, or move around widgets and add new ones to each of your panes and the Home screen? It's a breeze. The rest of this section shows you how.

Adding Widgets and Wallpaper

The Home screen and all its panes are much like a prepared canvas, waiting for your Picasso-like touches. Instead of paint, you can add widgets and wallpaper.

To do any of the above, the first step is the same: Press and hold your finger anywhere on the Home screen or a pane. Your current pane shrinks and gets outlined, and below it you'll see three options: Wallpapers, Widgets, and "Home screen settings." Here's what to do with each.

NOTE The Home screen and panes have limited real estate—there's only so much you can put on them. In fact, when the phone is factory fresh, the Home screen and panes may already be full. If you try to put something new on them, like an app or a widget, the S5 won't let you do it. Nothing happens when you hold your finger on the screen or pane. In that case, you have two options: delete apps or widgets (page 33) or create a new pane (page 34).

Wallpapers

Here's where the Picasso part comes in. You can add a wallpaper image to the background of your Home screen, just like adding wallpaper to your computer desktop. When you tap this option, you're asked whether you want to set wallpaper for your Home screen, Lock screen, or both.

Make your selection. When you do, you'll see representations of wallpapers you can use at the bottom of the screen. Swipe until you find one you want, tap it, and then tap "Set wallpaper." You've got new wallpaper.

But what if you find Samsung's selections dull and uninspiring? No problem—tap the "More images" icon on the bottom left of the screen, and you can use your own fabulous photos and pictures. After you tap, you choose where you want to grab a picture from—the Gallery on your S5, a cloud-based service such as Dropbox, or any others you've got on your S5. For example, say you want to take a photo from the Gallery, so you tap that choice.

The Gallery launches. Navigate until you get to the photo you want to use (for more detail on using the Gallery, see page 115.

NOTE When you add wallpaper to your Home screen, it also shows up as the background on all your panes. And when you add it to a pane, it shows up on your Home screen.

If you select a picture from the Gallery, you can crop the photo to fit the screen. The S5 suggests a crop for you. You can change it by moving any of the squares that define the crop. Make your selection, tap Done, and you'll see only the cropped area fill your screen.

Widgets

This option lets you add widgets to your Home screen or any pane. A *widget* is an applet that performs a small, specific task, often grabbing and displaying information from the Galaxy S5 or the Web. When you select this option, you see a list of widgets you can use. Swipe to see more widgets if there are more than can fit on one screen.

The same holds true for widgets. Tap the Widgets tab, hold your finger on the widget you want to add, and drag and drop it where you want it to be. If the pane you're adding it to is full of icons and widgets, you won't be able to add more. The Home screen usually fills up first, so consider adding the widget to a different pane.

Home screen settings

Tap this, and you won't get much to choose from. You can select the transition effect your Home screen and panes use, and turn My Magazine (Chapter 15) on or off. If you uncheck the box next to My Magazine, its pane disappears.

Adding Apps and Folders to the Home Screen

You can also add apps to the Home screen. To do it, tap the Apps icon to get to the Apps screen. Then drag the app's icon to the pane where you want it to appear and drop it there.

NOTE When you add an app to your Home screen or a pane, you're not actually moving that app to the screen or pane. Instead, you're adding a *shortcut* to the app, and that's a good thing. When you tap the shortcut, you run the app, just as if you had tapped it in the Apps screen. But there's a difference: If you delete a shortcut on the Home screen or a pane, you don't delete the app itself. It still lives on. But, if you delete the app *from the Apps screen*, it disappears from your S5.

Deleting and Moving

Once you've added widgets, folders, and shortcuts to your Home screen, you're not stuck with them, or with where you've placed them:

- **To move a widget or shortcut to an app,** hold your finger on it for a second or two. The pane or Home screen gets outlined, and a small highlight box appears around the widget, folder, or shortcut. Drag it to its new location and take your finger off. That's where it'll stay. You can even drag it to another pane—just move toward that edge of the screen. Some widgets can be resized as well. If so, small handles will appear on its outline. Move the handles until the widget is the size you want.

- **To delete a widget or app shortcut,** again hold your finger on it for a second or two until the highlight box appears. You'll notice a Delete icon in the shape of a trash can at the top of the screen. Drag the doomed item to the trash can. When you see it turn red, release it—it's gone.

Adding and Deleting Panes

Say you've got a pane tricked out with widgets, shortcuts, and folders. You decide that you'd like it all to go—every widget, every shortcut, every folder. Rather than deleting them one by one, you want to delete them in one fell swoop. Just delete the entire pane. So, for example, if you had the Home screen and six panes, you'd end up with the Home screen and just five panes. Fear not—you can always add a new pane back.

To delete a pane, when you're on the Home screen or a pane, hold your finger on an empty area of it. Then drag the current pane to the trash can icon at the top of the screen. Voilà—it's a pane no more.

To add a pane, hold your finger on an empty area of the Home screen or pane. Then swipe to the right past your final pane. There will be a big empty pane with a + sign on it. Tap the + sign. You've just created a new pane.

Controlling the Galaxy S5 with Your Fingers

WITH THE GALAXY S5, your fingers do the walking. They do all the work that you do on a computer with a mouse or keyboard. Here are the eight finger strokes you can use on the phone's screen.

Tap

Tapping is as basic to the S5 as clicking is to a mouse. This simple gesture is how you press onscreen buttons, place the cursor for text entry, and choose from menus. Note that's a *finger* tap; the screen is designed to detect a fleshy fingertip, not a stylus.

Touch and Hold

Touch an object and hold it for several seconds, and depending on what you're holding, an option menu may appear. For example, when you touch and hold the Home screen, a menu appears that lets you add an object such as a widget, change your wallpaper, and so on. You also touch and hold an object as a way to grab onto it if you want to drag the object somewhere.

Drag

After you've grabbed something, you can drag it with your finger—like dragging an icon to the Trash.

Slide

Slide your finger across the screen to perform some specific tasks, like unlocking your phone after it's been put into Standby mode, or answering a call if the phone is locked. You'll also use the sliding motion to move through all five panes.

Flick

Think of the flick as a faster slide, done vertically when scrolling through a list, like your contacts list. The faster you make the flicking motion, the faster your screen scrolls—sometimes too fast. You can stop the motion, though, by touching the screen again.

NOTE Flicks seem to actually obey the laws of physics, or at least as much as virtual movement can. When you flick a list, it starts off scrolling very quickly, and then gradually slows down, as if it were a wheel set in motion that gradually loses momentum.

To scroll through large lists quickly, you can flick multiple times.

Pinch and Spread

In many apps, such as Google Maps, Mail, Browser, and the Gallery, you can zoom in by spreading your fingers—placing your thumb and forefinger on the screen and spreading them apart. The amount you spread your fingers will determine the amount you zoom in.

To zoom out, put your thumb and forefinger on the screen and pinch them together. The more you pinch, the more you zoom out.

Double-Tap

When you're viewing a map, a picture, or a web page, you can zoom in by double-tapping. In some instances, once you've reached the limit of zooming in, double-tapping again restores the zoom to its original size.

The Magic of the S5's Gestures

LOOK MA, NO HANDS! No longer is that only the cry of a child showing off riding a bicycle without touching the handlebars. You can do the same thing with your S5. Amazingly enough, you can control it by just moving your hands without touching the screen.

To get to many of the S5's magic motion features, tap the Settings icon on the Apps screen, and then tap Motions and gestures. You'll want to try several features you find there.

Air Browse

Turn on Air Browse, and you can scroll through lists and other content such as the body of an email just by moving your hand over the screen in the direction you want to scroll. Once you turn it on, you can customize which apps it works with, such as email, the Gallery, the Web, and Music.

Direct Call

With this magical setting turned on, you can call someone whose message or contact details are currently on the screen, simply by bringing the S5 close to your ear.

Mute/Pause

This one mutes or pauses music or a call when you cover the screen with your hand, or turn the device over. On the same screen, you can turn on "Smart pause," which is a remarkable feature that detects when you're watching video, and will pause it when you look away from the screen.

Air View

This feature, which originated on the Samsung Galaxy Note II, lets you hover your finger over the S5 to get information from it. For example, hovering over a web page magnifies it, hovering over a picture in the Gallery opens it, hovering over a Calendar event reveals more details about it, hovering over a truncated text message reveals the full message, and so on.

To turn on Air View, see the full list of what you can do, and customize it, tap the Settings icon on the Apps screen, and then tap "Air view." Slide the "Air view" button to On or Off.

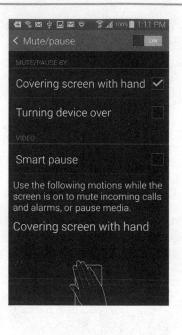

Using Multi Window

MULTI WINDOW IS AN S5 feature you could easily miss—but don't. It lets you do more than one thing on the phone at the same time. For example, watch a video while you're also checking your email. What could be handier?

To turn it on, on the Apps screen, tap Settings and select "Multi window." Then, when you're doing something, like browsing the Gallery or viewing a photo, press and hold the Back key, or else slide the arrow on the left side of the screen to the right. A menu appears down the right-hand side of the screen, with icons for a variety of apps: web browser, email, text messaging, and so on.

Drag the icon of the app you want to use (in addition to the one you're currently using) to a portion of the screen and then drop it there. The second app opens, so you have two apps open on your screen simultaneously.

Drag an icon from the tray to open that application.

Drag an icon from the tray to open that application.

Drag the separator between the two windows to change the relative size of each app onscreen. Hold down the separator and then release your finger, and you'll display a set of Multi Window controls. They let you switch the relative position of the windows, make one of the windows full screen, or close down either of them.

You'll learn to:
- Use the Samsung keyboard
- Have your S5 take dictation
- Copy and paste text
- Send and receive text messages
- Search the Web

CHAPTER 2

Typing, Texting, and Searching

A SMARTPHONE LIKE THE Galaxy S5 wouldn't be very smart without the keyboard. Of course the S5 is great for voice calls, but for text messaging, email, and web surfing, you need an easy way to enter text, and the S5 comes through with flying colors. It gives you two onscreen keyboards—but three ways of entering words into your phone. You can tap to type the usual way, swipe your way through words without lifting your fingertip from the screen, or use the S5's built-in microphone to speak what you want to type.

Whether you prefer to use your fingers or your voice, this chapter is about all the things the S5 lets you do with text. From basic typing, you move on to editing, text messaging, and chatting. Another important thing you need typing for is searching through all your stuff on the phone, so the chapter finishes off with that.

The keyboard automatically pops up when you tap somewhere you can enter text, like an email message, a text message, a web browser's address bar, and so on. You're not limited to tapping individual keys. Instead, you can tap a key and then drag your finger over each letter in the word, in order. This feature captures all the letters in the word using built-in intelligence to figure out what you're entering. It's much faster than tapping individual letters. It takes some getting used to, but you can master it in a few minutes. Once you get used to swiping, you may never go back. If even swiping feels like a bit too much effort, the Galaxy S5 understands. It lets you speak to enter text just as if you were talking on the phone.

Using the Samsung Keyboard

TAP WHEREVER YOU CAN enter text, and the keyboard appears. When you first tap in the text-entry box, a blinking cursor appears, indicating that you can start typing text. When you tap a key, a speech balloon pops up just above your finger, showing you a larger version of the letter you've just tapped.

Surrounding the letters are five special keys:

- **Shift.** Tap this key, and the letters all change to uppercase. After you type a key, though, the keyboard changes back to lowercase. To turn on Shift Lock so you can type multiple capital letters in a row, tap the Shift key twice. The blue arrow turns white, and the gray background turns blue. Press Shift again, and you're back to the lowercase keyboard.

- **Del.** This key deletes letters to the *left* of the insertion point, like the Delete key on a Mac keyboard. If you use a PC, where the Delete key is a *forward* delete key, you may find this behavior confusing at first. Just use the direction of the arrow icon on the key as a guide: Think *backspace*.

Tap the Del key once, and it deletes the letter to the left of the insertion point. Hold it down, and it keeps deleting letters to the left until you let it go.

- **Sym.** This key reveals a keyboard full of symbols, punctuation marks, and numbers. When you tap it, the same key changes to read ABC, to indicate that if you tap it again, you'll return to the letter keyboard.

- **Return.** Tap to move down to the next line, just as on a computer.

- **Microphone.** Don't want your fingers to do all the work? No problem. Tap this key, wait for the words "Speak now" to appear, and then speak into the Galaxy S5. For more details, see page 357.

Auto-Suggestions and the Dictionary

As you enter text, the Galaxy S5 helpfully suggests words that might match what you plan to type. As you type, the phone changes its suggestions based on the letters you enter. The suggestions appear just above the keyboard. Tap any one of the choices to enter it.

NOTE Auto-suggestions often spring into action even before you start typing. When you begin a new email, for example, the S5 thoughtfully suggests two words it thinks you're likely to start an email with: "The" and "You."

The S5 even makes suggestions if the text you've entered is obviously mis-spelled—great if you're ham-handed. So, for example, type *meeyibv,* and auto-suggest offers a variety of options, including *meeting.*

But there are more suggestions than the ones you see. Tap the right-facing arrow at the right of the screen, and more suggestions appear. Also, the keyboard fades out so you can't use it. All you can do is select one of the suggestions. To go back to writing, tap the arrow—which has now turned into a left-facing arrow—and the normal keyboard appears again. Or simply tap in the text input box to get the normal keyboard back.

You may notice something more amazing still: The Samsung keyboard doesn't just suggest words that you're currently typing, but it even suggests words *before you type them.* That's right; it's as though the phone is a mind reader of sorts. So if you type *I am going out of,* before you can even start typing the next word, the keyboard helpfully shows you the word *town.* Tap it if you want to use that word. The keyboard even adds a space before it.

Moving the Insertion Point

Once you get the hang of entering text, you'll come across another challenge—how to move the insertion point if you want to go back and edit, delete, or add words or letters. You can tap where you want to place the insertion point, but that's not always effective. Even if you have tiny fingers and fine-tuned hand-eye coordination, you'll rarely be able to tap in the precise spot where you want the insertion point.

There's a better way: Tap anywhere in the text, and you'll see a big arrow beneath the blinking cursor. Move that arrow to place the insertion point precisely.

Accented and Special Characters

You can easily type accented characters with the Galaxy S5 keyboard. (After all, don't we all have a friend named René Müller-Strauß?). When you press and hold certain keys—the ones shown in the table—a palette of accented characters appears, with a box around the first accented character. Move your finger to the one you want to use, and it gets inserted.

KEY	ACCENTED AND SPECIAL CHARACTERS
A	å, æ, ā, ă, ą, @, à, á, â, ã, ä
C	:, ç, ć, č
D	!, ď, đ
E	é, ę, ě, ĕ, ə, =, è, é, ê, ë, ē
G	/, ġ, ğ
I	ı, į, ī, ï, î, í, ì, >
K	ķ, (
L	ł, ĺ, ļ, ĺ,)
N	ñ, ņ, ń, ñ,,
O	œ, ő, ø, ö, õ, ô, ó, ò, [
R	%, ŕ, ř
S	$, ß, ś, š, ş
T	\, Þ, ť, ţ, ţ
U	ų, ŭ, ů, ū, ü, û, ú, ù, <
Y	ý, ǀ
Z	-, ź, ż, ž,

The Express Lane to Punctuation Marks

The Galaxy S5 letter keyboard doesn't have many punctuation marks on it, which can make for much annoyance as you have to constantly switch back and forth between the letter and number keyboards. There's a simpler way, though: Press and hold the period key. The most common punctuation marks and other common symbols, such as the @ sign, appear on the pop-up palette—11 of them. Tap the mark you want to use. If you tap the Sym button on the palette that pops up, you'll be sent straight to the symbols keyboard.

TIP If you want the keyboard—as well as all your menus, button labels, and so on—to use a language other than English, it's easy. Pull down the Notification panel, tap the Settings icon, and then select "My device"→"Language and input"→Language, and then select the language you want to use. You've got plenty of choices, including German, Spanish, French, Italian, and more.

Swipe Your Way to Better Text Input

The Samsung keyboard has an even niftier piece of magic built into it, one that you likely won't immediately notice: You can move your finger across the keys rather than tapping them, and input text that way. Rather than tap each letter individually, you put your finger on the first letter of the word, and then, with a single motion, move your finger from letter to letter of the word you want to input. As you do so, you'll see the path you've traced. Don't worry too much about accuracy, because the keyboard does an exceptional job of interpreting the word you want to input, using its dictionary. Just try to get near each letter; it's OK if you're off a little bit. When you've finished tracing the word, lift your finger.

There are times when the keyboard might not know precisely what you're trying to trace, and the trace might match multiple words. If that happens, just choose from the word choices that pop up. Tap the word you want. That's all it takes. Then keep swiping your fingers.

Tips for Swiping Text

Entering text this way can be much faster than tapping. Here's how to get the most out of it:

- **Don't use the space key.** After you enter a word, lift your finger and then enter another word. The keyboard automatically puts a space between the two words.

- **Circle or scribble for double letters.** If you want to enter the word *tennis*, then when you get to the "n," make a circle on the key with your finger, or scribble back and forth across the key. Then glide with your finger to the next letter.

- **Work quickly.** Don't slow down in an attempt to be more precise. Swype is built for speed. Move your finger quickly; you'll be surprised at how well Swype recognizes words.

The Magic of the Microphone Key

REMEMBER THE MICROPHONE KEY (page 43)? Tap it, and you can dictate text to your Samsung S5. But that's just the beginning of what this key can do. Tap and hold it instead of just tapping it, and a menu bar appears just above.

There are a bunch of cool things you can now do by tapping the appropriate icon. Here's what they do, from left to right:

- **Microphone.** Does what the icon says—lets you dictate text. Tap this key and start speaking. Say a few words. The Galaxy S5 thinks for a few seconds and then types what you dictated. If you decide you'd prefer to type, tap the little keyboard symbol.

  Speak clearly and distinctly. The S5's microphone works well for words and short phrases, but not so well for long sentences. You can, however, speak part of a sentence, let it input the text, and then speak the next part.

TIP Between the Microphone and Clipboard buttons, you may have a button that looks like a capital T with a pencil. Tap it, and you get a screen where you can write with your finger or a stylus.

- **Clipboard.** This lets you paste in something that you've previously copied to the Clipboard. (For more on copying and pasting, flip to page 51.) When you tap it, a list of your last several clips appears. Tap any to insert it.

- **Settings.** Takes you to a screen that lets you change the S5's keyboard settings.

- **Emoticons and pictures.** Are you a fan of smiley faces? Then tap this and you can embed them as colorful graphics. And it's not just emoticons you can put into your messages. There are plenty of other small graphics as well, such as pictures of animals, houses, and more. Just tap the appropriate button at the bottom of the screen.

- **Keyboard size.** The next icon lets you select what size keyboard to use. Out of the box, you're using the normal-sized keyboard. If you want to use the much smaller keyboard, tap the icon all the way to the right. A wee little keyboard appears, one you need mini-fingers to use. You can drag it around the screen by dragging the little tab at its top. When you're tired of working so small, hold your finger on the microphone key and press the keyboard icon again.

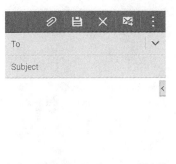

Copying and Pasting Text

WHAT'S A COMPUTER WITHOUT the ability to cut, copy, and paste? A computer at heart, the Galaxy S5 lets you do all that, even though it has no mouse. For example, you can copy directions from Google Maps into an email to send to a friend, paste contact information into a note to yourself, and so on.

You copy and paste text using the same basic techniques you use on a PC or a Mac. You select it, copy or cut, and then paste it.

To select text in an input box, double-tap the text you want to select. If you're lucky, the exact words you want to select are highlighted in blue with brackets on either side. Just above the keyboard, you'll see the words as well.

There's a good chance, though, that you won't be that lucky. No problem—just drag either or both brackets to select the exact text you want.

When you select text, a menu bar appears at the top of the screen. There's more than what you see at first; swipe the menu bar to see everything you can do. Here's what you can do from this menu:

- **Select all.** Selects all the text and graphics in the input box and pops up the same menu of choices you have when you select a word. The selected text is highlighted and contained within the brackets. Move any of them to limit the selection.

- **Cut.** Deletes the text and copies it to the Clipboard so you can paste it somewhere.

- **Copy.** Copies the text to the Clipboard so you can paste it somewhere but doesn't delete the text.

- **Clipboard.** Replaces the text you've selected with the latest text you've pasted to the Clipboard.

- **Dictionary.** Looks up the word in a dictionary. The first time you use this feature, you'll be prompted to download the dictionary.

As for pasting text once you've copied it to the Clipboard, it's a snap...well, a tap. Hold your finger where you want to paste the text, and then tap the Paste button that appears. You can also paste text by holding your finger on the microphone key and selecting the paste icon.

Copying Text from a Web Page

Chances are when you're browsing the Web, you'll eventually come across some text that you want to save for later use. The Galaxy S5 has a specific—but simple—procedure for copying text from a web page to the Clipboard:

1. **Hold your finger on the text you want to copy.** A magnifying glass appears, and the word is highlighted in blue.

2. **Take your finger off the screen.** The word is bracketed and a menu bar appears above the text. Move either one or both of the brackets to include all the text you want to copy. A menu bar appears.

3. **Tap the Copy icon.** The text is copied to the Clipboard. You can also tap the Select All icon to select all the text on the page; tap "Share via" to share it via Bluetooth, email, Facebook, or several other ways; tap Dictionary to look up the word; tap Find to find the word in the page; and tap "Web search" to perform an Internet search for the text. Not all the icons will be immediately visible on the bar, so you'll have to swipe to see them.

Text Messaging

WHAT? YOU USE YOUR smartphone to make phone calls? That's *so* early 21st century! Fittingly, the Galaxy S5 is a messaging monster. Not only can you send and receive plain old text messages, but you can send and receive pictures and videos along with them as well.

When you send text messages, you use the SMS (Short Message Service), which limits you to 160 characters (including spaces and punctuation), which comes out to a sentence or two. That may sound short, but in a world where Twitter limits you to messages of 140 characters, 160 characters can suddenly seem like a lot of space.

NOTE Text messaging is different from a chat program. A chat program establishes a direct connection between you and another person or people, and in addition to letting you chat with one another via the keyboard, you can do videochats and more. For details on how to chat with Google Hangouts and Samsung's ChatON program, see page 274.

Text messaging doesn't come free. You'll have to pay extra, either for a monthly plan or for individual text messages. Check with your wireless provider for details.

NOTE The charges for text messaging are for messages you *receive* as well as those you send.

Receiving a Text Message

When you get a text message, the S5 plays a notification sound. What happens next depends upon whether the phone is active or asleep:

- **If you're using the phone,** you hear a notification sound, and a message appears across the top of your screen. A notification also appears in the status bar.

- **If the phone is asleep,** it wakes up, you hear a notification sound, and you get a notification that you've got a text message (at the top of your screen).

TIP When someone sends you a text message with links in it, the links are live. Tap a web address to visit it in your browser, or tap a phone number to dial the number for a voice call.

In either case, pull down the Notification panel and tap the notice. If you've got more than one text message, the notice tells you so. You go straight to a list of your most recent text messages, those you've sent as well as those that have been sent to you. You see only the last text message in a conversation. So if you exchanged four text messages with someone three days ago, you see only the last message listed here.

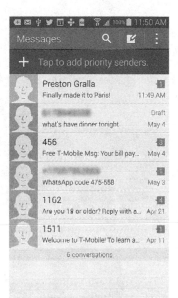

To read the message you were just sent, tap it. You see the message in a text balloon, and if it's part of an ongoing conversation of messages, you see each message.

Text messagers are encountering an unpleasant fact of texting life—spam. It's not nearly as prevalent as email spam, but you'll most likely get some at some point in your messaging life.

To respond, tap in your message using the keyboard, and then press the Send icon next to your text message. Off your message goes, instantly. You see the record of your message appear in a text balloon. If your friend texts back, you see it in a text balloon...and so on.

Sending a Text Message

To send a text message if you haven't received one, tap the Messaging icon on the Home screen or the Apps screen. The list of all your messages appears. Tap the pen icon at upper right, and a screen appears where you create your text message. There are several ways to tell the Galaxy S5 where to send your text message, both accessible from the To field:

- **Type a name into the field.** The phone looks through your contacts and displays any matches. Tap the contact to whose cellphone you want to send a text message.

- **Tap a phone number into the field.**

- **Tap the icon of a person** next to the recipient field, and you're sent to your Contacts list, where you can choose a recipient.

After that, type your message in the message field and tap the Send icon, and your message goes on its merry way.

TIP If you prefer to talk rather than type, press the microphone key on the keyboard, and then speak your message (page 48). Yes, it's odd to send a text message that starts out as spoken, but welcome to the 21st century.

There are plenty of other places on the Galaxy S5 where you can send text messages. Here are the most common ones:

- **When you're viewing a contact.** Tap the Message icon next to a phone number to address a text message to that number. Anywhere you view your contacts, you're only a tap or two away from sending a text message.

NOTE Make sure when you tap the Message icon that the phone number is a *cellphone* number. If it's a landline, the message won't go through.

- **When you're viewing pictures or video.** You can share these things via text messaging much the same way you can share them via email. When viewing the picture or video, tap it so the top menu appears, and then tap the Share button. From the screen that appears, tap the Messages icon. The photo will be embedded into a text message. Type any text you want, and then add the recipient and send it as you would any other text message.

NOTE If the photo or video is too large to send, the S5 will compress it for you. It will take a few seconds to compress, depending on its size.

Adding Pictures, Audio, and Video

On the Galaxy S5, the term "text message" is an understatement, because you can send a whole lot more than text using the SMS service. It's a breeze to send a photo, an audio snippet, a video, an entire slideshow, a name card with contact information on it, and more. You can even take a photo or record a video and embed that as well. When you're composing your text message, tap the Insert icon (it's the picture of a paper clip) to choose any of these items and others from a menu that appears. Depending on what you choose, you'll come to a different menu—for example, all your photo albums if you choose to include a photo. From the menu, you can also take a picture, or record audio or video, which you can then send.

You end up back on the text-messaging screen, where you see an attachment icon on the left side of the screen. Tap Send, and the S5 sends your picture. After a moment or two, you'll see the message you just sent, including the picture, audio, or video.

Text Messaging Tricks

When you're composing a text message, you're in the text input box, and you tap the Menu button, you have more options than just inserting a picture, audio, or video. You can even create a slideshow. Here are your primary options when you tap the Menu button:

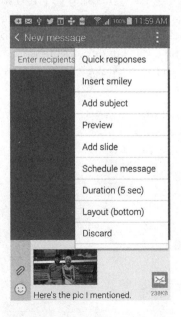

These options don't appear unless you're in the text entry field. Also, other options may appear as well, depending on the person you're contacting.

- **Quick responses.** Tap this to pop in preset text messages, such as "How's it going," and "What's up." No, it's not Shakespeare, but it gets the job done.

- **Insert Smiley.** If you're a fan of smileys, also called *emoticons*, tap here to see a long list of ones you can insert. (If smileys set your teeth on edge, avoid this option.)

- **Add Subject.** Creates a subject field so you can add a subject line to your text.

- **Preview.** Previews the text you're going to send, when you've created a slideshow using the "Add slide" option, or if you've embedded a picture or video into the text. (This option appears only under those circumstances.)

- **Add slide.** This tricky option is fun once you get used to it. Tap it and a slide doesn't actually get added—instead you see a dotted line of text with "1/2" at the right. That means you've created a two-slide show and one of the slides is already done—the text you initially put into the message. To add a picture to the slide, tap the paper clip icon and select what you want to put there. You can keep adding slides in this manner, by choosing "Add slide" from the menu and placing what you want in each slide.

- **Remove slide.** Lets you delete one of the slides from the show. This option appears only if you've already created a slideshow.

- **Schedule message.** Lets you select a later time for the message to be sent.

- **Duration.** Sets how long each slide should display in the slideshow.

- **Discard.** Tosses out the message.

- **Font size.** Lets you select a different font size.

Searching Your Galaxy S5

LOOKING TO FIND THE proverbial needle in a haystack on your Galaxy S5? It can seem like an insurmountable problem. After all, the S5's haystack is rather large, including contacts, maps, social networking sites like Facebook, and the entire Web.

It could take you quite a long time to find a needle in all that hay if you didn't have the S5's universal search, which searches all of the above in one fell swoop. Here's what universal search scans to find matches for you:

NOTE This list will vary according to the apps installed on your S5.

- **Contacts.** Search through first and last names, and also company names. It lists names as well as phone numbers in the results.

- **Browser.** Looks through your bookmarks and web history.

- **Music.** Searches artist names, album names, and track names.

- **Kindle.** If you have the Kindle book-reading app from Amazon on your S5, then universal search looks through the titles and authors of the books you've downloaded.

NOTE When you first unpacked and used your Galaxy S5, it may not have had the Kindle app on it, and you may never have downloaded it. Yet the app may be on your Galaxy S5 all the same. If so, that's because it may have been installed during one of the software updates performed on your phone wirelessly. (It's called an *over-the-air* update, or OTA.)

- **Google search.** Lists popular Google searches that include your search term. It also includes search terms you've already used on Google, even those that you've used on a computer, not on your phone.

- **Titles of installed apps.** It searches through the names of apps you've downloaded. Tap a name to launch the app.

- **Contacts on social media sites.** Universal search doesn't just search through the contacts on your phone—it also searches through contacts on social networking sites whose apps you've installed, such as Facebook.

- **Text messages.** It searches through text messages you've sent and received.

Performing a Search

To launch a search from the Home screen, tap in the Google search box. Tap in your text, and the Galaxy S5 does its magic. As you tap, search displays its results, narrowing the results as you type and your search term gets more specific. In addition, you'll also see Google recommendations for your search.

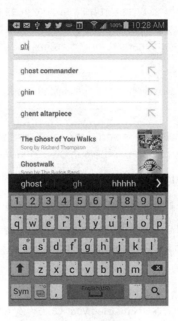

As you type, just beneath the search box, you'll see Google recommendations for searching the Web, and then any partial matches of apps, contacts, and other matches from your phone. So, for example, you might see individual music tracks and individual contacts there as well.

To search the Web, tap the Search button; to choose any Google suggestions, tap them; and to launch any matching app, open a contact, and so on, just tap it. And to search your phone, tap Search Phone (naturally). Why do you need to search your phone, when the S5 has just searched it? Tapping Search Phone does a deeper search. It lists the search results by category. If there are too many to show for each category, there's a Show More button at the bottom of the category. Tap it to see more matches.

Look down at the bottom of the screen. There's a set of icons for many different kinds of searches, including Books, Videos, Apps, Shopping, and more. You won't be able to see them all, so swipe to the side to see more. Tap any to launch a search. The search, though, will be Web-focused—for example, tapping Images uses Google image search, and tapping Places searches Google Places. Tapping Phone, though, searches your phone yet again. And tapping More brings up a whole host of new Google searches, ranging from News to Books to Shopping to Video and more.

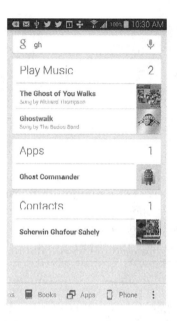

Voice Search

WANT TO SAVE WEAR and tear on your fingers? Use voice search. It works like regular search, with one very important difference: Rather than typing your search, you speak it. Other than that, everything is the same.

To perform a voice search, tap the microphone icon to the right of a Google search box, or else press the Search button and choose Voice Search from the screen that appears. Talk into the phone clearly. Your S5 gamefully tries to interpret what you've said. It then displays results. (For more detail on searching by voice, see page 357.)

The S5 can also perform a very nifty trick—listen to a piece of music, and then tell you what it is and link to it. While doing a voice search, tap "Listen to Music" and hold the phone close enough to the music source so the S5 can hear it. After a little bit, if Google can figure out the music, it shows a match, including a link to buy the music or to listen to it if you own it. This feature is really useful if you're listening to music and want to know who is singing.

TIP This feature can be somewhat flaky. When I tried it with what many people believe is the best rock song ever written, Bob Dylan's "Like a Rolling Stone," the S5 failed to recognize it.

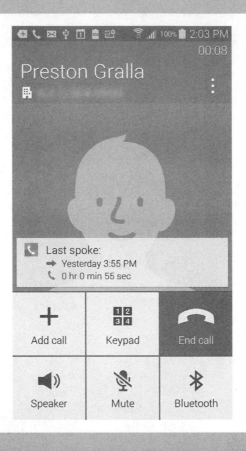

You'll learn to:

- Use the dialer and Contacts app to make calls

- Use Favorites as your speed dialer

- Manage, add, and delete contacts

- Use the S5 for conference calls

- Use caller ID, call forwarding, and call waiting

CHAPTER 3

Phone Calls

THE SAMSUNG GALAXY S5 can do so much, you may forget it's a phone as well. Among all the amazing things this device can do, though, it's great for making phone calls. When texting just won't do, the Galaxy S5 offers everything from simple voice calls to nifty features like visual voicemail and call waiting—and that's what you'll learn in this chapter.

Once you see by the bars in the Galaxy S5's upper-right corner that you've got cellular reception, you're ready to make calls. You can place a call in any of five ways. Don't be daunted by the variety—all methods are easy, including a "Look, Ma, no hands" approach to calls that lets you call someone by talking into the phone rather than by using your fingers to tap keys.

Placing a Phone Call

THE GALAXY S5'S PHONE App is Command Central for making phone calls. On the Home screen, tap the phone icon (at lower left). The Phone app opens, with four buttons at the top, representing the four ways you can make a call:

- **Keypad.** You'll be pleased to see that the virtual buttons on this dialer are a whole lot bigger and easier to tap than the cramped keypads on most cellphones. Even if you have fat fingers or iffy coordination, tapping the right number is a breeze. Tap the number you want to call, and then tap the green Call button at the bottom.

- **Logs.** On this list of recent activity, icons indicate calls that you've made ⤴, received ⤵, or missed ⤵. You also see more information about the call, like the date and time. To repeat or return a call, tap its listing in the log. When the call screen appears, tap the green phone button.

TIP You can also send a text message from the Logs area. Tap the listing and then tap the text message icon on the screen that appears.

- **Favorites.** The Galaxy S5's version of speed dial. The Galaxy S5 lists the people you call or contact frequently. Tap the person's name, and then on the screen that appears, choose how you want to get in touch—phone, email, text message, and so on.

- **Contacts.** Tap a contact, and you can choose from among making a call, sending a text message, sending an email, sending an instant message via Google Talk, and more. The options you see here depend on the information you have for that contact. If you don't have someone's email address, for example, you won't get that option. You'll find out more about all these options later in this chapter.

You may see more contacts here than what you originally tapped into your phone. That's because, if you have a Gmail account, the S5 imports those contacts into its Contacts list. It can also import contacts from other services, like Facebook. You'll see how it works later in this chapter (page 77).

Dialing a Call

MAKING A CALL WITH the dialer is straightforward: Tap the virtual buttons,
and then tap the green phone button to place the call. You'll find the keypad
easier to use than a normal cellphone keypad because its buttons are larger.

If you want to call in to your voicemail instead (see page 88), tap the voicemail
button at lower left. (It looks like a cassette tape from an old-school answering
machine.)

When you make a call, the Dialing screen pops up showing you the phone number you're dialing. If you have a picture of the person in your Contacts list, you
see that photo here. A timer begins, showing you the elapsed time of the call.

There are also buttons for putting the call on the Galaxy S5's built-in speaker, muting the call, and connecting to a Bluetooth headset. And, of course, to end the call, tap the "End call" button.

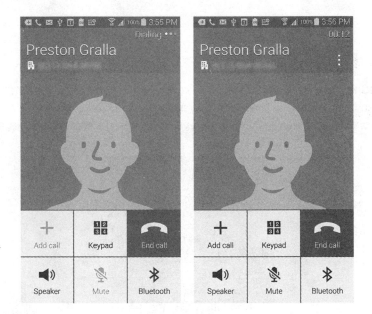

Next to the "End call" button is another button whose purpose seems baffling at first—Keypad. Why would you need a keypad when you're already on a call? For that most annoying means of modern communication—the phone tree. Press the keypad button, and you can experience all the joys of having to "Press 1 for more options."

The Dialing screen offers a bit more Galaxy S5 phone magic. Hit the "Add call" button and presto—you've created your own conference call. For details, check out page 86.

Choosing from the Logs

The Logs list shows you every call you've made or received—and lets you make phone calls right from the list. Tap the Logs button at the top of the screen, and you see your call history listed in chronological order. You see the name, phone number, and time each call was made. Icons next to each call listing provide further details:

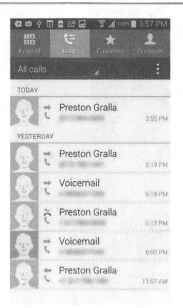

- ☏ means a call you made.
- ☏ means a call made to you.
- ☏ means a call you missed or didn't answer.

NOTE For calls you made, the log doesn't tell you whether or not anyone answered; only that you placed the call.

You can also get more information about each call in the Logs list by tapping anywhere in the log entry (except on the contact's picture—more on that in a minute). A screen then appears with more details about the call, including the exact date and time it was made and its duration. You even see all your recent history of calls and communications with that person. From here you can also call her (tap the phone icon), send her a text message, add her to your Contacts list, view her info in Contacts if she's already there, and more.

Back on the Logs list, if you tap the contact's picture (or if there's no picture, the person icon), a pop-up screen appears. Tap any of the icons on it to contact the person in the following ways, among others:

- Call the person.

- Open his record in Contacts.

- Send him a text message.

- Send him an email.

- Contact him via a social networking site such as Facebook. You see this option only if you've installed the appropriate social networking app on your Galaxy S5 as described in Chapter 11.

- Locate the person on Google Maps by using the address information in your address book.

TIP Tap the Menu button for ways to manage the Logs list, including deleting individual entries, searching for a person on the list, and more.

Choosing from Your Contacts

The Phone app gets phone numbers, pictures, and other information by tapping into your main Contacts list. The Galaxy S5 gets these contacts from multiple places. For example, if you use Gmail, the S5 automatically imports your Gmail contacts into its list. And if you use S5 along with Facebook, your Facebook friends join the party as well. You can also add contacts directly to the S5. You'll learn all the ins and outs of Contacts in the next section. Suffice it to say that if you've ever interacted with someone by email or social media, chances are your S5 already has her phone number.

> **NOTE** You may notice that on your Contacts list, many people have pictures next to their names, even though you never took their pictures. Is the Galaxy S5 pulling hidden camera tricks? Of course not. If you use Facebook on your Galaxy S5, it pulls in pictures from Facebook for any of your contacts who have them. It also pulls in pictures from Google+ as well.

When you first load Contacts, you'll notice something odd and potentially annoying—the S5 arranges your contacts alphabetically by first name, not last name. So if you know a lot of Joes and Marys, you're going to spend a little more time than you'd like scrolling.

Why does the Galaxy S5 alphabetize by first name, rather than by last name? It's a Google thing. Google wrote the Android operating system that powers the phone, and Gmail alphabetizes its contact list by first name. As Gmail does, so does the Galaxy S5.

You likely know more than one screenful of people, and you can navigate through the list in several ways:

First, you can flick through the list. You'll see the alphabet down the right side of the screen, and you can tap any letter to get sent to that letter immediately.

You can also search the list. Type into the search box at the top, and as you type, the list gets pared down, hiding everyone whose first name, last name, company name, or title doesn't match what you've typed. It's a great time-saver for quickly paring down a big list. You also see the words you're typing, just above the keyboard, so you can more easily track what you type.

TIP How do you find a contact whose name you can't recall? If you know someone's place of work, type that in, and you'll see a list of all your contacts who work at that company.

When you've gotten to the person you want to call, tap the person's contact listing. You'll see all the information you have about him — phone numbers, email addresses, home and work addresses, and more. From this screen you can make a call, send an email or text message, and so on by tapping the appropriate icon.

Managing Contacts

THE GALAXY S5'S PHONE, Messaging, and IM apps all use the same master Contacts list. In fact, you can go directly to the list by tapping the Contacts icon on the Apps screen.

NOTE Although the Contacts app has its own launch icon, it simply sends you to the same Contacts list you see in the Phone app. Everything you learned in the previous section applies everywhere you use your Contacts on the Galaxy S5.

The Galaxy S5 is nothing if not thoughtful. If you use Gmail or Google+, the phone grabs all your contacts from there and pops them into your Contacts list. And it's not just a one-time transfer of contacts, but it happens every time you add, edit, or delete a contact. Whenever you change or add a contact in Gmail or Google+, those changes are synced to your S5, and vice versa. So, if possible, it's better to create new contacts in Gmail on your computer, and then let the phone import that new information when you sync up. It's much easier to type on a keyboard than it is to tap on your S5.

Adding a Contact

It's easy to add a contact right on your Galaxy S5. Tap the + button at the top of your Contacts list (the button stays there even when you scroll) and a screen pops up asking where you want to save the contact. The available locations may vary depending on the apps you have and your S5 setup, but at a minimum you'll be able to choose from saving to your SIM card, to the device, to your Google account, or to a Samsung account if you've set it up. No matter where you save the contact, though, it'll show up in your Contacts list. However, if you save to your device or SIM card, the contact won't sync with your Google account, so your best bet is to go for the Google option.

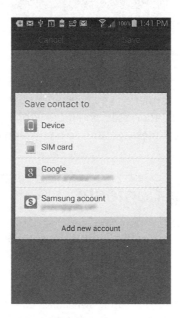

After you choose where to create your contact, you arrive at a screen where you fill in contact information. Type the person's first name, last name, address information, and so on. If she has more than one email address, phone number, or address, tap the + button next to the entry to add more. Make sure to scroll through this whole screen—there's plenty of information you can add here.

One more trick—you can add a photo to the contact information. At the top of the screen, tap the icon that looks like a person's head with a + on it, and a screen appears that lets you add a photo. If you already have a photo on your phone, tap Image and you can browse through the Gallery (page 115) for the picture. If the person happens to be right there with you, tap "Take picture," and the Camera app launches. Use it to take a photo. There are several other options available for adding pictures, but none are as easy as browsing the Gallery or snapping a photo on the spot.

If you want to change the location where you're saving a contact, tap the same triangle on the right side near the top of the screen that shows the location you're saving to. When you tap the triangle, you'll get a choice of other locations where you might want to save.

The Contact screen also lets you do way cooler things than typing in basic information. You can choose a specific ringtone and even tell your phone to vibrate in a certain way when that contact calls. So pay attention to those fields. And there are plenty more fields you can add as well. Tap "Add another field," and you'll get plenty of options, like Relationship, Notes, and so on.

Editing Contacts

Already have a contact and want to edit his information? Tap the Edit button at the top of a contact, and then edit to your heart's content. You can change or add any of the same things as when you first added the contact.

For even more contact-handling options, tap the Menu button when you're viewing a contact. You'll be able to do things like these:

- Delete the contact.

- Combine two different bits of contact information into one (if one comes from Gmail, for example, and another from Facebook).

- Add a shortcut to the contact to the Home screen.

- Share the contact information via Bluetooth, email, text message, and other ways.

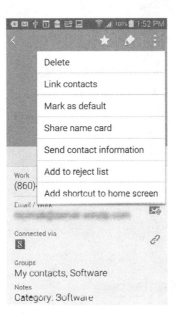

Working with Groups

Like most folks, you probably have a long list of contacts, and although Contacts lets you flick through them quickly, you might have a hard time zeroing in on the person you want. There's a simpler way—Groups. The Galaxy S5 lets you put contacts in various groups—Family, Work, and so on—making it easier to find the person you want. You can view just the group rather than the entire Contacts list.

The Groups button appears to the right of the search box when you're viewing all your contacts in a list. Tap it to see your Groups. Tap any group in the list to see all its members. To create a new group, when you're viewing the list of your groups, tap the + button. Type a name for the group and then start putting people in it. Tap Add Member, and your entire contact list appears, with a check-box next to every contact. Tap that box for each contact you want to add to the group, and when you've added everyone, tap Done.

> **TIP** From the screen that lets you create a group, you can also select a ringtone for when anyone from that group calls you. (Beyoncé for your ring-theory group, perhaps?)

Fancy Tricks with Contacts

The Galaxy S5 has a few more tricks up its sleeve when it comes to working with contacts. To see them, open a contact, and then press the Menu button. The choices vary according to the contact information you have. Here are the choices you'll see, and what each does:

- **Delete.** Deletes the contact from your Galaxy S5.

- **Link contacts.** Combines two separate listings for a contact into a single listing. For example, if you've imported a contact from both Gmail and Facebook, they'll usually show up as separate contacts until you combine them using Join.

- **Share name card.** Lets you send information about a contact using many different sharing methods, such as via Bluetooth, email, WiFi Direct, and others. You can send all the information about the contact or just some of it. Follow the onscreen prompts after you make your choice about how you want to share.

- **Remove from favorites.** This option appears only if the person is in your favorites list.

- **Add to favorites.** Adds the person to your Favorites—the Galaxy S5's version of speed dial.

- **Send contact information.** Lets you send information from the contact via email.

- **Add to reject list.** Puts the person on a list of callers you don't want to hear from. Your phone won't answer calls from numbers on this list.

- **Print contact info.** If you have a wirelessly enabled printer that works with your Galaxy S5, you can print the person's namecard.

- **Add shortcut to home screen.** Puts a link to the contact on your Home screen.

TIP If you're viewing a contact, you can get to some of the same choices by tapping the Menu button.

Designating Favorites

WHAT IF YOU WANT to quickly call your best friend, your spouse, your lawyer, one of your children, or your weekly tennis partner? Scrolling through hundreds of contacts is a complete waste of time. You need a way to quickly jump to the contacts you frequently call.

That's where the Favorites list comes in. Think of it as the Galaxy S5's speed dial. The S5 puts people on the list based on how often you communicate with them. Other than that, it works the exact same way as the normal Contacts list.

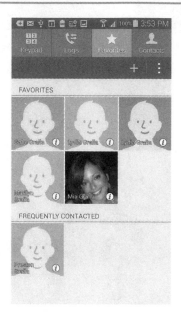

Although the S5 automatically adds your frequently used contacts to the Favorites list, you can also add your own. Just open the contact and tap the star at the top of the screen. The star turns gold, and the person shows up on your Favorites list.

NOTE To remove someone from your Favorites list, open the contact and then tap the gold star. It loses its gold color, indicating that the person is no longer one of your Favorites.

Answering Calls

ONE RINGY-DINGY, TWO RINGY-DINGIES...when you get a call on your Galaxy S5, you'll know in no uncertain terms that someone is trying to reach you. Depending on how you've set up your S5 to handle incoming calls, you'll hear a ring, feel a vibration, and see the caller's name, photo, and phone number onscreen.

NOTE For information about how to choose a ringtone, and whether to use Vibrate mode, see page 373.

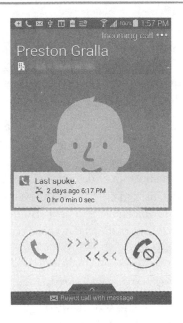

The way you find out when a call is coming in, and the way you answer it, depends on what you're doing when you get the call:

- **If you're doing something else on the Galaxy S5,** you'll hear a notification, and a screen appears telling you that you've got a call. Slide the green button from left to right. When the call is over, tap "End call." If you don't want to answer the call at all, drag the red button from right to left.

- **If the Galaxy S5 is asleep or locked,** you get the same call screen and the same red and green buttons. Even if you've added a password to your phone, you answer the phone the same way—no password required to answer a call.

- **If you're wearing earbuds or listening to music on an external speaker,** the music stops playing and you hear the ringtone in your earbuds or speaker. Slide the green or red button. After the call ends, the music starts playing again.

Turning Off the Ring

If the Galaxy S5 starts to ring at an inopportune time, you can turn off the ringtone without turning off the phone or dropping the call. Just press the volume switch at the phone's upper-left side. The ring goes away, but you can still answer the call in any of the usual ways.

Ignoring the Call

Suppose you're just getting to the juicy part of a book you're reading, or you simply don't want to talk to the annoying person calling. You can ignore the call. After five rings, the call goes to voicemail. (It does so even if you've silenced the ring with the volume switch.)

If you prefer, you can send the call straight to voicemail, without further ado or further rings. And not only that, but you can also send a text message to the caller, explaining why you can't answer the call. To do it, pull up the "Reject call with message" button at the bottom of the screen, and select from any of the messages that appear, such as "I'm driving," "I'm in a meeting," and so on. The caller will be sent straight to voicemail, and he'll also get the text message from you. You can also write your own text—as long as, of course, you're *not* driving— by tapping "Create new message."

Conference Calling

HERE'S A FANCY PHONE trick that's great for business and personal use: conference calls. Sitting at a Starbucks, but want people on the other end to think you're in an office with a fancy phone system? The Galaxy S5 lets you conference in multiple people with no extra charges or software, depending on your carrier. And you can also use it for conferencing in friends when you're all trying to decide whether to meet at 6 p.m. before the Red Sox game so you can catch Big Papi at batting practice.

To make a conference call, first make a call as you would normally. Then tap "Add call." A screen appears where you can dial the second number, or else get the number from your Logs list, Contacts, or Favorites. At upper left, you'll see an indication that you're on a call, and a timer shows you how much time has elapsed.

After you make the second call, you'll see a series of new icons labeled with text. One shows the name of the original caller and shows he's on hold; another, called Merge, lets you merge both calls into a single conference call; and the final one, Swap, lets you switch between the calls. As you switch to one call, the other one is placed on hold.

To end the call, tap "End call." If you're in a conference, both calls will be ended. If you're talking to just one of the people on the line, only that call will end, and you're automatically switched to the other call.

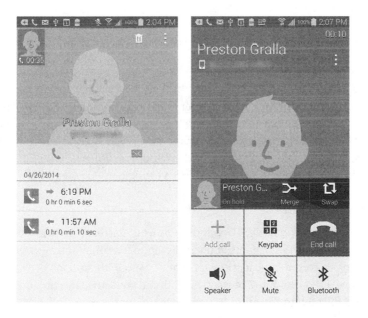

Voicemail

YOUR GALAXY S5 HAS built into it all the usual voicemail capabilities you'd expect. You know the drill: Dial in to your voicemail, enter a password, and listen to voice messages. To dial in to voicemail on the Galaxy S5, hold down the "1" key on the keypad (it has a voicemail icon on it.) If you're using voicemail for the first time, follow the prompts for setting up your voicemail box, including choosing a password and selecting or recording a message.

Visual Voicemail

Looking for something niftier? Depending on your carrier, the Galaxy S5 may have *visual voicemail*, which lets you see, listen to, and manage all your voicemails in a neat, chronological list instead of dealing with a bunch of prompts. For example, if you've got 17 messages, and you want to listen to number 17, you don't need to listen to the other 16 first. Just tap message 17.

When you're playing a voicemail, you get visual controls for pausing, restarting, and calling back. Tap the menu button at the top of the screen, and you can forward the call. There are several ways to delete a call. While you're listening to it, or after you've heard it, tap the Delete button at the top of the screen. When you're viewing the complete voicemail list, you can also delete one by holding your finger on it and selecting Delete from the menu that appears.

For details, check with your carrier. You may be charged extra every month to use this service, often a fee of about $3. To use the service, select Settings from the Apps screen, and then tap Visual Voicemail.

Call Waiting

THE GALAXY S5 OFFERS call waiting, so it lets you know when you have an incoming call while you're already on a call. You can choose to either answer the new call—and put the first call on hold—or ignore it and let it go to voicemail. If you're a real fast talker, you can even keep both calls going at once and switch back and forth.

When you're on a call and another call comes in, your screen shows you the phone number of the second caller. The phone won't ring or vibrate, and at that point, you're still on the call with your first caller.

You have two choices:

- **Answer.** Answer the call as you would normally, and you can accept the incoming call. You get an "Answer call" notification message on your screen that gives you two choices: Put your first caller on hold and answer the call, or end the first call and answer the incoming call. If you answer the call and put the first caller on hold, you'll see the same screen as you do for conference calling, and you can switch back and forth between the calls or merge them.

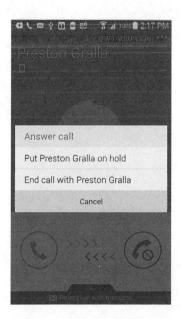

- **Ignore.** You can ignore the call as you normally ignore an incoming call, and proceed with your first call.

Call Forwarding

CALL FORWARDING LETS YOU have your Galaxy S5 calls rerouted to a different number. That way, when you're at home, you can have your cellphone calls ring on your landline and have to deal with only one phone. Even if the S5 is out of commission, you can still forward its calls to another phone and never miss a call.

If you haven't used call forwarding before, first make sure that the service is available from your carrier and activated. Check with the carrier for details.

Once you've done that, turning on call forwarding is a breeze. On the Apps screen, tap Settings, scroll to the Applications area, and tap Call→"Additional settings"→"Call forwarding." From the screen that appears, you can turn call forwarding on and off and set rules for when to have call forwarding turn on automatically—for example, when your phone is busy or you don't answer it. When you turn on call forwarding for the first time, you enter the number where you want your calls forwarded.

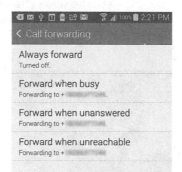

Caller ID

CALLER ID IS BUILT into the very guts of the Galaxy S5. That's why you see the phone number, and at times the caller's name, every time you get a call. And when you call someone, she sees your phone number as well. There's a way to block your number from being displayed, although as with call forwarding, you can't do it on the phone, but have to go through your carrier. Check your account to make sure you have the capability. Then when you want to block your phone number from being displayed when you make a call, tap *67, and then make the call. Your number won't be displayed on the receiving end. Instead, the person will see "Private" or "Anonymous" or something to that effect. When the call ends, Caller ID is reactivated; you'll have to tap *67 again to enable it on your next call.

You can also turn off outgoing Caller ID on your carrier's website, log into your wireless account, and turn it off there. You may see an "Add/Change features" section, for example, where you can turn on the checkbox for Caller ID Blocking.

Bluetooth Earpieces

BLUETOOTH IS A SHORT-RANGE wireless technology designed to let all kinds of devices connect with one another, exchange or sync files and photos, or let a cellphone serve as a wireless modem for a computer.

With a little work you can get the S5 to do all that. Mostly, though, the phone's Bluetooth capabilities come in handy for hands-free talking with an earpiece.

If you've ever seen someone walking down the street, apparently talking to an invisible friend, you've seen Bluetooth in action (unless he really *was* talking to an invisible friend). The small device clips to your ear, and you talk into its microphone and listen in the tiny speaker in your ear.

NOTE The earpiece you use for making phone calls is typically monaural, and not designed for listening to music. If you're a music lover, invest in a *stereo* Bluetooth headset.

Pairing with a Bluetooth Earpiece

To use a Bluetooth earpiece with your phone, you'll need to *pair* them—that is, get the two of them talking to each other. The process is a bit geeky, but not difficult. The exact steps may vary a bit depending on the earpiece you're using. But, generally, these are the steps you'll take:

1. **On the earpiece, turn on Bluetooth and make it discoverable.** In other words, set the earpiece so your Galaxy S5 can find it. Check the earpiece's documentation on how to do so.

2. **On your S5, turn on Bluetooth there, too.** You have several ways to do this. The simplest is to pull down the Notification panel and tap the Bluetooth icon, if Bluetooth isn't already turned on. You can also turn it on by tapping Settings in the Apps screen, and in the Network Connections area, tap the Bluetooth icon. Once Bluetooth is on, the S5 will start scanning for any nearby Bluetooth equipment. Your earpiece should show up on the list.

3. **Tap the earpiece's name and type a passcode.** You'll find the passcode in the earpiece's manual. The passcode is for security purposes, so that no one else can pair with the device. The number is usually between four and six digits, and you'll need to type it within a minute or so. You only need to enter the passcode once. After that, the pairing will happen automatically.

You should now be connected. You still dial using the Galaxy S5, but you can talk through the earpiece. Check the earpiece's documentation on how to answer calls, control the volume, and so on.

Having trouble getting your new Bluetooth earpiece to work? Search the Internet for the make, model number, and the word *setup*. If you're having trouble, someone else likely had trouble as well, and you'll probably find a solution.

Bluetooth and Car Kits

An increasing number of cars include built-in Bluetooth so that you can pair your S5 with it. This way, you can make calls directly from your car's control panel and hear calls over your car's speakers. You can do other nifty things, such as play music from your phone on your car's entertainment system.

If your car doesn't have built-in Bluetooth, there are plenty of Bluetooth car kits out there. Generally, pairing your S5 with a Bluetooth car kit is much the same as pairing it with a Bluetooth earpiece. How you use the car kit varies, of course. In some instances, you can dial a number on the car's touchscreen or answer the phone by pressing a button on the steering wheel.

Don't be lulled into thinking that driving with hands-free calling is safe. Studies show that the danger in talking on a phone while driving isn't related to holding the phone—It's the distraction of holding a conversation while driving.

The Built-In Features

CHAPTER 4:
Music

CHAPTER 5:
Camera, Photos, and Video

CHAPTER 6:
Maps and Navigation

CHAPTER 7:
Calendar

You'll learn to:

- Use the built-in Music app
- Create playlists
- Play Internet radio stations
- Play music on nearby devices
- Use the Google Cloud Music Player

Music

THE GALAXY S5 DOES a great job of playing and managing music, so much so that you may no longer feel the need to carry around another music player. It includes an excellent built-in music player and manager, and a 3.5 mm headset stereo jack that you can connect to headphones or external speakers. You can connect wirelessly to Bluetooth speakers as well. Read this chapter and get ready to plug in and turn up the volume.

Where to Get Music

BEFORE YOU PLAY MUSIC, of course, you first need to get it onto your Galaxy S5. For details about how to do that, turn to page 319. You can also buy or download music from Google's Play store or other S5 apps. (The Play Music app is a Google music subscription service that also lets you play music you own on a computer—it doesn't let you buy individual music tracks. For more info, see the Note on the next page.)

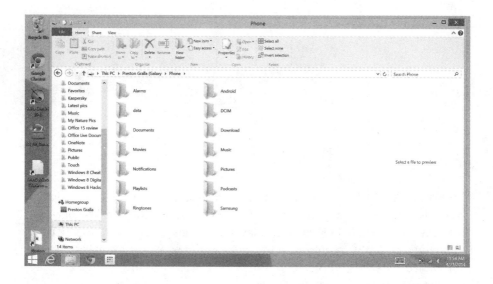

NOTE If you tap a download link on a web page for a music file in the Galaxy S5 browser, the file doesn't download to your phone. Instead, the S5 plays the music file but doesn't add it to your collection.

Using the Music App

YOU PLAY AND MANAGE your music by using the Galaxy S5's Music app. Tap the Music icon on the Apps screen to launch it. The app organizes your music into seven different lists, through which you scroll like all other lists on your phone. Simply swipe to the right and left to see all of them, and then tap any you want to view or play:

- **Playlists.** Here's where you'll find all your *playlists*—groups of songs that you've put together in a specific order, often for a specific purpose. For example, you might have several party playlists, a playlist of songs you like to listen to while you work, another for the gym, and so on.

NOTE In addition to the Music app built into the S5, Google also has a *cloud-based* music player app. With it, you can upload music from your PC or Mac to big Google computers (called *servers*), and then play that music on your phone, without actually having to store it on the phone. (Because your music lives in the cloud—get it?) The service and app are free and work like a charm. The app is called Play Music and is likely already on your S5. If it's not, though, download it from Google Play. There's also a for-pay version that's a streaming music service in which you pay a monthly fee and can stream music to your S5. See page 111 for details about the cloud music player.

To see the contents of a playlist, tap the playlist. Tap any song to play it from that point until the end of the playlist. To add a song to the playlist, press the Menu key, tap "Add to playlist," and then select songs to add from the list that appears. (You can also add songs to playlists while you're playing them, and in other ways as well. See page 107 for details.) When you press the Menu key, you get other ways to manage your playlist, including removing songs from the playlist, searching through the playlist, and changing settings (for the entire music app, not just for playlists).

- **Tracks.** An alphabetical list of every song in your music collection. It shows the song names and artists. Tap a song to play it.

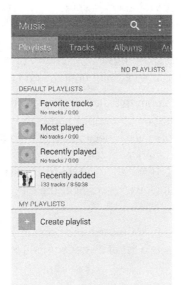

NOTE When you're in the Music app, at the bottom of the screen, you see the name of the song you're playing. If you're not playing a song, you see the last song you played, along with a control for playing the song. Tap it and you're sent to the full player. (See page 102 for details.)

- **Albums.** Lists all the CDs (albums) in your music collection. If a thumbnail picture of the album is available, you see it next to the album listing. Each album lists its name and its singer, composer, band, or orchestra. Tap the album to see a list of all the songs in the album. To play any song, tap it. The Music app then plays from that point until the end of the album.

  To add songs from an album to a playlist, when you're viewing an album, hold your finger on the song you want to add, and a screen appears with all the tracks on the album with checkboxes next to them. The song you're pressing on has a checkmark next to it. Tap to put a checkmark next to other songs you want to add. Then tap the "Add to playlist" button at the top of the screen (it has a + sign on it) and select the playlist you want to add it to or create a new one.

- **Artists.** Lists every singer, composer, and band in your collection. Tap the artist's name, and you see a list of all her songs. To play any song, tap it.

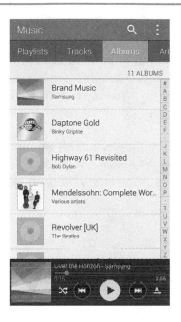

NOTE The Galaxy S5 can play a wide variety of music files, including AAC, MP3, WAV, WMA, OGG, AAC+, and MIDI. Android by itself won't play WMA (Windows Music Audio) files, but Samsung gave the S5 a special piece of software called a *codec* so it can play them. For the same reason, it can also play WMV (Windows Media Video) videos.

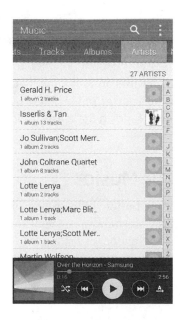

- **Music Squares.** This unique-to-Android feature examines all your music and arranges tracks in different squares onscreen depending on the emotion of the music—Calm, Exciting, Passionate, and Joyful. It gives you a way to suggest the sort of music you want to listen to without having to come up with specific songs or artists. You can choose a mix of these music moods by tapping any square on the grid.

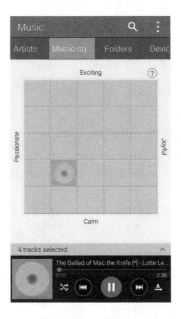

- **Folders.** Lists all your music by folder. Tap the folder to display all its files, and then tap a track to play it. The track will play, as will all the others from that point until the end of the listing.

- **Devices.** Lists all nearby devices on your network that have music on them. Tap a device to see the music on it. You can then play the music on the device, using the player, by tapping the music using the normal controls.

Playing Your Music

TAP A SONG TO play it. At the bottom of the screen, you see the usual controls for playing and pausing music and moving to the next or the previous track. If you want to play your music in random order, tap the Shuffle icon at the bottom left of the screen.

If you tap the picture of the music note and three horizontal lines at the lower left of the screen, the picture at the top of the music player vanishes and is replaced by a listing of all the tracks on the album or playlist. And if you hold the music player sideways, you'll see a compact version of the player, plus recommendations for other music you might like, based on the track you're listening to.

The music player screen, when you're holding your S5 vertically, is loaded with controls and widgets. Among other controls, you'll find these:

- **Pause/Play.** When music is playing, the button looks as it normally does on any music player. Tap it to pause; tap it to play again.

- **Previous, Next.** These controls work just as you'd expect. Tap Previous to skip to the beginning of the song you're playing or, if you're already at the beginning, to go back to the last song you just played. Tap Next to skip to the following song.

   Hold down one of the buttons, and you rewind or fast-forward through the song. As you hold, the rewinding or fast-forwarding accelerates. You'll hear the music as you speed forward or backward, sounding like experimental, avant-garde music.

- **Slider.** Underneath the picture of the album from which the song is taken, you'll see a slider that shows you the song's progress. It includes the song's total length and how much of it you've already played. Move the slider to go to a specific location in the song.

- **Song and album information.** In the middle of the screen you'll find the name of the singer, the name of the album, and the song being played.

- **List.** Tap the small musical note at lower left, and the big album image or musical note changes to the current song list. For example, if you're listening to a playlist, you'll see the entire playlist, and if you're playing an album, you'll see the whole album. From here, you can tap any other song to play it. To bring back the picture of the album or musical note, tap the button again, which has turned into a picture.

- **Shuffle.** The Galaxy S5 music player normally plays the songs in your playlist or album in order, from first to last. Tap the Shuffle button at lower left to play the songs in your current album or playlist in random order—you never know what's coming next. Tap it again to stop the shuffle.

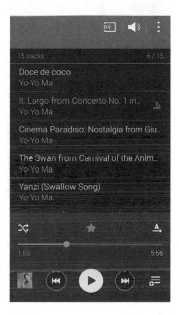

- **Loop.** Can't get enough of the current album, playlist, or song? Tap the Loop button. This button starts out as an A with an arrow next to it. Tap it, and it changes into an A with a loop around it, signifying that the album or playlist will keep repeating. Tap it again and that changes to a number 1 with a loop around it, signifying that the track you're currently playing will keep repeating. When you've had your fill, tap it again, and you get back to the A with an arrow, which means that looping is off.

> **TIP** Want to play a stupid music player trick? Tap the picture of the album when you're playing a song. Bubbles pop out from the picture. Why do this? Because you can.

- **Volume button.** Tap this upper-right button, and a volume slider appears. Drag to increase or decrease the volume. Tap the small icon at the bottom of the volume slider and you can select from a variety of built-in sound modes—Normal, Pop, Rock, Dance, Jazz, Classical, and so on.

- **Other buttons.** There are other buttons as well. The button just to the right of the volume buttons shows you nearby devices on your network whose music you might want to play. Tap the star just above the slider to turn it gold and identify the track as a favorite. That puts it on a playlist called, unsurprisingly, Favorites, that you can then play when you want. Tap the button with a + and three vertical lines to add the current song to a playlist.

Select device

AVAILABLE DEVICES

My phone
Preston Gralla (Galaxy

Dining Room - Sonos
CONNECT Media
Renderer
Via home network

Living Room - Sonos
CONNECT Media
Renderer
Via home network

Master Bedroom - Sonos
PLAY:3 Media Renderer
Via home network

Office - Sonos PLAY:3
Media Renderer
Via home network

Cancel   Refresh

More Music Controls and Features

Want even more music controls and features? Tap the Menu button, and you'll be able to do all the following:

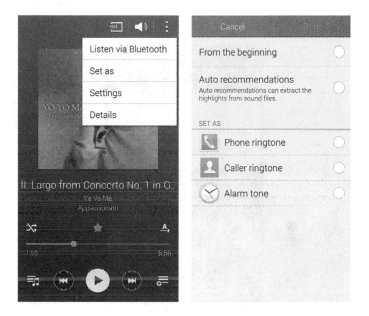

- **Listen via Bluetooth.** Lets you share the song via Bluetooth (see page 91)

- **Set as.** This very nifty feature lets you set a song as a ringtone or alarm tone.

- **Settings.** Lets you change many settings; sound effects, music menu items, and so on.

- **Details.** Provides all kinds of information about a song, including its title, artist, track length, recording date, genre, and so on.

More Song Options

And, yes, you've got even more options when you play songs. Hold your finger on a track on a list, and boxes appear next to each track, with a checkmark on the current track. Tap the boxes on all the songs you want to select. You can then add them to Favorites or a playlist, or delete them.

Creating Playlists

MAKING YOUR OWN PLAYLISTS is a breeze on the S5. The easiest way to do so is to tap the Playlist button at lower right when you're playing a song (it's a +

and a series of three horizontal lines), and then tap "Create a playlist." A screen appears that lets you name your list. Type in a name and tap OK. A playlist is created, with that track added to it. If you already have playlists, then when you tap the Playlist button, you'll see all of them, so that you can add the current song to an existing playlist or create a new one.

You can also create playlists from the Music player's main screen. Tap Playlists at the top of the screen, and then tap "Create playlist" toward the bottom of the screen. A screen appears that lets you name the list. When you're done, you'll be sent to a screen that reads "No tracks." Tap the + sign at the top of the screen, and you'll see a list of all of your songs with empty boxes next to them. Turn on the boxes next to the music you want to add to the playlist, and then tap Done to add all those songs to the list. If you want to find specific music on your S5 to add to the playlist, tap the Search button.

The S5 creates several playlists automatically for you—"Favorite tracks," "Recently added," "Most played," and "Recently played." These playlists don't show up when you try to add music to a playlist, because they're created and managed by the S5.

To edit a playlist, when you're in the list, hold your finger on a song. Boxes show up next to all the songs. Check those you want to manage in some way, and then perform your action—delete them by tapping the trash can icon, or add to other playlists by tapping the "Add to playlist" button.

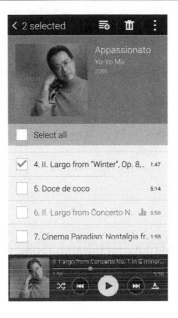

APP ALERT

Galaxy Radio

Another way to play music by using your Galaxy S5 is to use an app that turns the phone into an FM radio or streams music to the phone wirelessly. To use your S5 as an FM radio, head to Google Play and download any one of many apps, like Tune-In Radio (*www.tunein.com*).

There are also many apps that play streaming music to your S5, like Pandora (*www.pandora.com*) and Spotify (*www. spotify.com*); search for them by name in Google Play. In fact, if you already have a Pandora account that you use to play music from the Web, all your stations will already be set up when you use the S5's Pandora app. How's that for convenient?

Services like Pandora and Spotify have the seemingly psychic ability to learn what kind of music you like from the choices you make, and play similar songs for you. Spotify also lets you share music over Facebook, Twitter, and other services. With the S5, you can truly enjoy and share your tunes wherever you go.

Using Your Galaxy S5 While Playing Music

BECAUSE THE GALAXY S5 is built for multitasking, you can play music even when you're doing something else. Open the Music app, start the music, and then feel free to use other apps and features. The music keeps playing. While music is playing, a small button appears in the status bar. Drag down the Notification panel and tap the song playing, and you see a miniature set of controls for playing, pausing, and jumping forward and back in music. To head to the music player, tap the picture of the album.

Even when your phone is locked, if you were listening to music before the Galaxy S5 locked itself, it keeps playing. Turn on the screen, even though the phone remains locked, and you'll see music controls. You can pause and play music, as well as skip to the next song or go back to a previous song, without having to unlock the Galaxy S5.

Playing Music and Media on Other Devices

THE GALAXY S5 LETS you share, view, and play music, videos, and photos using a standard called DLNA—short for Digital Living Network Alliance. The S5 is DLNA-compliant, which means that it can share media with other DLNA devices, such as TVs, computers, and mobile devices. When you buy a device, look in the documentation to see if it's also DLNA compliant. You can also look for this logo on packaging or documentation: dlna.

NOTE If you're not sure whether you have a device that's DLNA-compliant, go to *www.dlna.org*. In addition to finding out more information about DLNA, you can do a search for your device and see if it supports DLNA.

Here's just some of what you can do with your Galaxy S5 and other DLNA devices:

- Stream your music, videos, and photos from your S5 to a DLNA device, such as a TV, PC, Xbox, or PlayStation 3.

- Transfer music and picture files from your phone to your PC.

- Stream videos from the phone to your TV.

- Browse any videos you have stored on your PC, using the Galaxy S5, and then stream the video to your TV by using an HDMI cable (see page 136 for details about HDMI).

And that's just a few of the possibilities and permutations with your Galaxy S5 and DLNA; this section can't cover them all.

Out of the box, the S5 is set up to use DLNA. In the Music app, when the phone scans your network to see if there are nearby devices from which it can play music, it's actually using DLNA.

For sharing with other devices such as TVs, check the device documentation for how to share via DLNA. And you can also customize your DLNA settings on your S5. To do it, tap Settings from the Apps screen, scroll down to "Connect and Share," and tap "Nearby devices." You'll then be able to change your DLNA settings, such as what media content you want to share, what devices you want to share with, and so on.

Google Music Cloud Player App

THE GOOGLE MUSIC CLOUD Player may forever change the way you manage—and even think about—your music. It lets you play music on your phone that isn't actually *on* the phone, but instead lives in the *cloud*—basically big Google computers called servers that store your music and stream it to your Galaxy S5 (or any other device, for that matter).

The app's official name is Google Play Music, and it should come installed on your S5. If it isn't, you can download it from Google Play. Then install the Play Music software on your PC or Mac (whichever computer houses your music collection). You then tell the software to upload the music to the cloud. After that, you install Play Music on your S5 (or, indeed, any other Android device). At that point, you can listen to your music from the cloud—as long as you have a 3G, 4G, or WiFi connection.

Once you've got everything installed, just tap the Play Music app and start playing. It integrates with the S5's normal music player, so it plays any music you've got installed there, as well as music from the cloud.

And you can also subscribe to unlimited music streaming and play thousands of tracks for a $9.99 monthly fee, much like the streaming Spotify music service. Play Music will give you all the details if you tap "Try it Free" when you first run the app. If you don't want to try the for-pay version, and only want to listen to your own music, instead tap "Not now" when you run the app.

TIP If you sign up for the pay service, you can download tracks for offline listening. That's a great way to avoid eating up your data allowance by streaming music.

Keep in mind that there will be times when your music isn't available from the cloud—because you're not connected to the Internet—so you can choose to hide streamed music at that point. You can also set a variety of other options, such as whether to stream music only when connected via WiFi rather than via 3G or 4G. That way, you won't eat up data from your data plan.

The cloud player is a fabulous player, especially if you have a digital music collection on a PC or Mac. Check it out and listen to your beloved music anywhere!

You'll learn to:

- View photos and videos in the Gallery
- Create slideshows
- Take photos and videos
- Use photo modes
- Use the S5 as a universal remote

CHAPTER 5

Camera, Photos, and Video

THE SAMSUNG GALAXY S5 has a big 5.1-inch screen for a good reason—it's designed to excel at displaying photos and videos, and capturing them as well. It has a built-in 16-megapixel camera, so you can take photos in very high resolution, as well as a 2.1-megapixel front-facing camera for videoconferencing. It can even shoot and play HD (high definition) video. (For techies, it records video at 4K resolution, which stands for horizontal resolution of 4,000 pixels. What does that mean in plain English? Two words: spectacular videos.)

In other words, you've got more than just a phone in your pocket—you've got a multimedia marvel as well. And with a bit of mucking around and tweaking, you can even watch videos from it on a big-screen TV.

This chapter gives you all the details about taking and viewing photos and videos with your Galaxy S5, viewing pictures and videos transferred to your S5 from your computer, and viewing photos and videos from your phone on TVs and other monitors.

Opening the Gallery

THERE ARE SIX MAIN ways to get photos or videos into your Galaxy S5:

- Transferring them from your PC or Mac (see Chapter 13 for details).

- Taking them using the Galaxy S5's built-in camera.

- Downloading them from the Web.

- Getting them in email attachments.

- Using Google's Picasa app.

- Using the Dropbox cloud-based file storage service.

No matter how you get them, though, you view them the same way, by using the Gallery app. Here's how:

1. **In the Apps screen, tap the Gallery icon.** The Gallery app launches. You'll see photos organized by individual albums. Even if you haven't yet taken a single photo with your S5 (or transferred any), you may still find albums there, because the S5 automatically imports photos from Google's Picasa photo service and the Dropbox cloud-based file-storage service. So if you've used those services, you've got photos.

   When you first run Gallery, it organizes your photos by album. But you can view them in other ways as well. To change your view, tap the three horizontal lines next to Albums and choose how they're organized. The Gallery has a lot of smarts built into it, because it can automatically show you just photos of people, scenery, pets, vehicles, and so on

---

TIP If you use photos a lot, drag the Gallery icon to your Home screen (page 32).

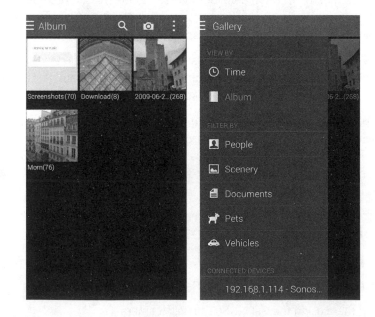

2. **Tap any of the albums.** The screen fills with thumbnails of photos in the album. You can view the thumbnails, as well as entire albums and individual photos, either vertically or horizontally. Just turn the phone in the direction you wish to view them.

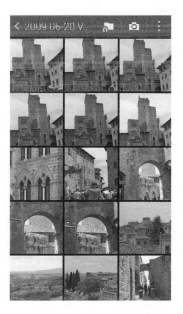

3. Tap the photo you want to view.

The phone displays the photo on its big, beautiful screen. Now you can see why you wanted the Galaxy S5—that extra screen real estate pays off when viewing photos.

A variety of buttons appear onscreen for a moment or two, and then disappear. Tap the photo to make them appear again.

NOTE Depending on the photo's length-to-width ratio, it may not fill the entire screen. If it doesn't, you'll see black space along the sides or at the top and bottom.

4. Tap the arrow button at the top left ◀ and you move up a level in the Gallery. Keep tapping the arrow on subsequent screens to get all the way to the top. The button to its right lets you show pictures from the gallery onto another device on your network. Tap the button and choose from any compatible devices. Tap the Share button ◀ and you share your photos in many different ways, from email to text messaging, via Bluetooth, using social media, and more. The exact ways you can share will vary according to what apps you've got on your S5.

The next button is a trash icon and will delete the photo. Next comes the Camera button . Tap it to launch the camera to take photos or videos. (You'll learn how to do both later in this chapter.) The final button, the menu button , has a whole lot of features—so many that there's an entire section devoted to it. Go to page 123 for details.

Look down at the bottom of the screen when the icons appear on the photo. You'll see thumbnails of all the photos in the album you're viewing. Tap any thumbnail, and you'll jump straight to that photo.

Viewing Pictures

Now that you've got photos on your screen, the fun begins—viewing them in different ways and flicking through them:

- **Zooming** means magnifying a photo, and you've got the power to do that at your fingertips—literally. Double-tap any part of the photo, and you zoom in on that area; double-tap again and you zoom out. You can also use the thumb-and-forefinger spread technique to zoom in more precise increments. Once you've zoomed in this way, you can zoom back out by using the two-finger pinch technique. (Flip back to page 34 for a refresher on all these techniques.)

- **Panning** means to move the photo around the screen after you've zoomed in, so you can see different areas. Use your finger to drag the photo around. As with zooming, panning works the same whether you're holding the phone horizontally or vertically.

- **Rotating** means to turn your phone 90 degrees so it's sideways. When you do so, the photo rotates and fills the screen using the new orientation. This technique is especially useful when you have a horizontal photo that looks small when your S5 is in its normal vertical position. Rotate the phone and, like magic, the picture rotates and fills the screen properly. Similarly, if you're viewing a vertical picture while holding the phone horizontally, simply rotate the phone 90 degrees, and your photo rotates as well.

- **Flicking** advances you to the next or previous photo in your list. Flick from right to left to view the next photo, and from left to right to view the previous one.

Tagging Faces in Photos

ONE OF THE NIFTIEST things you can do on social media sites such as Facebook is to share *tagged* photos of yourself, family, and friends. It's a great way to share. In any photos on the S5 with pictures of people's faces, you can identify the people in the photo by name—that is, tag them. Then, when you put the photo up on a social media site, people can see the names of the people in the photos. More amazingly, people who've been tagged in the photos get a notification that a tagged photo of them is available, and they can then view it.

Tagging photos is easy, but first you have to turn the feature on. In the Gallery, whether you're looking at an individual photo or an album, tap the Menu button and select Settings. At the bottom of the screen, tap the box next to "Face tag" so it turns green. Now open a photo as you would normally, and then tap it. Boxes appear around the faces of every person in the photo. The S5 will then do some photo magic and automatically tag any people whose faces it knows—for example, you. For other faces, tap "Add name" and then follow the onscreen instructions for tagging the person.

That's all it takes. Now when you and your friends look at photos on your favorite social media site, you'll be able to remember who's who.

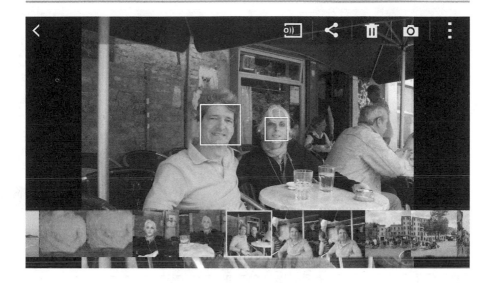

More Photo Options

WHEN YOU'RE VIEWING A photo, you've got even more options available when you tap the Menu button:

- **Edit.** Gives you a solid set of tools for editing photos, including dropping, rotating, changing colors, adding effects, and more. You can also add some cool effects—see the box on the next page.

- **More info.** Shows you all kinds of details about the photo. You'll find the size, resolution, time it was taken, focal length, exposure time, and much more. The first screen you come to gives only the basics, such as the date the photo was taken, the location where it was taken, and any tags associated with it. Tap Details at the bottom of the screen and prepare to be overwhelmed with more technical details about the photo than you've ever imagined.

- **Copy to Clipboard.** Does just what it says: Copies the entire photo to the Clipboard so you can paste it somewhere, like into an email.

- **Rotate left.** Rotates the photo 90 degrees to the left.

- **Rotate right.** Rotates the photo 90 degrees to the right.

- **Crop.** Lets you cut away part of the photo.

- **Rename.** Lets you give the photo a new, more descriptive name.

- **Slideshow.** Runs an onscreen slideshow of the photos in your current album or view. You can choose transitions between slides, choose music to accompany the show, adjust how long each photo should display, and choose whether to show the oldest photo first or the newest one first.

Edit Away

The S5 gives you surprisingly powerful photo-editing tools right on the phone. They're worth checking out. True, they're not up to the level of a high-powered, expensive piece of software like Photoshop, but you can't beat free. And with each iteration of the software they've gotten more and more powerful, so if you've tried a previous version—or never tried them at all—you owe it to yourself to check out the tools you've got.

For a start, there's a great auto-enhance feature that first appears when you open the editor. Just tap and it does its magic, adjusting the brightness, colors, and so on. If you're looking for a no-muss, no-fuss way to fix your photos, auto-enhance is a great place to start.

If you prefer digging right in and doing the work yourself, tap the X button at upper right. You can rotate, crop, and resize any photo. The Rotate tool is surprisingly robust. Tap it and you can rotate the photo to the right or left, as well as flip it horizontally or vertically.

The Tone tool gives you eight ways to edit the color—adjusting the brightness, the contrast, the color saturation, and so on. And there are tools for adding special effects like sepia, grayscale, negative, fisheye, engraving, and more. The Portrait tool focuses on face fixes like removing red eye, brightening, and so on. You can even draw right on the image and add extras like stickers and frames.

- **Set as.** This nifty choice lets you do lots of things with the photo, such as setting it as your Home or Lock screen, or as a contact photo. Make your choice, and you can then crop the section of the photo you want to use. The S5 does the rest.

Working with Multiple Photos

IN THE PREVIOUS SECTION, you learned about ways to work with individual photos. But what if you want to work with multiple photos at once—delete them, share them, and so on? On the S5, it's easy.

When you're viewing photos in an album, by time, or other grouping, tap the Menu button and then tap Select. Double-headed arrows appear on each photo. Tap the photos you want to select—a green checkmark appears on them.

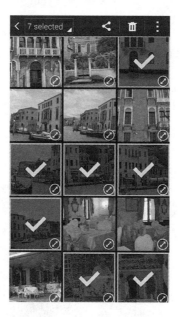

When you select photos, the top of the screen displays the number of photos you've selected. Tap that top box, and on the screen that appears you can select all the photos, or deselect them all. To deselect individual ones, tap the checkmark, and it goes away.

Now you can perform actions on the photos you've selected. At the top of the screen are the usual buttons for sharing them and deleting them. You get many of the choices that you get when you are looking at an individual photo—see page 123 for details. But you also get a few others:

When you tap Details, you'll see information about all the photos you've selected, including how many items you've chosen and the dates of the first and last photos taken.

- **Copy.** Lets you copy them to a different album.

- **Move to album.** Lets you move them to a different album.

- **Add to event.** Adds the photos to an event.

- **Studio.** Launches the Studio app that lets you create collages, make video clips, trim videos, and more.

- **Slideshow.** Creates a slideshow out of the selected photos. You get to choose the transition effects, apply filters to the photos, and add music.

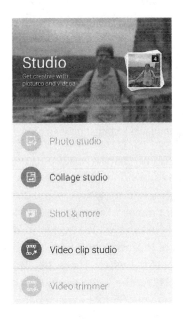

Videos in the Gallery

THE WAY YOU VIEW and work with videos in the Galaxy S5 is essentially identical to the way you work with photos, with a few minor differences:

- **You can spot videos in the Gallery** by the right-facing triangles on their thumbnails.

- **Rotate your S5 by 90 degrees** when you're viewing videos, since they're usually taken with a horizontal orientation (as are the ones you shoot on your S5).

NOTE Do you, a friend, or a loved one suffer from "vertical video syndrome"? This fictitious disease afflicts people who hold their phones vertically when taking videos, which means they will look small and squashed when played the way videos are supposed to be viewed—in horizontal orientation, like on a television or in a movie theater. In June 2012, a tongue-in-cheek public service announcement was uploaded to YouTube warning about this threat. It's received five million views!

- **When you tap a video,** it opens with a right-facing triangle—the Play button. Before you play the video, buttons appear at the top right of the screen to let you share the video with others, trim the video, and delete it. If you tap the Menu button, you'll get a selection of options, including renaming it, creating a slideshow with it, getting details about it, and changing video settings.

NOTE When you tap the video, you may be asked which app you want to use to play it, depending on what apps you have installed on your S5.

- **Tap the triangle to play the video.** When the video starts plays, a circle moves along a progress bar to show where you are in the video. Drag the circle forward or back to move forward or back in the video. Tap the Pause button to pause the video; tap the Play button to start playing it again. You'll also see the total time of the video, and how long the current video has played. You can also mute the video. There are also buttons for playing the video full screen and playing the video on another device, such as a TV. (For details about connecting your S5 to a TV, see page 136.) All the buttons and controls vanish after a few seconds; to bring them back, tap the video.

Here's a handy video feature for multitaskers: Tap the video when it's playing to bring up the player controls, and then tap the small icon on the lower-right side of the screen. The current video plays in a small screen inside the larger screen. That way you can use the Gallery to look at photos, for example, and keep watching the video. Tap the X on the mini video window to close it.

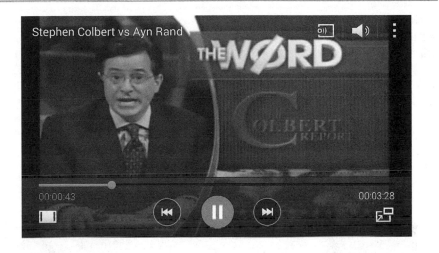

Taking Still Photos

IF YOU'RE USED TO no-frills smartphone cameras that do little more than let you point and shoot grainy, low-resolution photos, you're in for a surprise with the Galaxy S5. It sports a 16-megapixel camera that takes sharp, vivid photos. And it also has a front-facing camera that takes photos at 2.1 megapixels. Although you'll mainly use it for videochats, it's also useful for taking selfies and the S5's great Dual mode feature that lets you take a combined photo with both cameras simultaneously. (See the box on page 133 for details.)

Front-facing camera

Camera

Heart rate sensor with LED light

Camera flash

Fortunately, using the camera is still point-and-shoot simple. Tap the camera icon on the Home screen or Apps screen. Frame your shot on the screen. You can use the camera either in the normal vertical orientation, or turn it 90 degrees for a wider shot. Zoom in by spreading your fingers apart on the screen and zoom back out by pinching them together. Then tap the button on the right side of the screen to take the photograph.

> **TIP** The camera also includes a handy onscreen zoom feature. To zoom in, pinch your fingers together; to zoom out, spread them apart.

You'll hear the familiar snapping sound of a photo being taken. A small thumbnail of your new photo is displayed in the lower-left corner of the viewfinder. Tap it to view the big image. You can zoom in and out of the image by using the normal zoom in and zoom out finger motions.

> **NOTE** When you're not taking pictures, you can also get them onto your S5 by transferring them from your computer. See page 319.

Using the Onscreen Controls

THE CAMERA HAS A variety of convenient onscreen controls.

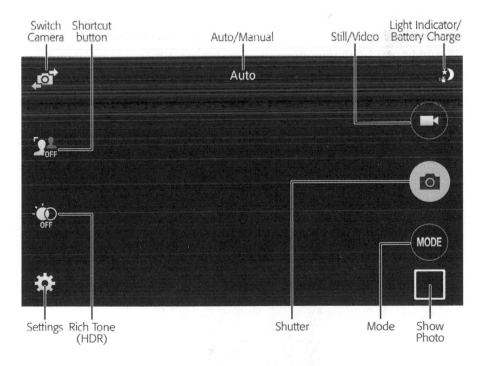

Switch Camera   Shortcut button   Auto/Manual   Still/Video   Light Indicator/ Battery Charge

Settings   Rich Tone (HDR)   Shutter   Mode   Show Photo

- **Switch camera** toggles between the normal camera and the camera facing you. Use the camera facing you for a self-portrait (think of it as the "selfie" button) or during video chats.

- **Shortcut** can be customized, letting you put any of a number of modes and features from the Settings screen on it—for example, face detection or selective focus. The icon that appears here will change according to what mode or feature you've attached to it. Out of the box, it's a shortcut to **Selective focus**, which lets you adjust the focus to make nearby objects stand out from the background.

NOTE For selective focus to work, the focal object must be within 1.5 feet of you and at least three times that distance from the background.

- **Rich tone (HDR)** is a special mode that lets you take multiple photos of the same image or scene, at different exposure levels, and then combine them to create a richer photo with a greater range of tones. It's good for compensating for scenes that are underexposed or overexposed.

- **Settings** lets you choose from a variety of features and modes, including picture stabilization, face detection, selective focus, and more. Tap the Settings button, and then tap the option you want to use. From this screen, you can also add any setting or mode to the Shortcut button—just drag the icon toward the top of the screen and place it on the Shortcut button.

- **Light indicator and battery charge.** If you're in low-light conditions, a low-light indicator appears. A battery icon shows you your current battery level. Typically, if the low-light indicator is on, you won't see the battery icon.

- **Still/Video** lets you choose either the still camera or the video camera.

- **Shutter** snaps the picture.

- **Mode** lets you select from many different modes of taking photos—for sports photos, night photos, panoramas, and more. (For details, see the next section.)

- **Show Photo** shows a strip of other photos you've taken. Tap any to open it.

Challenge to a Dual Shot

The Galaxy S5 lets you take photos of images with your front and back cameras simultaneously. Think of the interesting effects you can come up with—a picture of the band onstage juxtaposed with your own rapt reaction. A picture of the summit that includes you in your climbing gear. Imagine a kind of postcard effect, with a scenic vista as the background (taken with the camera you normally use to take photos), and then an image from the front-facing camera as a stamp.

To use it, select Auto mode and tap the Dual Shot icon—It's an overlapping image of the front and back of the camera symbol. You can play around with choosing borders other than a stamp for the image you take with the front-facing camera. To do so, tap the arrow at the bottom of the screen and choose which one you want to use.

Using Different Modes

THE CAMERA'S PRESET SHOOTING modes represent one of its most powerful features. They automatically take the best pictures for what you're currently shooting. Tap the Mode button to see them all. To use them, just follow the onscreen directions. Make sure to play around with them, because you get a number of amazing ones.

- **Auto** mode chooses what the camera thinks are the best settings for the current conditions. For example, on a bright, sunny day, it will adjust to prevent the picture from getting washed out.

- **Beauty face** takes a photo using an airbrushed effect that smooths over what Samsung believes to be facial imperfections. It may not work if the image is too dark.

- **Shot and more** is actually a misnomer — it should be called something like "burst mode features." It puts the camera into burst mode, where it takes a series of photos of a scene automatically one after another and then lets you take a variety of actions on those five photos. For example, the Drama feature creates a truly striking effect. It lets you take a series of photos of a moving subject and then merges them into a single shot with multiple images showing the movement over time. Or you can select the best one and have the rest of the photos deleted. (For more advice on using Drama mode, see the box on the next page.)

- **Panorama** mode lets you stitch together a panorama from multiple photos so that you'll literally get the big picture.

- **Virtual tour** does what the name says: Lets you take multiple photos and stitch them together to create a virtual tour.

- **Dual camera** lets you take photos with your front and back cameras simultaneously. See the box on page 133 for details.

- **Download** lets you download even more modes to use on your camera, such as "Sound & shot" mode, which lets you add a few seconds of background sound to a picture, and Sports mode for taking pictures of fast movements, so that rather than showing a blur of motion, your photos will be crisp. (You'll need to sign into your Samsung account before downloading.)

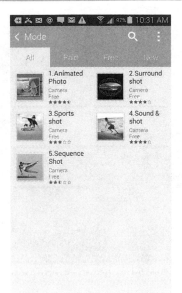

Drama Mode

Drama mode, one of the "Shots and more" options, is a bit hard to describe, but once you get the hang of it, you may get hooked. Turn it on, and the S5's camera takes a continuous set of frames of a location for about 5 seconds—for example, your daughter doing a handstand. The S5 detects the person moving in the photos and stitches together multiple pictures of the person against the static background, so you see the person's movements over time in a single photo. Sort of a time-lapse effect.

To get the best results with Drama mode, you need to make sure that the person in the frame isn't too large or too small, and that she doesn't move too slowly or too quickly. But it should take you only a few minutes to get it right. Once you do, you may never stop playing with it.

Taking Video

TO TAKE THE VIDEO, tap the camera/video button at upper right. The video immediately starts recording. At the upper left, a red button with the word REC appears, and a number next to it tells you how much time in your video-taking has elapsed. At the upper right, a number tells you how much memory the video is taking up as you shoot.

The Pause button lets you discontinue recording. You can zoom in and out in the same way that you can with the still camera, by pinching or spreading your fingers, or using the volume buttons.

NOTE If you want to change video options, such as using a video stabilizer, you can't do it from video mode. Instead, you have to switch back to the still camera and select your options, as outlined on page 132.

Playing S5 Video on Your TV

THE S5 INCLUDES A somewhat secret feature that you might find extremely useful: You can play video from it on your TV. And it's not just video you can play there. You can also display photos on your TV and even play games on your S5 and see them on your TV. In fact, anything that you see on your S5, you can send over to your TV.

To do it, you rig up a way to connect your S5 to a TV. Alternatively, if you have a Samsung TV, you may be able to connect wirelessly.

Connecting to the TV by Cable

First, you need to buy a special cable from Samsung, an HDTV HDMI adapter. (You can get it from Amazon at this URL: *http://www.amazon.com/Samsung-MHL-2-0-HDTV-Adapter/dp/B00BTCPQ5C*. To buy it elsewhere, just look for

Samsung's part number ET-H10FAUWEGWW.) Then buy an HDMI cord, available from any electronics store or online. Now follow these steps:

1. Plug one end of the HDMI cord into the HDTV HDMI adapter. (Only one end of the adapter fits.)

2. Plug the other end of the HDMI cable into your TV.

3. If you want your S5 to get external power while you're using it with your TV, connect your S5's power charger to the HDTV HDMI adapter, and then connect the power charger to a power source. (Note: This step isn't required, but it'll prevent losing power in the middle of watching a long video.)

4. Plug the HDTV HDMI adapter into the port where you normally plug your power charger—at the bottom of the S5.

5. On your TV, switch the input to the HDMI port where you've just plugged in the HDTV HDMI adapter. You should now see whatever is on your S5 mirrored onto your TV.

This method generally provides better audio quality than a wireless connection, and you also won't tend to experience laggy video. On the other hand, your S5 will have to be near enough to your TV so the wires reach.

Connecting to a Samsung TV Wirelessly

This method works only if you have a specific kind of Samsung TV—called a Smart TV. Even then, setting up a wireless connection is a bit dicier. In theory, you merely need to change a setting on your S5 and, like magic, its screen gets mirrored to your nearby TV. But practice rarely works as well as theory. Suffice it to say that you shouldn't go buy a Smart TV just for this one purpose. And if you do, double-check the documentation to ensure that it will work.

Say you do have the right Samsung TV. On the S5, tap Settings from the Apps screen, scroll to the Connect and Share section, and tap Screen Mirroring. Make sure it is turned on. When you turn it on, your S5 automatically looks around, searching for a device that will let it do screen mirroring. Your TV will show up on the list. Tap it and you'll be mirroring what's on your S5 onto your TV.

Using Your S5 as a Universal Remote

THERE'S ONE MORE PIECE of TV magic your S5 can perform—you can use it as a universal remote to control your TV, streaming music player, and more. It's not always easy to do, and it may not work at all, but it's worth a shot.

To do it, tap the Smart Remote icon in the Apps screen. You'll go through a series of setup screens: choosing your country and Zip code, personalizing the kinds of content you like to watch, and so on. It takes only a minute or two.

Now that you've done that, it's time to pair your S5 with your TV and cable box. Tap the remote icon in the top right and select your TV brand. Then tap the onscreen power button to check whether the remote works with your TV. If it does, tap Yes. If not, tap No, and you'll test the next potential code for connecting the Smart Remote to your TV.

If no codes work, you're out of luck. However, if you manage to make the connection to your TV, you may be able to select the manufacturer of your set-top box. You'll go through the same procedure as you did for connecting to your TV. If it works, you'll not only be able to use it as a remote, but take advantage of extra features as well. For example, you can use the Smart Remote guide rather than your TV guide for finding what you want to watch, you can stream from your Netflix account, and plenty more.

You'll learn to:

- Use Google Maps to map anything

- Fly around the world with Google Earth

- Get directions for walking, driving, biking, and for public transportation

- Use the GPS with turn-by-turn navigation

CHAPTER 6

Maps and Navigation

WHAT'S THE MOST-USED SMARTPHONE feature these days? Quite possibly maps and navigation. And they can do much more than show you where you are or how to drive to your next destination. They can help you find a great nearby restaurant, pull up the fastest route to your friend's house via public transportation, show you which highways are clogged with traffic, and more.

Google Maps

GOOGLE MAPS ON THE Galaxy S5 is the mobile version of the renowned Google Maps website (*http://maps.google.com*). In fact, the S5's Maps app is even more powerful than the web version, since it can incorporate GPS information.

Type any address or point of interest in the U.S.—or in many places all over the world—and you see a map. You can choose a street map, an aerial satellite photo, or a combination of the two (more on that on page 143).

But don't settle for looking around. You can also find nearby businesses, points of interest, and traffic congestion. Maps also offers turn-by-turn directions, even including public transportation in some cities. There are even bike-friendly maps.

Browsing Google Maps

Tap the Maps icon on a pane or in the Apps screen, and Google Maps launches. At first launch, if it finds your location, it will show a map of your neighborhood, with a pointer to your location. If it can't find you, you'll likely see a map of the United States, but you can work your way down to street level.

Navigate the map by dragging or flicking. Rotate the map's orientation by putting your thumb and second or third finger on the map and twisting. Zoom in by spreading your thumb and your second or third finger or tapping twice with a finger. Zoom out by pinching your fingers or by tapping the screen once with two fingers (the amazing two-finger tap).

> **NOTE** If you've turned on GPS (page 19), instead of displaying a map of the United States, Google Maps locates you and displays a map of your current location.

As you zoom in on the map, you'll see locations of interest—museums, libraries, schools, parks, restaurants, and so on. Tap any, and a balloon appears over it, and at the bottom of the screen you see information about it, including ratings if people have reviewed it. There's also an icon of a car that you can tap to get driving directions to it.

Tap the balloon or the description at the bottom of the screen, and you get a lot more details, including a Street View photo of the location (if available), photos people have taken, and more. You can also call the establishment, read (and write) reviews, get directions, search for nearby businesses, and so on. For even more details, swipe up from the bottom of the screen, and a screen full of information about the location appears over the map. Swipe back down to return to the map.

> **NOTE** Google frequently updates its Maps app. The Maps app described here is the latest version as of the writing of this book. So if you have an older or newer version of Maps, it may vary from what you see here.

Changing Your View

Just being able to zoom in and out of a map down to the street level, or all the way out to the continent level, is pretty cool, but you have still more view options, which Google Maps calls *layers*. A layer is a specific type of view, or information superimposed over a view. To change a view to a different layer, look down at the bottom left of the screen for a small vertical rectangle with three lines inside it. Swipe that rectangle to the right. A menu swoops in from the left that shows you a bunch of choices, including a satellite view, a real-time traffic map, a link to Google Earth (more on that on page 147) and so on. Your current view will be highlighted with a dark band. To switch to any other view, tap it.

The satellite view, unsurprisingly, is an actual satellite photo of the location. Layered on top of it is the normal Google map, making it easy to see streets, street names, and landmarks. As you zoom in, the photo may at first appear blurry, and it may take a little while for the image to resolve itself, so be patient.

NOTE The layers on Google Maps sometimes change, as Google adds new information, and as it makes deals with other companies to add their layers. So check layers often to see what new things Google has in store.

Traffic

The map can show you how bad the traffic is on highways and major metropolitan thoroughfares. Turn on the Traffic layer and, where available, the app indicates traffic congestion with the following color coding:

- **Green** means the traffic is flowing very nicely—at least 50 miles per hour.

- **Yellow** indicates slower-moving traffic, between 25 and 50 miles per hour.

- **Red** means a traffic jam; avoid it if you can. It means that traffic is moving at less than 25 miles per hour.

Make sure to look for icons on the map, such as a symbol of a man at work, or of a car accident. Tap any of the symbols, and you get more information about it.

NOTE You can help Google get more accurate information about traffic in your area. Before you start driving, turn on GPS. That way, your phone sends information about your location and driving speed (anonymously) to Google, which then uses it to help figure out the current traffic conditions.

Google Earth

For a truly awesome piece of mapping technology, check out the Google Earth layer. Google Earth lets you fly over anywhere on the planet in full, realistic 3D. It uses satellite photography, so you can virtually visit realistic pictures of anywhere on earth. Want to visit the Colosseum in Rome, the Grand Canyon in Arizona, the Taj Mahal in India? You can do that and more. It also integrates with Google Maps so that you can overlay street names on top of satellite maps. There are even built-in "tour guides" to take you on tours of many places on earth. Make sure to look at the bottom of the screen for a small tab. If it's there, pull it up. You'll see photos of interesting places to visit. Tap any to see a video tour of it.

> **NOTE** Google Earth is a companion app to Google Maps and may not be preinstalled on your S5. If it's not, then the first time you tap that layer to use it, you'll be sent to Google Play to download and install it.

Street View

Street View is a full, 360-degree panoramic, photographic view of streets and an entire area—an entire city, if you like. Street View is a great way to plan, for example, a walking tour of downtown Boston. (Make sure to visit the State House and its golden dome on top of Beacon Hill if you head there.)

To use Street View, hold your finger on any location on a map, until the address appears at the bottom of the screen. Pull up the location from the bottom and select Street View. Once you're in Street View, drag and flick to move around to change your view, or explore nearby streets.

More Layers

As Google updates Maps, it continually adds (and sometimes takes away) layers, so you'll find plenty of layers to try out. Transit Lines shows public transportation on the map, and Bicycling shows bike paths.

Layers also change depending on how you use Google Maps. If you use Google Maps to find businesses (see page 152), it puts listings of businesses you've viewed online in layers. And if you've searched maps, it lists those searches as well, so you can quickly relaunch the search directly from layers.

The Compass Button

See that compass button on the bottom-right corner of the screen? It's a magic find-me button. If you're looking at a map that isn't your current location—for example, if you're in Boston and you're looking at a map of San Francisco—just tap the compass, and it shows a map of your current location, with an indicator in the center of the map showing where you are. So if you're viewing a map of a place halfway across the world, you can always tap this button to go to your current location.

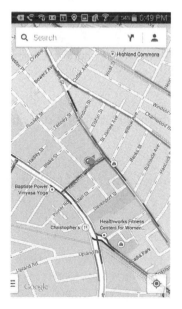

For even more magic, if you're already looking at a map of your current location and tap the compass, it becomes a *live* compass so you can see the direction in which you're viewing your map. Not only that, but you can also tilt your Galaxy S5, and the map orientation follows the direction of the tilt.

How the Galaxy S5 Finds Your Location

Google Maps' usefulness really comes into play when it's combined with the S5's ability to find your location. The phone finds where you are in one of three ways:

- **GPS.** The S5's built-in GPS chip works just like the one in a Garmin or TomTom, although it's not quite as accurate. (Hey, those devices do *only* GPS, not phone calls or games, so cut your phone some slack.) GPS works best when you have a good view of the sky. If not, the S5 switches to one of the other two location methods.

- **WiFi positioning.** The phone's WiFi chip can do more than just connect you to a WiFi network—it can also help determine your location. It does this by using information (from a large database) about WiFi networks near you. Then, using the information about the WiFi locations and your distance from them, it calculates your location. It's not as accurate as GPS, but it still works pretty well.

- **Cellular triangulation.** If GPS or WiFi positioning doesn't do the trick, then the S5 calculates your location based on how close you are to various cell-phone towers near you. It's not as accurate as GPS or WiFi positioning, but it's nice as a backup.

TIP GPS and WiFi can use up a lot of juice from your battery. When you don't need them, turn them off.

Now that you know how the Galaxy S5 finds you, it's time to tell it to do its tricks.

You'll need to tell the S5 to find your location if you're going to use any of its location-based services, such as giving you turn-by-turn directions. Doing it is simplicity itself: As explained earlier, tap the compass button in the lower right. Google displays a blinking blue arrow to show your location.

NOTE If the Galaxy S5 is not exactly sure about your precise location, it draws a blue circle around the blinking arrow, to show that you may be anywhere inside that location. The larger the circle, the less certainty Google has about your location.

As you walk, drive, bicycle, or move in some other way, the blue arrow moves as well. The arrow changes direction to show the direction in which you're moving.

Searching Maps

Google Maps makes it easy for you to search for a business or other location. Given that Google is the premier search site on the Internet, would you expect anything less?

To search, tap the Search button at the top of the screen, and then type your search term into the search box that appears at the top. When Maps finds what you're looking for, it displays the location and shows a little pushpin in it.

There are countless ways to search the maps. Here are some of the most common:

- **Address.** Just type an address, including the state or Zip code. Don't bother with commas, and most of the time you can skip periods as well. You can use common abbreviations. So, if you type *157 w 57 ny ny*, you'll do a search for 157 West 57th Street, New York City, New York.

- **Intersection.** Type, for example, *massachusetts ave and cogswell cambridge ma*, and Google Maps displays the location at the intersection of Massachusetts Avenue and Cogswell Avenue in Cambridge, Massachusetts.

- **City.** Type, say, *san francisco ca*, and you'll see that city.

- **Zip code.** Type any Zip code, such as *02140*.

Cambridge, MA 02140

As you enter search terms, Google Maps displays a likely list of matching results. You can speed up entering your search by choosing from the right search term when it appears, rather than tapping in the entire address.

- **Point of interest.** Type *central park*, *boston common frog pond*, or *washington monument*, for example.

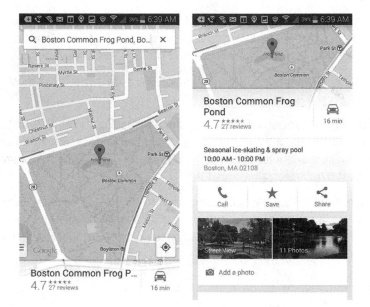

- **Airport code.** If you know the three-letter code, you can type, for example, *sfo* for the San Francisco International Airport, or *bos* for Boston's Logan Airport.

When Maps finds the location, it marks it with a pushpin and shows the address at the bottom of the screen. Pull the address up from the bottom of the screen to get more details about it.

Finding Businesses and Contacts

GOOGLE MAPS CAN EASILY find local businesses. Any business that you can find with a Google search, Maps can find, too. But Maps can also find the home and business addresses of your friends, which it does by tying into your Contacts list.

M.F. Dulock Pasture-Rai...
3 reviews · $$$ 4 min

If you want to search for a business near your current location or any other place, first navigate to the area where you're looking for businesses. Then do a search for the kind of business you're looking for—restaurants, for example. What happens next depends on your search results. You may see icons representing all the businesses matching your search. And it also may put a pin on the one closest to you, with details about it at the bottom of the screen. You may see details about a single result, with a small series of vertical lines next to the search term in the search box. Or the screen may go gray, with a single white circle, and the text "Tap here to see a list of your search results."

To see a list of all matching searches—again, in this example, restaurants—tap the white button, or else tap the series of vertical lines in the search box. You'll see a listing of all matching businesses, including ratings and recommendations from various services or customers of those various services such as Zagat (which Google happens to own). To get more information about any business, tap the listing. Information appears at the bottom of the Maps screen. Pull that information up, and you'll see complete details about the business.

NOTE You may notice that when you search for a business, ads sometimes appear in various locations—for example, at the top of the screen that gives you a business's details. That's one of the ways Google makes money—by selling ads related to your map searches.

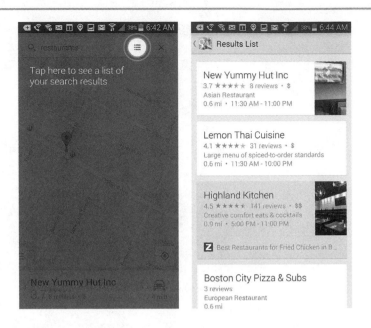

Which details you get vary according to what the business is and what information Google has about it. For restaurants and other businesses that have been reviewed by Zagat, for example, you'll get a detailed review. For a restaurant, you'll also see an overall rating; cost; and category ratings for food, decor, and service. There may be photos of the restaurant, and you can also upload photos yourself.

All businesses have three buttons associated with them: Call, Save, and Share. Tapping Call takes you to the S5's phone app and places the call. Tap Save, and the Save star turns gold. You also see the star on the map, in gold. From that point on, whenever you're using Maps, you'll see the gold stars of all businesses you want to visit again, right onscreen. Tap the star, and you see the description of the business in the usual way. To take away the star, when you're viewing its description, tap the gold star to turn it back to blue. Tap Share, and you can share information about the business via email, Bluetooth, chat, and other means. Next to the name of the business, you'll see an icon of a car. Tap it, and you get turn-by-turn directions to the business by foot, car, bicycle, or public transportation.

Locating the address of your friend's home or business is easy. You can do it, though, only if the address is in your Contacts list. In Maps, search for the friend's name. If you have an address for the friend, it appears in the search results. Tap it, and you'll see the location on a map.

You can also do it straight from the Contacts list. Find the person in your Contacts list (see page 75 for details). Next to the person's address or addresses, you see a small pushpin icon. Tap the pushpin to go to the location on Google Maps, complete with another pushpin.

Getting Directions

YOU'VE HEARD THE OLD cliché: Ask a Maine resident for directions, and the answer is inevitably, "Can't get there from here." Fortunately, Google Maps is much more helpful. Ask it the same question, and you get to choose how you want to get there: driving, walking, biking, or public transportation. Google provides directions for all four, or as many as it can find. (Not all types of directions are available to all places, but you'll have more choices in major metropolitan areas.)

You can get directions in many places throughout Maps, and throughout the Galaxy S5, because that capability is embedded very deep in the phone. So expect to find directions in many different places; for example, when you search for a business, find the location, and look at the page that gives you information about the business.

One surefire way to get directions anywhere in Maps: Tap the Directions icon just to the right of the search box at the top of Google Maps. A screen appears with a starting point, possible destination points, and icons for finding directions via car, public transportation, bicycle, and on foot. You'll also see a list of places you've just been to or searched for.

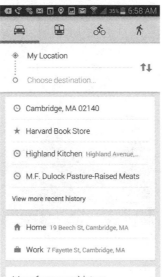

If the S5 knows your current location, it uses that as the starting point and puts the words "My Location" in the starting point box. If you want a different starting point, tap My Location and then type an address into the text box that appears.

Next, choose your destination. Either choose from the list of recent searches and locations or tap "Choose destination" and type where you want to go. Once you've set the starting point and destination, you're ready to go. Tap which kind of directions you want. Next you'll see one of two things, either a map with the directions in blue, or else a list of various options for getting there, each showing the amount of time it will take, the distance in miles, whether there's traffic, and the main routes you'll use. To choose one of the routes, tap it. You'll see a map with the directions laid out. Pull up the directions from the bottom of the screen to see the turn-by-turn directions. This example uses driving directions, but the other types of directions work much the same way. You can scroll through the entire list of directions. To zoom in on a specific section of the route, tap it on the direction list.

Tap the arrow buttons to get to the previous or next driving instructions. You can also return to your master list of instructions by tapping the S5's Back button. In this way, you can switch back and forth between your overall directions and your current one. When you're looking at the list of overall directions, tap any instruction, and you'll see a closeup of the directions on the map.

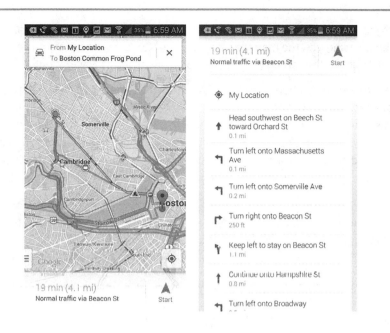

Turn-by-Turn Navigation

GETTING TURN-BY-TURN DIRECTIONS IS helpful, but the Galaxy S5 offers something even more powerful—turn-by-turn navigation, just like the GPS gizmos made by Garmin and TomTom.

To use it, when you've typed in your location and final destination and are on the screen showing you the map view of your directions, tap the Start button at the bottom right of the screen (or, in the Apps screen, select Navigation).

You've turned your phone into a full-blown GPS navigator, complete with the usual annoying robot-like female voice. But it does the job. It tracks your location as you drive and displays it on a map. When you're approaching a turn, it tells you what to do ahead of time. It shows you all the information you need, including distance to your next turn, current location, time to your destination, and more. So forget buying that $300 GPS unit—it's built right into the S5.

NOTE The turn-by-turn navigator requires your GPS to be turned on. You don't need your GPS turned on if you want to get normal directions on Google Maps, though.

Turn-by-turn navigation includes lots of other nice features. Want to avoid highways or avoid tolls when you drive? Press the Menu key while you're in the Navigation app and select Options. You can choose to avoid either or both.

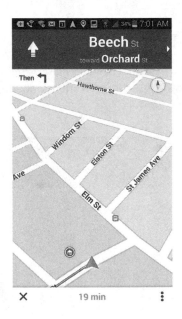

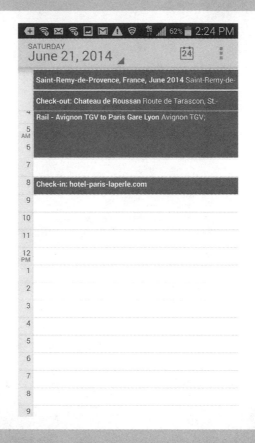

You'll learn to:

- Use different calendar views
- Create new appointments
- Accept an invitation
- Use multiple calendars
- Sync your calendar with Outlook

CHAPTER 7

Calendar

OF ALL THE WAYS you can use your Galaxy S5 to keep track of your life, the calendar may be the most important. Need to remember the meeting this afternoon, the dinner date tonight, the tennis game tomorrow morning? Forget paper-based calendars—the S5 puts them to shame.

Better still, the Galaxy S5's calendar is actually Google's Calendar, so whether you're looking at your calendar on your phone or on your PC, you see the exact same thing, because the S5 syncs with Google Calendar. So no matter where you are, you know where you need to be today, tomorrow, and beyond.

Using the Calendar

TO RUN THE CALENDAR, tap the calendar icon in the Apps screen...well, things aren't quite that easy. The S5 comes with two calendar apps. One is the true-blue Google Calendar, and that's the calendar you'll read about in this chapter. The other, with a green icon, is a calendar from Samsung. The Samsung calendar can sync with Google Calendar, so they can work together. (For more information on the differences between the two calendar apps, see the box on page 163.)

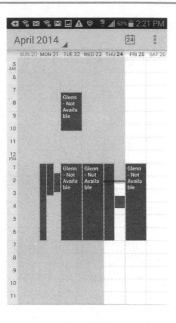

When you tap the calendar, it immediately opens. You're looking at events from Google Calendar, so if you're already using Google Calendar, you see your appointments instantly. If you've never used Google Calendar, you see a blank calendar.

You should see the most up-to-date calendar information on your S5, because it syncs with Google Calendar on the Web. Syncing means that not only will your S5 calendar grab the latest information from your Google Calendar on the Web, but when you make any changes to your calendar on the S5, Google Calendar gets updated with that information as well.

If you have more than one calendar in Google Calendar, you can see information from all calendars in one unified view.

NOTE When you first set up your phone, you either chose to set it up with an existing Google account or create a new one. If you set it up with an existing account, your Galaxy S5 calendar automatically syncs with your existing Google Calendar and displays all its events. If you created a new account, you start with a blank Google Calendar.

Calendar Views

There are four different ways you can look at your calendar, all within easy reach: Day, Week, Month, and Agenda. To get to any of them, tap the triangle to the right of the date on the top left of the screen.

Google Calendar vs. Samsung Calendar

On your S5, you've got a choice of which calendar to use, the Samsung Calendar or Google Calendar. This book strongly recommends going with Google, for several reasons. Perhaps most important is the fact that Google Calendar has become a standard for working with others, and using the same calendar that coworkers, family, and friends use is a big plus. Although the two calendars sync automatically, there's a lag when you use the Samsung Calendar rather than the Google Calendar, which could prove problematic if you need to update your events with others quickly.

In addition, Google Calendar is designed to work with all of Google's services—not just today's services, but tomorrow's as well. There's no guarantee how well the Samsung Calendar will work with all of Google's services, including future ones.

Google Calendar is one of Google's most important services, and so Google spends plenty of time adding new features. But calendaring is far from being one of Samsung's most important services, so it's not as likely that Samsung will update it as frequently as Google updates its calendar.

One final note: Google Calendar may not be on your S5 when you first run it. Each cellphone provider decides which apps go on and which don't. So if it's not on yours, head to Google Play and download it.

Here's what each does:

- **Day.** Tap here to see the calendar for the day you've highlighted, arranged by hour. Flick up and down to go through all hours of the day. Swipe your finger to the left or right to see the next day's calendar or the previous day's calendar.

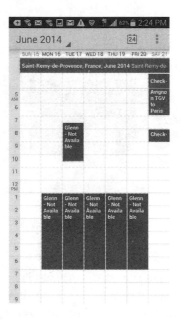

- **Week.** Here you get a weekly view. Swipe left or right to see the next week or previous week, and flick up and down to see later or earlier in the day.

- **Month.** This view shows you the entire current month. Horizontal colored bars indicate appointments and events, and show you their duration. Flick up and down to see the next or previous month.

- **Agenda.** This scrolling view displays a list of all your events and appointments, not just for today or this week or next month, but years into the future, and years back in the past. It's a great way to see what's on the horizon or to get an overview of where your time is going. Scroll through them all by flicking. To see the details of any event or appointment, tap it, and the appointment opens.

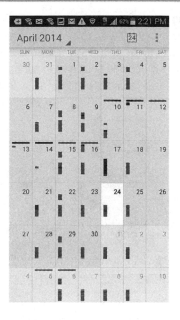

Making an Appointment

There are two ways to create an appointment (which Calendar calls an *event*):

- **In Month, Week, or Day view,** hold your finger on the time you want to make an appointment. Then tap "New event" and follow the instructions.

NOTE When you run the Galaxy S5 calendar, you're not actually looking at Google Calendar on the Web. Instead, the Galaxy S5 calendar syncs with Google Calendar on the Web, but holds the information in the Galaxy S5 itself. So if you're in an area without reception, and you've previously updated Google Calendar on the Web but not yet synced it to your phone's calendar, the S5 calendar won't have any information you added since the last sync.

- **In any view,** tap the small button with three dots on the upper right of the screen, and tap "New event."

In some instances, like when you create a new event from the Month view, you only need to fill in a name. In other instances, like when you create a new event from the Day view, a much more detailed form pops up, with plenty of information to fill in:

- **Event name.** Type a name for the event.

- **Location.** Tap here and enter the location for the event. As you type, Calendar looks in your address book for places that match the location as you're typing. That way you don't have to type an entire address. Type part of it, and then pick from the list.

- **From and To.** Tap this to choose the starting and ending times.

- **Time Zone.** Choose your time zone.

- **Guests.** Type in the name or names of the people you're inviting. As you type, the Calendar looks in your Contacts to find matching names. Select any that match to cut down on your typing.

- **Description.** What will you be doing? Having lunch? Meeting with your accountant? Skydiving? Tap in a description. If you're inviting other people, keep in mind that the invitation will be sent to them, so make the description clear (and keep it clean).

- **Repetition.** Will this be a one-time event or one that repeats? If it repeats, the calendar gives you a lot of flexibility about how to choose that. You can choose an event to repeat every day at the same time, every weekday at that time, once a week at that time and day of the week, monthly, or even yearly on that date. And there are more options as well.

- **Reminders.** After you create the event, the S5 can flash reminders before the event, letting you know that it's about to happen. You can choose how far in advance to send the reminder, in any increment you want. Create as many reminders as you like by tapping the "Add reminder" button and filling in the details.

    When you set a reminder time, you get a notification in the Notification panel when the time comes. Tap it to see the full reminder details. You can then Snooze the reminder so it'll disappear, and then pop up later according to what interval you've set. Or you can dismiss it, which means it will vanish forever, never to be heard from again.

    To get even more event details, tap the reminder, and you see who organized the appointment, who will be attending, the time, and the reminder interval. You can also accept the invitation, decline it, or tentatively accept it.

- **Show me as.** This option lets you choose whether you appear to be available or not, if someone else wants to schedule you for an event held at the same time. Unless you change the default setting, the calendar assumes that you're not available—after all, you're already attending an event. But you can choose to make yourself available. For example, you may want to schedule an event for yourself tentatively but be willing to change it in case someone needs to schedule an important appointment with you.

- **Privacy.** Sometimes, you want others to see an event you put on your calendar ("Board meeting"), and other times you won't want them to see it ("Dog grooming"). This option lets you make the event private, so only you can see it, or public, so others in the group calendar can see it.

Now you're ready to save your event. But there's one more thing you can do—color-code it. Tap the small icon of the palette near the top of the screen and, from the colors that appear, choose one.

When you've done all that—and don't worry, it goes a lot faster than it sounds—tap the Save button. Your event now shows up on your calendar.

NOTE For more information about using a group calendar and how to set all its options, head to your Google Calendar on the Web: *www.google.com/calendar*.

Getting Notifications about Who Has Accepted

If the appointment you created includes someone else—a dinner companion, let's say—he gets an email, and either accepts the invitation or not. You don't need to do anything to send the email; it gets sent automatically. (All of life should be so easy.) Once someone has accepted, you get a notification, and the acceptance is noted in the calendar.

Editing, Rescheduling, and Deleting Events

To look at one of your appointments, tap it. You see a summary of the appointment, including the date and time, place, attendees, and any reminders you've set. You also see whether attendees have confirmed that they'll attend.

To edit something you've scheduled, tap the Edit button at the top right of the screen. (It looks like a pencil.) You're now at the familiar screen you used to create the event. You can edit everything about the event—name, location, place, duration, and so on. When you're done, tap Save.

Accepting an Invitation

If you're a social kind of guy or gal, you'll not only invite other people to events, but people will also invite you. If they use Google Calendar (or the Samsung calendar), they can use it to invite you to events.

You'll get the invitation by email, and it'll contain all pertinent information about the event, including the time and place, who scheduled it, who else is attending, and so on. Tap "More details" to get still more information. When you do so, you can choose to get more details via either your web browser or the calendar itself. In practice, both options have the same result—they launch your browser and take you to a Google Calendar page showing more details about the event.

Down at the bottom of the screen, you can say whether you're going—Yes, No, or for those unable to commit to anything (you know who you are), Maybe. Tap your response, and you go to a Google Calendar page confirming your choice. There you can write an additional note or change your response. The person creating the event gets notified of your status via email (or Outlook or whatever calendar program she uses).

NOTE   You can accept invitations sent via email not only in your S5's email program, but also via your normal email service. So, for example, if you're a Gmail user, you can accept the invitation on Gmail either on the Web or on your phone.

Calendar and Geolocation

THE GALAXY S5 CALENDAR beats a paper-based one in many ways, and none better than geolocation. When you create an event, send an invitation, or receive one, the S5 turns it into a live link that, when clicked, shows its location in Google Maps—as long as an address is provided, or it's located at a business or landmark such as a restaurant, park, health club, and so on. Tap the Maps link to see it.

So when folks get your event invitation, they can see exactly where to go on Google Maps. And you can use all of Google Maps' capabilities, including getting directions, getting additional information about the business or area, seeing it in Street View, and more. (For more details about using Google Maps on the Galaxy S5, see page 142.)

Working with Multiple Calendars

GOT MORE THAN ONE Google Calendar? You can use them on your Calendar app on the S5 the same way you can use them in Google Calendar on the Web.

Whenever you create a new event, you see a downward-pointing arrow next to your name in the Calendar area at the top of the event screen. Tap the arrow, and you see all your Google Calendars. Tap the calendar where you want the event to appear.

When you look at all your available calendars, you may notice one you don't re-member creating, the Samsung Calendar. That's a calendar created for you automatically if you create a Samsung account (page 22). It's also the main calendar used by Samsung's built-in Calendar app. It syncs automatically with your Google Calendars.

Your calendars are color-coded, so as you look at your schedule, you can see at a glance which calendar each event is on. The color appears just to the left of the event itself.

If you'd like, you can turn off the display of one or more of your calendars. When you're in the calendar, press the Menu button on the upper right of the screen (it looks like three buttons), and then tap "Calendars to display." You see a list of all your calendars, along with the color-coding for each. Next to each calendar is a checkbox. If there's a checkmark next to it, the calendar is visible. If there's no checkmark, it's hidden. To make it visible, turn on the checkbox next to it; to hide it, take the check away. Don't worry: when you hide the calendar, you haven't deleted the calendar itself. You've just hidden it.

You can't change which calendar automatically appears in the Calendar area when you create a new event—it's the same one every time. So even if you choose a different calendar to create an event, the next time you create a new event, that first calendar is the one that automatically shows up. The same holds true for Google Calendar on the Web. Whichever calendar you created first is the calendar that automatically shows up.

Calendars to sync

More Calendar Options

TAP THE MENU BUTTON, at the top of the screen and you'll find a few more options for your calendar:

- **New event.** Tap here to create a new calendar item as described on page 165.

- **Refresh.** In theory, this should sync your calendar with Google Calendar on the Web. In practice...well, it's a bit mysterious what it actually does in practice. You may end up with a blank new event at a random time on the day you're viewing. As the saying goes, your mileage may vary.

- **Search.** This option gives you a nifty way to search your calendar. Tap it and type a search term. As you type, your calendar pulls up matching calendar entries. Select any calendar entry to search your calendar, or type in a different term. The calendar then displays matching results. Tap any calendar entry to go to the event.

- **Calendars to display.** As explained in the previous section, this option lets you decide which calendars to show.

- **Send feedback.** Got a problem or complaint with Google Calendar? Here's a way to get in touch with the folks at Google about it. You may or may not hear back from them. (Still, it's always good to get something off your chest; you'll live longer that way.)

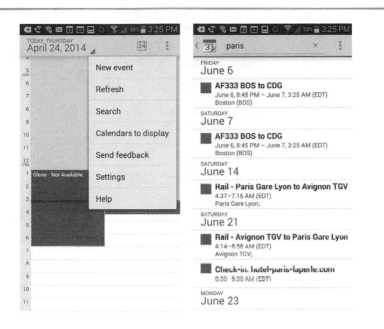

- **Settings.** Settings, settings, and more settings. That's what you'll find here. You'll be able to change settings for all your calendars (choose General settings for that), or for individual calendar accounts (choose an individual calendar account for that). You can also create a new account by tapping "Add account" at the top of the screen.

  General settings control options such as whether to hide events that you or others have declined, which day should display as the first day of the week, whether to receive calendar notifications, whether your phone should ring and vibrate when you get a calendar notification, and so on. The settings for individual accounts are as bare-bones as it gets: You decide whether to show the account or any individual calendars in the account.

NOTE There's a difference between an account and an individual calendar. It's possible to have multiple calendars under a single account. (Confusing, isn't it?) So your main Google account, for example, may have three calendars if you've set up three of them: Work, Home, and Travel. So what's an account? If you have more than one Google account, each is a separate account. And if you've signed up for a Samsung account, that's a separate account as well.

Google Calendar on the Web

THE WEB-BASED VERSION OF Google Calendar lets you set many of the options for your calendar that you can't set on the Galaxy S5. So in your S5's browser, head over to *www.google.com/calendar* to set those options. Sign in, and you'll see a version of Google Calendar on the Web specifically designed to display nicely on the Galaxy S5. You can create new events, but you won't be able to change all the options that you can change if you use your computer to visit; it's somewhat stripped down.

What Happened to Google Tasks?

If you're already a Google Calendar or Gmail user, you may have used Google Tasks, a very simple and very useful way to keep track of all your to-dos. When you use Google Calendar on the Web, your task list appears at the right side of the screen.

But the Tasks feature is nowhere to be found on either the Galaxy S5 calen-

dar, or on the Google Calendar version designed to be viewed on the Web with your phone's browser.

Ah, but that doesn't mean you can't get to it on the S5. You can. It's just that Google has put it somewhere you didn't expect. Go to *http://gmail.com/tasks*. You'll find Google Tasks there, in all its glory.

Google+ Gmail **Calendar** Drive   more

Today   Day   Month   C   +

April 2014   ◀ ▶

S	M	T	W	T	F	S
30	31	1	2	3	4	5
6	7	8	9	10	11	12
13	14	15	16	17	18	19
20	21	22	23	24	25	26
27	28	29	30	1	2	3
4	5	6	7	8	9	10

Wednesday, April 16, 2014   ◀ ▶

	Preston Gralla (TripIt)
All day	**San Francisco, CA, April 2014** San Francisco, CA
	Preston Gralla (TripIt)
12:00 AM	**Drop-off Rental Car: Hertz** 780 McDonnell Road, San Francisco, CA US 94128
	Preston Gralla (TripIt)
12:00 AM	**Drop-off Rental Car: Hertz** 780 McDonnell Road San Francisco (), CA, US Phone Number: 650-624-6600 Fax Number: 650-624-6683
	Preston Gralla (TripIt)

Synchronizing Your Calendar with Outlook

WHEN YOU SET UP your Galaxy S5 calendar, you either hooked it to an existing Google Calendar or you had to create a new one. But not everyone in the world uses Google Calendar. Plenty of people use other calendars—notably, Outlook.

There's no direct way to synchronize your S5 Calendar with Outlook, so you may think you have to manually keep two sets of calendars in sync, by adding and deleting appointments in both places.

You don't—there's a workaround. It's a bit kludgy, but it works. First, synchronize Outlook with Google Calendar on your PC. That way, Google Calendar and Outlook will stay in sync. Then sync your Galaxy S5 with Google Calendar. So you're essentially using Google Calendar as a go-between—it shuttles information between Outlook and your S5.

Here's where things get complicated. In the past, one way to do this calendar two-step was to download the free Google Calendar Sync app and use that to synchronize. Unfortunately, though, Google and Microsoft have been fighting like the Hatfields and McCoys, and so that app no longer works. However, if you use the Google for-pay service called Google Apps, you can use Google Apps Sync for Microsoft Outlook (*https://tools.google.com/dlpage/gappssync*) to do the trick.

An even better bet, if you're willing to pay a little bit of money, is Companion-Link for Google (*www.companionlink.com*). Not only does it sync your calendar, but it also syncs your Outlook contacts with your Gmail contacts, which means you can keep your contacts in sync between your Galaxy S5 and Outlook. You can try it for free for 14 days. If you decide it's worth paying for, it'll cost you $49.95 for a one-time license, or $14.95 per three-month subscription.

> **TIP** Neither of these pieces of software work for syncing Google Calendar with Macs and iCal. However, Google has posted instructions for syncing iCal with Google Calendar at *http://bit.ly/a2if0E.*

Corporate Calendar and Microsoft Exchange

WOULDN'T IT BE NICE if we could all get along? Yes, it would. And wouldn't it be nice if your Outlook calendar at work synced with your Google Calendar? Yes, it would.

Sigh. But it probably won't work...unless it does. That pretty much sums up the confusing state of the conflict between Microsoft and Google when it comes to having their calendaring technology work with each other. Once upon a time, a piece of technology with the daunting name Microsoft Exchange ActiveSync worked with Google Calendar. The IT gods could set it up so that if you used an Outlook calendar at work, you'd be able to view that calendar right on your Android phone (like a Galaxy S5).

Ah, those were the days. Back in early 2013, though, Google stopped supporting Microsoft Exchange ActiveSync. So any company looking to use it for the first time to sync Outlook with Google Calendar is out of luck. However, companies that were already using it may still be able to keep doing so.

Does yours? There's only one way to find out. Call up IT and ask them. Then cross your fingers, follow their instructions, and hope for the best.

The Galaxy S5 Online

CHAPTER 8:

Getting Online: WiFi, 3G/4G, and Mobile Hotspots

CHAPTER 9:

The Web

CHAPTER 10:

Email and Gmail

CHAPTER 11:

Facebook, Twitter, Google+, Chat, and Videochat

CHAPTER 12:

Downloading and Using Apps

You'll learn to:

- Connect to a WiFi network
- Turn your S5 into a WiFi hotspot
- Configure WiFi calling and Download Booster
- Use Airplane mode

Getting Online: WiFi, 3G/4G, and Mobile Hotspots

THE SAMSUNG GALAXY S5 is filled with plenty of cool features, but it really comes to life when you take it online. With it, you've got the whole Internet in your hand—and on a screen larger and more vivid than on other smartphones, along with a blazing fast 4G Internet connection. Whether you need to search, get maps and directions, watch YouTube videos, or do pretty much anything else on the Internet, the Galaxy S5 lets you do it.

But first, of course, you need to get connected. You'll get the rundown on how to do that in this chapter, along with learning about one of the Galaxy S5's more amazing capabilities—the ability to turn into a WiFi hotspot to give computers and other devices an Internet connection.

How the Galaxy S5 Gets Online

WHENEVER IT'S POWERED ON, the Galaxy S5 is ready to hop onto the Internet. Whenever your carrier's high-speed third-generation (3G) network or even faster, state-of-the-art 4G network is available, the phone uses it—you can tell by the symbol in the status bar. The 3G and 4G networks were built for data and the Internet, so you can quickly send and receive good-sized email attachments, download music, watch YouTube videos...pretty much everything Internet.

POLITICS

Obama Spends Another Night Searching Behind White House Paintings For Safes

» Elite Congressman Trained To Kill Legislation In 24 Different Ways

» 4 Senators Mauled During Congressional Tiger Show

» G7 Unable To Get Deposit Back On Shipment Of 'G8 Summer Getaway' T-Shirts

» White House Sends Obama To 3-Day Management Seminar At Washington Marriott

LOCAL

With your carrier's 3G or 4G coverage, you'll be able to hitch a ride in most places you use the S5. When the 3G or 4G network isn't available, the Galaxy S5 drops down to the older network used for voice calls, indicated by the bars in the status bar. It's much slower than 3G or 4G, but at least you're not cut off from civilization completely. 3G and 4G connections do run through your battery charge pretty quickly, which was a problem on earlier smartphones, but Samsung gave the S5 a battery that's up to the challenge. (If you are worried about running out of juice, however, you can carry a spare. Try that with an iPhone!)

To connect via 3G, 4G, or the voice network, there's nothing you need to do. The Galaxy S5 connects automatically depending on what's available. WiFi, the fastest connection of them all, takes a little more work, as you'll see in the next section.

Connecting via WiFi

WHEN YOU CONNECT TO the Internet via a WiFi hotspot, you've hit the mother lode of connection speeds. WiFi hotspots can be as fast as your cable modem connection at home.

If you've ever taken a laptop on the road, you may already know where the best WiFi hotspots are. Some coffee shops and hotels, for example, offer customers free WiFi, while others make you pay for it. More and more, you'll find WiFi coverage in airplanes, libraries, and even entire cities. In fact, if you connect your computers to the Internet at home using a wireless router, you have your own WiFi hotspot, and you can connect your S5 to the Internet via your home network.

Your actual connection speed varies from hotspot to hotspot. When you're at a public hotspot, you're sharing the connection with other people. So if a lot of people are using it at once, and the hotspot isn't set up to handle that many connections, your speed may suffer. Also, WiFi isn't a good bet when you're in motion. Hotspots have a range of only about 300 feet, so you and your phone can quickly move right past them.

NOTE   When you're connected to a WiFi hotspot, the S5 uses it for more than just Internet access. It also uses WiFi for finding your current location in apps like Google Maps (unless you turn off GPS, as described in the box on page 19). The phone uses a clever technology that finds nearby WiFi networks and uses fancy algorithms to determine your location. It's not as precise as GPS, but it's still pretty good. And as you'll see on page 196, the S5 can also use WiFi to make phone calls, so you'll use up fewer minutes of your calling plan.

Unlike the 3G/4G connection, which happens automatically, WiFi doesn't work unless you turn it on. That's a good thing, since WiFi connections sap much more battery power.

Once you're ready to hook up to a hotspot, here's how:

- **Use the widget.** To get to it, pull down the Notification panel, and it's at the upper left of the screen. The leftmost button controls your WiFi radio. If the button is gray, tap it and it turns green, meaning you've turned on WiFi. If it's already green, you don't need to do anything. (If it's on and you want to turn it off, tap it.)

- **Use connection settings.** Pull down the Notification panel, tap the Settings icon, and from the screen that appears, tap Wi-Fi at the top of the Quick Settings section.

What happens next varies according to whether you're connected to a WiFi network. If you're already connected, and your settings are all aligned, you don't need to do anything—you'll automatically connect to one of your preferred WiFi networks, like the one you use at home.

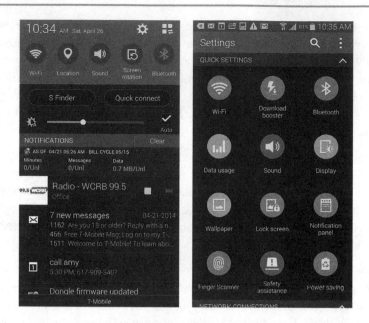

However, if you've never connected to a network before and you're in range of an open WiFi network, or if networks you've connected to before are out of range, then the S5 needs to ask you which network you want to join. When you turn on WiFi, a list of all nearby networks appears. For each network, you see its name, as well as the relative strength of the connection: the more blue waves, the stronger the connection. In addition, some networks have lock icons on them. A lock means that the network is encrypted and password-protected, and so you'll need the password in order to connect to it. No lock means that you can connect without a password.

On the screen that lists all nearby WiFi connections, you'll also see a list of networks you've connected to in the past, even those out of range. Those networks won't show an icon with waves on it, and the words "Not in range" appear underneath them in the listing.

Tap any network on the list, and a connection screen appears. Tap Connect if it's open or, if it's protected, type the password and tap Connect. Either way, after a few seconds, you make the connection. The network to which you just connected shows up in your list with the word "Connected" underneath it.

NOTE In some instances even though a network shows that it doesn't require a password, you'll need a password in order to use it. In those cases, you can connect to the network without typing in a password, but in order to use the network, you'll have to open your browser and register or type in a password. Ask the manager or whoever owns the network. Often, these kinds of networks are for-pay, so you'll have to use a credit card. In some instances, a business (like a coffee shop) will give you a password for free, sometimes for a limited amount of time.

At the very top of the WiFi screen, you'll find a setting called Smart Network Switch. It's normally turned on, and if it isn't you should do so by turning on the checkbox next to it. With Smart Network Switch turned on, you'll enjoy uninterrupted Internet access when you move in and out of range of WiFi networks. When you're on a WiFi network and go out of range, your cellular data connection takes over, *without* dropping your Internet connection. And when you're on your cellular connection and go within range of a network to which you've already connected, your Internet connection gets handed over to the WiFi network.

If you find yourself getting disconnected from WiFi networks, try adjusting your connection settings. From the Home screen, pull down the Notification panel, tap the Settings icon, and then tap Wi-Fi. Press the Menu key at the upper right of the screen and then select Advanced. Make sure the "Keep Wi-Fi on during Sleep" setting is set to Always. That way, your WiFi won't go to sleep when the

S5's screen turns off. Select "Only when plugged in," and WiFi won't go to sleep as long as your phone is plugged in.

What if for some reason a screen doesn't appear showing you all the available nearby networks? That might mean that there are no networks within range... or it might just be some odd temporary glitch. To check whether there are any available networks nearby, on any page, pull down the Notification panel, tap the Settings icon, and then tap Wi-Fi. You come to the screen that shows you all the nearby WiFi networks so you can make a connection.

TIP If your cellphone plan includes a limit on the amount of data you can use every month, and charges you more if you go over the limit, the S5's WiFi capabilities can be your best friend. When you're sending or receiving data via WiFi, it's not counted as part of your data plan. So using WiFi whenever possible can help make sure you don't bump up against your limits. And if you know you're going to be downloading large files, such as songs or movies, try to do it via WiFi. In addition to not racking up data use, it'll be faster than 3G or 4G.

Disconnecting and Reconnecting

To disconnect from a WiFi network, turn off WiFi. If you want to keep WiFi on, but want to disconnect from the network, go back to the screen that lists the nearby WiFi networks, tap the network to which you're connected, and then tap Forget. Boom—you're disconnected.

There's a downside to disconnecting this way, though. Normally whenever you connect to a WiFi network, the Galaxy S5 remembers that connection. So the next time it's in range, it automatically connects you, including using the network's password. If you tap Forget, though, it won't log you in automatically the next time you're in range.

NOTE   The S5 tells you in the Notification panel that there's a nearby WiFi network if that network is an open one—that is, one that doesn't use security. It won't notify you if you've previously connected to the network and your phone is set to remember it and connect automatically. If you want to turn off ever being notified, on any pane, pull down the Notification panel, tap Settings→Wi-Fi, press the menu button, and select Advanced. Then turn the checkbox off next to "Network notification."

Connecting to For-Pay WiFi Networks

Some WiFi hotspots require you to pay a fee for their use. In those instances, you'll have to take one more step when connecting. First make the connection in the normal way. Then launch the Galaxy S5's web browser by tapping its icon on the Home screen or in the Apps screen. A screen appears, delivered by the network, asking you to first register and pay.

Some free WiFi networks require you to agree to terms of service before you can use them. In that case, when you launch the browser, those terms of service will appear. So if you're at a free WiFi hotspot and connect to it, but can't get an

Internet-based app like Pandora to work, it might be because you haven't yet launched your browser and agreed to the terms of service.

Connecting to an "Invisible" Network

For security reasons, some people or businesses tell their network not to broadcast its name—its *Service Set Identifier* (SSID). That way, the network may appear invisible to people passing by. (Dedicated hackers, though, can easily detect it.)

If you need to connect to a network that isn't broadcasting its SSID, you can still connect, as long as you've been provided with its name, the type of security it uses, and its password. Pull down the Notification panel, tap the settings icon, tap Wi-Fi, and from the screen that appears, scroll to the bottom of the screen and tap "Add Wi-Fi network." Type the network's SSID, choose the security type, type the password, and then tap Save to connect to the network.

Boost Your Download Speed

WiFi is typically faster than a 3G or 4G connection, but let's face it: No matter how fast your connection is, it's not fast enough when you're downloading something from the Internet. Everybody wants instant satisfaction.

The S5 has an ingenious way to bring you closer to download satisfaction—it can combine your WiFi connection with your cellular data connection into one big download pipe when you're downloading big files. As a result, you'll download things at the speed of WiFi *plus* the speed of 3G or 4G.

To do it, pull down the Notification panel, tap the Settings icon, and then tap "Download booster." Move the setting from Off to On. When you do that you'll get a warning that you'll be using your data connection in addition to WiFi for large downloads, which could mean additional charges if you go over your data plan limits. Proceed if you don't care. Note that the Download booster goes into effect only when you download files over 30 MB.

The WPS Alternative

All this fiddling around with WiFi network connections can be confusing and time-consuming. So the Galaxy S5 has a built-in feature for making the connection easier—as long as the WiFi hotspot to which you want to connect uses a standard called WPS (WiFi Protected Setup). Find out from your provider whether your home router has it, and if it does, follow the instructions that came with the router for setting it up. Then, on your phone, pull down the Notification panel, and then tap the settings icon. From the screen that appears, tap Wi-Fi. Tap the Menu button and, from the menu that appears, select either "WPS push button" or "WPS PIN entry," depending on the way you've set up WPS on your router. (Again, check the WPS instructions for doing this.) Then just follow the S5 instructions onscreen. You'll make the connection automatically—no muss, no fuss.

Turning Your Galaxy S5 into a WiFi Hotspot or Tethering It

The Galaxy S5 can do more than just connect you to a hotspot. It can create its own hotspot, so other computers, cellphones, and devices can connect to the Internet through it. That means, for example, that if you've got a computer that you want to connect to the Internet but there's no WiFi hotspot or Internet service nearby, you can connect using your phone. So from now on, wherever you are, you've got Internet access as long as you've got your Galaxy S5 with you. The S5 calls this setting up a *mobile hotspot*.

Doing this, you can provide Internet access not just for one PC, but for up to five—that's right, count them, five—devices. (Note: The number of devices you can connect to may vary according to your carrier, so check with it for details.)

Not only that, but a related feature lets you share your Internet connection by simply connecting a USB cable between your computer and your S5. That's called *tethering*. And you can also connect the devices to the WiFi hotspot via Bluetooth as well.

 If you don't have a 3G or 4G connection, you won't be able to set up a mobile hotspot. So try doing this only when you see the 3G or 4G signal in the status bar.

To perform this magic, the Galaxy S5 connects to a 3G or 4G network as it normally does, using its 3G or 4G radio. Then it uses its WiFi radio to set up a WiFi hotspot and lets multiple computers, phones, tablets, and similar devices connect to it. They connect to it as they would connect to any other hotspot, and share its single 3G or 4G connection. So don't expect blazing speed if several people use it simultaneously. Still, it's a high-speed connection.

Be aware that this does come at a price. As of this writing, you'll generally have to pay an extra $20 per month or so in addition to your normal data fee to be able to use this feature. (Again, check with your carrier.) And there may be maximum data limits imposed as well. That will apply only to data sent and received via the 3G or 4G hotspot, not toward your normal data plan.

OK, enough introduction. Here's how to do it: First, make sure WiFi is turned on and you've got a 3G or 4G connection. Once you've done that, pull down the Notification panel, tap the Settings icon, and from the screen that appears, scroll down to the Network Connections area and tap "Tethering and Mobile HotSpot." What you do next varies according to whether you want to tether your phone or turn it into a hotspot.

Setting Up a Hotspot

If you want to set up a hotspot, tap Mobile HotSpot on the screen that appears, and at the top of the screen, slide the setting to On. A screen appears titled "First time HotSpot configuration." As the name implies, you'll see this screen only once, so don't despair—you won't have to fill it in every time you want to set up a hotspot.

Here's what you'll fill out:

- **Network SSID.** Type the name that you want your hotspot to have. The box will be filled in for you already, with something really exciting like "Samsung Galaxy S 5529." Make the name anything you want. Go crazy....or don't. But make it something that you'll remember.

- **Broadcast network name (SSID).** This box will already be checkmarked for you. It means just what it says: Anyone will be able to see the network's name because it's being broadcast, which is the way networks normally work. But if you're paranoid, uncheck the box. No one will be able to see that your network exists. However, you can still connect to it. For details, see page 190.

- **Security.** This drop-down menu lets you choose the type of security you want your network to have. WPA2 PSK will be chosen for you. Most of the time, you'll want to stick with it, because it gives you a high level of security. Whatever you do, though, don't choose Open. If you do that, anyone can connect to your hotspot. Not only will they suck up your bandwidth, but they could also possibly steal your files.

- **Password.** Select the password that you or anyone else will have to type in in order to connect. Please, whatever you do, don't use the word "password" as a password. When choosing a password, use a mix of numbers and letters, including capital letters. You'll have to make it at least eight characters long.

That's it. Tap Save, and you'll be ready to go. If you're feeling super-techie, tap the "Show advanced options" box. A number of new options appear, including choosing the network's broadcast channel (if you need to ask what that is, then you don't need to select it), the maximum number of devices that can connect to the hotspot, and the timeout settings, which is the number of minutes of inactivity it takes before the connected device will get bumped off the network.

> **NOTE** Changing the maximum number of devices that can connect using the "Show advanced options" menu may not actually change the number of devices that can connect. The maximum number of connections is set by your carrier, so increasing the number beyond that won't actually change how many devices can connect.

When a device connects to your hotspot, you'll get a notification.

When you don't want the hotspot to be active anymore, get back to the screen where you set it up, and then flip the On switch to Off.

Setting Up and Using Tethering

If you're going to connect only one device to your phone in order to give it Internet access, such as a PC, you might instead want to use the USB tethering feature. With it, you connect your PC and your phone with a USB cable, and your PC then uses the phone's Internet connection.

To tether your PC to your phone, first connect your PC to your S5 (page 319). Windows will install a special driver that lets your PC recognize your phone. Next, from the "Tethering and Mobile HotSpot" screen that you used to set up your mobile hotspot, turn on the USB Tethering checkbox. You will now be able to use the S5's Internet connection. Your phone can be connected via 3G, 4G, or WiFi, and your PC will share that connection.

NOTE When you connect your S5 to your PC with a USB cable, you can't use tethering and transfer files at the same time. Also, when you use tethering, you won't be able to use the S5's memory card.

Configuring Wi-Fi Direct

YOUR GALAXY S5 CAN use a helpful technology called Wi-Fi Direct that makes it easy to connect directly to other WiFi devices *without* having to use a WiFi network. So, for example, you can connect directly to a PC that also uses Wi-Fi Direct in order to share files.

Only devices that meet the Wi-Fi Direct standards and certifications can use Wi-Fi Direct, and your Galaxy S5 does that. To use Wi-Fi Direct to connect to another device, pull down the Notification Panel, and tap Settings→Wi-Fi. Tap the Menu button and select Wi-Fi Direct. Your phone scans for nearby Wi-Fi Direct devices. Once it finds any, follow the onscreen prompts to connect.

NOTE For more information about Wi-Fi Direct, and to see what other devices use it, go to *www.wi-fi.org/Wi-Fi_Direct.php*.

Wi-Fi Calling

WHEN YOU'RE CONNECTED TO a WiFi network, the S5 can make your phone calls via WiFi rather than over the normal cellular network. What's so great about that? When you make calls using WiFi, they don't count against the number of minutes on your calling plan. So you'll be able to make more calls than if you make connections only using your normal calling plan.

To turn it on, pull down the Notification panel, tap Settings, and scroll down to the Applications area. Tap Call, and on the screen that appears, turn Wi-Fi Calling from Off to On. That's all it takes—you're done. If you want to get techie and fancy, you can customize how it works. With Wi-Fi Calling turned on, tap the Wi-Fi Calling entry, select Connection Preferences, and on the screen that appears, select from the following:

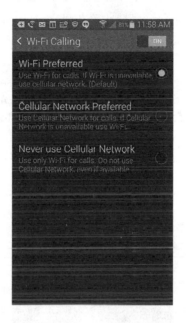

- **Wi-Fi Preferred.** When you're connected to a WiFi network, the call will go over WiFi, and when you're not connected to a WiFi network, the call will go over your normal cellular network.

- **Cellular Network Preferred.** Your calls will normally go over your cellular network, even if you're connected to a WiFi network. However, if you're connected to a WiFi network and your cellular network isn't available, the call will go over the WiFi Network.

- **Never use Cellular Network.** Your phone will make or receive calls only when you're connected to a WiFi network, and will never use your cellular network.

Airplane Mode

AIRLINES BAN THE USE of cellphone signals during flights. But they don't actually ban the use of phones. So you can still use your Galaxy S5 to run apps, play games, and so on, as long as its radios aren't turned on.

That's where Airplane mode comes in. It turns off all your S5's radios but lets you use your phone for everything else.

> **NOTE** You might also want to use Airplane mode even when you're not in flight in order to save power.

To turn on Airplane mode, pull down the Notification panel, tap the Settings icon and scroll down to the Network Connections area. Tap "Airplane mode," and from the screen that appears, turn the switch from Off to On.

> **TIP** An increasing number of airplanes have WiFi connections. If you want to connect your S5 to the plane's WiFi network, turn on Airplane mode, and then turn on WiFi alone. Make a connection as you would normally. That way you've turned off all the S5's radios except for WiFi.

You'll learn to:

- Browse the Web
- Use multiple browser windows
- Create and manage bookmarks
- Save and view online pictures and graphics

CHAPTER 9

The Web

ONCE YOU'VE USED YOUR Samsung Galaxy S5 to skim movie reviews on your way to the theater, check out an online menu before you choose a restaurant, or find a newspaper to read on the train, you may wonder how you ever got along without having the Web in the palm of your hand. The big 5.1-inch screen gives you an awesome Web experience wherever you go. With more and more web designers making their sites look good and work well on mobile devices like the Galaxy S5, you may find yourself using the Browser more than any other app.

The Galaxy S5's Browser

THE S5'S BROWSER HAS plenty of goodies, much like those in a computer browser, including bookmarks, AutoComplete for web addresses, cookies, password memorization, the ability to save and share pages, shortcuts, the ability to select and copy text...just about the whole nine yards. However, the browser itself is fairly bare bones, and its simplicity can at first be off-putting.

But once you know your way around a bit, you'll be browsing at warp speed. Here are the main controls you need to know about:

- **Address bar.** Here's where you enter the URL—the web address—for a page you want to visit.

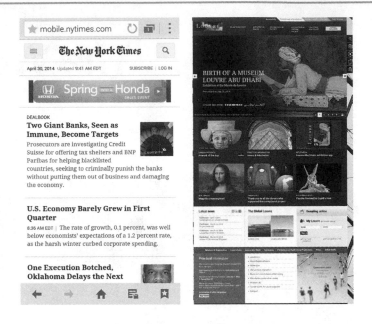

- **Windows open.** Tells you how many websites you've got open. Tap it to see thumbnails of them all. Then tap any thumbnail to visit it, and tap the – key to close any site.

- **Bookmarks.** Tap this button and you'll add the current page to your Bookmarks list and also be able to see pages you've visited frequently, and the history of your web browsing. See page 209 for more details.

- **Navigation buttons.** Tap these to go forward or backward in your browsing session.

- **Saved pages.** You can save entire web pages and then browse them on your S5 at any point, even if you're not connected to the Internet.

- **Menu key.** This key is in the same place that it is on all other places on the S5—on the screen's upper right. Tap it to get at most of the browser's features, including opening a new browser window, setting your homepage, adding a shortcut of the current web page to the S5 Home screen, managing your bookmarks, and more.

There are plenty of choices when you tap the Menu key. To open a new browser window, tap "New window." To share the page with others, tap "Share Page via." To find text on a page, tap "Find on page" and then do a search. There are also plenty more options, as you'll see in the next sections.

You may notice something odd and confusing as you use your browser. Sometimes the address bar and the buttons near it, and the buttons down at the bottom of the screen, disappear. These tools appear when you first visit a web page, but they scoot out of your way as you scroll down through the page. To make them appear again, scroll back toward the top.

Basic Navigation and Managing Windows

JUST LIKE A DESKTOP browser, your phone's browser lets you open multiple windows and visit multiple sites. It's just harder to tell that you're visiting multiple sites, because the S5's browser doesn't have enough room for tabs. Instead, the S5 opens multiple windows, one for each site you're visiting. When you're in the browser, tap the Window button (it's on the upper right of the screen, just to the left of the Menu button) to see thumbnails of your open windows superimposed on your existing page. It's a cool effect. Swipe up and down to see other open windows. Tap any window to view the site full screen. Tap the minus sign at its top to close the window. And tap the + sign at the top of your screen to open a new window.

Navigating a Web Page

HEAD TO A WEB page, and most of the time you see an entire page, laid out with the same fonts, links, pictures, and so on, as if you were visiting it using a computer with a much larger screen. Of course, looking at an entire web page on the S5's screen isn't the same thing as looking at a web page on a 21-inch monitor. The type is minuscule, the photos small, the links hard to detect. But letting you see the entire screen at once makes a good deal of sense, because at a glance you can see what section of the page you want to view.

Browsing for Browsers

The S5 gives you not just one, but two browsers: the standard one that runs right out of the box, and Chrome, which is the smartphone version of Google's house browser. They're similar, but with a few differences, notably in the way that Chrome handles tabs. This chapter focuses on the S5's built-in browser. It's the browser that runs whenever you tap the Internet icon. If you prefer to run Chrome, tap its icon in the Apps screen.

If you use Chrome on other computers or devices, it will sync bookmarks and other information with Chrome on the S5. If you use Chrome on a desktop computer, you may want to opt for using Chrome on the S5, and not just because it syncs information between the desktop and S5 versions. Its interface on the S5 is somewhat similar to the interface on the desktop version. For example, you can see and switch between multiple tabs, although unlike the desktop version, the tabs aren't arrayed horizontally, but instead vertically on top of one another.

There's also a nifty feature that lets you see all the sites open on your other devices that use Chrome, like desktops and laptops or Android-based tablets.

Not only can you see a list of sites, by device, but if you tap any, you head straight to it on your S5. To use the feature, press the Menu key and select "Other devices" from the screen that appears.

All that said, if you're not already a Chrome user, it can take some getting used to, particularly its tab handling. So which should you use? As the saying goes, you pays your money and you takes your chances—although in this instance, both browsers are free.

Furthermore, you're not just limited to the S5's built-in browser and Google Chrome. You can download other popular browsers—like Opera and Firefox—from Google Play.

These alternative browsers often add features that the built-in one doesn't have. Firefox, for example, will sync your Galaxy S5 bookmarks with the bookmarks on your PC or Mac. Opera is faster than the built-in browser because it compresses graphics before downloading them to your phone. It also syncs bookmarks with PCs or Macs and offers other extras as well.

That's where the fun begins. You can use the S5's zooming and scrolling capabilities to head quickly to the part of the page you want to view, and then zoom in.

You've got two ways to do so:

- **Use the two-finger spread.** Put two fingers on the screen on the area where you want to zoom in, and move your fingers apart. The web page stretches and zooms in. The more you spread, the greater the zoom. Pinch your fingers together to zoom back out. You may need to do the two-finger spread and pinch several times until you get the exact magnification you want.

- **Double-tap.** Double-tap with a finger on the section of the page where you want to zoom. Double-tap again to zoom out. You can't control the zoom level as finely with the double-tap as you can using the two-finger spread.

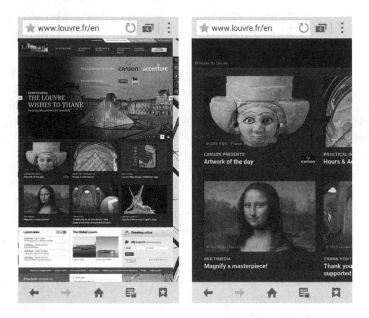

Once you've zoomed in, you scroll around the web page by dragging or flicking your finger—the same kind of navigation you use for other S5 apps.

Web Pages Designed for Mobile Phones

AS YOU BROWSE THE Web, you may come across sites that differ significantly when viewed on the Galaxy S5 (or other smartphones) compared with the exact same sites viewed on a computer. That's because web designers have created pages specifically designed to be viewed with mobile phones, taking into account that mobile phones have smaller screens than computers.

CNN, for example, has sites designed especially for mobile viewing. Head to the same site at the exact same time of day with a smartphone and a computer, and you see very different pages, even though the content of the pages is much the same.

These pages are formatted to be read on the phone, so very often they don't include complex layouts, and instead present articles and other information in scrollable lists. They generally don't allow you to zoom in and zoom out. You'll navigate primarily by scrolling and clicking links.

The Address Bar

THE ADDRESS BAR IS the box at the top of the browser where you type the URL of the website you want to visit. When you type an address and head to a page, a small bar above the address bar shows you the status—how much of the page has loaded and how much is left to go. To the right of the address bar, you'll find the Window button that indicates how many windows you have open and for navigating to them, and then the Menu button.

NOTE The bar indicating your page's loading status is only an approximation, so don't take it for the absolute truth. Also, if you're on a fast connection, you may not see the bar because pages may download so fast that the bar will appear and disappear in the blink of an eye.

Typing an Address

To type a URL into the address bar, first tap the bar. The current URL is highlighted in blue. Then use the keyboard to type an address. As you type, the S5 displays sites you've visited that match the letters you type. So when you type the letter *C*, for example, it may display Computerworld.com (*http://Computerworld.com*), CNN.com (*http://CNN.com*), and so on. It will also display search terms you might want to use, because the address bar does double duty as a search box. So it may be a very long list of URLs and suggestions you see.

NOTE As you type, you'll also see suggestions for sites you might not yet have visited. Google is trying to be helpful and displays popular sites that match the letters you're typing.

You'll notice, though, that it might also display URLs that don't start with the letter C. If you've previously visited a site about the international opera star Cecilia Bartoli, you may see that site come up when you type *C*. That's because the Galaxy S5's browser looks through your browsing history and Bookmarks list (see the next page), and looks for *all* matches to that letter, not just in URLs but also text in the page's title. When it displays its list as you type, it includes both the page's title and the URL.

As you continue to type, the list narrows down and includes only those sites that match the letters you're typing. So if you type *com*, cnn.com (*http://cnn.com*) no longer appears on your list, but computerworld.com (*http://computerworld. com*) does. When you see the site you want to visit, just tap its listing. You head straight there. If there's no match on the list, you'll have to type the entire URL.

You can also use the address bar to search the Web. Just type your search term, but don't add a .com ending. Your browser will search the Web for the term, using (what else?) Google.

NOTE Don't bother to type the *http://* part of a web address. The browser knows to put that in for you. You do, however, need to type in the .com or other ending, such as .edu. After you type in the address, tap the arrow button, and you head to the page.

Bookmarks

YOU CAN SAVE FAVORITE sites as *bookmarks*—sites you can easily visit again without having to retype their URLs. In fact, the S5's browser comes installed with bookmarks for a few popular sites, including Yahoo, Facebook, Twitter, CNN, ESPN, and more. The exact bookmarks you get depend on your cellphone carrier, which is usually in charge of that. Can you guess why? Right—because it puts its own web page there as well.

To see your bookmarks, tap the Bookmarks icon at the bottom of the screen. You see all your bookmarks, either displayed as a list or as a group of thumbnails of each of the bookmarked pages, so that you can distinguish them visually. To switch back and forth between the views, tap the Menu button and then select "List view" or "Thumbnail view."

No matter which view you use, to go to a bookmarked site, tap its thumbnail or listing. Voilà—you're there.

> **TIP** If you sometimes find yourself with a slow Internet connection, and wish there was a way to browse the Web faster, here's a bookmark you should add to your list: *www.google.com/gwt/n*. It hides most graphics, letting you browse the Web much more quickly on a slow connection. In the small box near the top of the screen, type the site you want to visit.

Adding a Bookmark

Whenever you visit a web page you want to add as a bookmark, tap the small star at the far left of the address bar. A screen appears that includes the web page's title and its URL. In the Name box, type a different title if you wish. You can even edit the URL in the Location box to go to a different website, but most of the time you won't want to. Then tap Save. The bookmark is added to your list.

The S5 has an oddball Bookmark feature that you'll no doubt find confusing. Sometimes when you add a bookmark it doesn't seem to appear, but if you try to add it again, you'll be told it's already in your Bookmarks, because...well, it is. You just haven't noticed. The S5 has already figured out that you visit that web page a lot and taken the liberty of adding it to a subfolder of Bookmarks called My Best.

Managing Bookmarks

The Galaxy S5 lets you do more than just go to bookmarks. You can delete them, share them, edit them, and so on. There are several ways to do this, each of which has different options. For the first way, head to Bookmarks and then tap the Menu button. You get these options:

- **Select.** Choose this option if you want to delete one or more bookmarks or move them to a specific folder. When you tap this option, boxes appear next to all of your bookmarks. Put checkmarks next to those you want to take action on. Then tap the trash icon to delete them, or tap the Menu button and tap "Move to folder" to move them to a different folder.

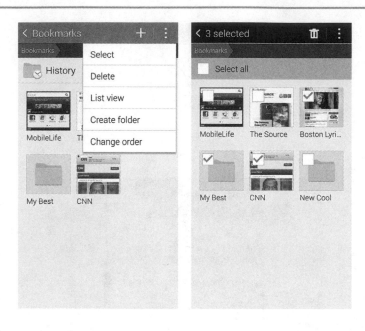

- **Delete.** Select this option, and a screen appears that lets you select bookmarks you want to delete. After you select them, tap Delete to delete them, or Cancel if you change your mind and don't want to delete any.

- **List view/Thumbnail view.** Switches between the list and thumbnail views.

- **Create folder.** If you've got a lot of bookmarks, you may want to organize them by folders—news, entertainment, and so on. Tap here and from the screen that appears, name your folder and tap OK. When you go to your Bookmarks, that folder will show up. Tap it to view any bookmarks in that folder.

- **Change order.** Lets you change the order in which your bookmarks appear in a list or thumbnails. Tap it, and from the screen that appears, drag the bookmarks to be in a different order on the list or thumbnail.

There's another way to manage your bookmarks. When you're on the bookmarks page, hold your finger on the bookmark you want to edit or manage. Boxes appear next to all of your bookmarks, with a checkmark next to your current one. Turn on the checkboxes of all the bookmarks you want to take action on. Then take your action; for example, tap the trash icon to delete them. Your choices vary depending on whether you've chosen only a single bookmark or multiple ones. If you select multiple bookmarks, your choices are limited to two: "Move to folder," and "Add shortcut to home screen." For single bookmarks, you get more possibilities.

Assuming you have only a single bookmark checked, here are your choices when you tap the Menu key:

- **Share via.** Tap to share the link of the bookmark by a variety of methods, including email, text message, Bluetooth, and more.

- **Edit.** Brings up a page that lets you edit the name and location of the bookmark. It looks much like the page for adding a bookmark.

- **Move to folder.** Lets you move it to the folder of your choice.

- **Add to Quick Access.** This adds the site to a floating toolbox you can have always available to you wherever you are on the S5. The toolbox holds your favorite apps as well as any websites you add to it. For details, go to page 378.

- **Add shortcut to home screen.** Tap this option, and a shortcut to the book-marked page is added to your Home screen. When you tap the bookmark, it opens the browser to that site. You can move and delete the icon after you add it, as you can see on page 33.

NOTE If you add a shortcut to your Home screen, and then delete the shortcut, the bookmark still remains in your browser's Bookmarks list.

- **Set as homepage.** Tap this, and from now on whenever you open a new window, it opens to that site.

The History List

DID YOU VISIT A website earlier today, or sometime within a week, but can't remember what it was? No problem! The S5's browser keeps track of sites you've visited. It's a great way (in addition to Bookmarks) to head back to sites you've visited before without having to type—or even remember—the web address.

To see it, tap the Bookmarks button, and then tap the History button at the top of the screen. You'll see a list of websites you've visited previously. The History list shows you not just sites you've visited today, but yesterday, in the last seven days, and a month ago. Rather than show you all the sites you visited before today, the browser shows the day (Yesterday, "Last 7 days," and so on), with an arrow next to it. Tap the arrow, and you see the full list of sites for that day.

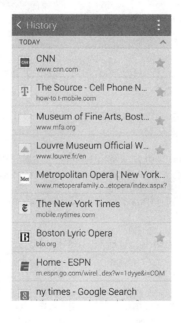

NOTE The History list doesn't give you the option of viewing sites as thumbnails, only as a list.

The list works much like the Bookmarks list—tap the site you want to visit. You'll notice one difference between these lists and the Bookmarks list: Some of the sites here have a gold star next to them. That indicates that the site is on your Bookmarks list.

Editing and Managing the History List

You can manage your History list in similar ways as with Bookmarks. Tap the Menu button and choose Select, and then choose sites you want to manage. As with the Bookmarks list, if you choose only one site you get more options than you do if you select multiple ones. If you choose one site, you can share it, copy it, add it to Quick Access, add it to your bookmarks, or set it as your homepage. If you choose multiple sites, all you can do is copy them to the Clipboard.

There's one thing you can do to your History list that you can't do with the Bookmarks list: You can clear your entire history. If you feel guilty about visiting sites for any reason, or just want them cleared out, you can get rid of them all. While in the History list, press the Menu key, and then select "Clear history." Your slate will be wiped clean.

Tapping Links

LINKS ON THE WEB couldn't be simpler or more convenient. Tap the link, and you get sent to a new web page. But this is the Galaxy S5, so there's a lot more you can do with links than just tap them. Hold your finger on a link, and a menu appears with these options:

NOTE Sometimes when you click a link, instead of loading a web page, the Galaxy S5 may take a different action. For example, if the link is to an email address, it will open the Email app, with a new message addressed to the link's email address.

- **Open.** Opens the linked page in the current window.

- **Open in new window.** Opens the linked page in a new window.

- **Save link.** Saves the linked page to the Download folder. To view the link and anything else in the Download folder, see page 218.

- **Copy link.** Tap to copy the link's URL to the Clipboard, so you can paste it somewhere else, such as in a document or email.

- **Select text.** Most links are text links—that is, they are words that, when clicked, send you to a web page. When you choose "Select text," you select that text and then have options for doing more things with it, such as searching for the text and more. For details, see page 221.

If you hold your finger on a graphic that's also a link, several other options having to do with the image appear. You can save the image, copy the image to the Clipboard, or view the image.

Other Things to Tap

The Galaxy S5 is smart enough that you can take action based on what you see on web pages, without even having to use links:

- **When you see a phone number** on the Web and want to call it, just tap it. The Galaxy S5 dialer launches, with the number already entered. Tap the phone icon to make the call.

- **When you see an address** on the Web and want to see a map of its location, tap it. Google Maps launches, centered on the location.

- **When you see an email address,** even if the address hasn't been created as a link, tap it and the Email app opens, with a new message already addressed to that address.

Saving Online Images

WHEN YOU'RE BROWSING THE Web, sooner or later you'll come across a picture you'd like to save. For example, if a friend posts a picture from your birthday party on Facebook, you can save it on your Galaxy S5 and then share it with others.

There's a quick and easy way to save that image. Hold your finger on the picture for a second or two, and a menu appears with the following three options:

- **Save image.** Downloads the picture to your Download folder. See the next section to learn how to go back and view all the pictures in this folder.

- **Copy image.** Copies the image to your Clipboard.

- **View image.** Opens the image in its own page. As a practical matter, this option doesn't do much, because it doesn't make the image any larger or smaller—you're seeing the same image, just on its own rather than on a web page.

TIP If the picture is also a link, the menu shows the usual options for bookmarking the link, saving the link, and so on.

Viewing Downloaded Images

Now that you've got graphics saved on your S5, how can you view them? It's simple. Open the Gallery (page 115) and go to the Download folder. Then view and manage them as you would any other pictures.

Finding Text, Sharing Pages, Getting Page Information, and More

THE GALAXY S5'S BROWSER has a lot more tricks up its sleeve than you've seen so far. To get to them, when you're on a web page, press the Menu key. You'll find a menu of options:

- **Homepage.** Sends you back to your homepage.

- **New window.** Opens a new window to your homepage.

- **Add to Quick Access.** Adds the site to your floating toolbox (page 378) so you can quickly hop to the site.

- **Add shortcut to home screen.** Adds a shortcut to the web page on your Home screen. The shortcut will be to the specific page you're on, not to the general website.

- **Save page.** Saves the entire web page, graphics included, on your S5. How to view it once you've saved it? At the bottom of the screen, tap the Saved Pages icon — it's the one with the disk on it, to the left of the Bookmarks icon.

- **Share via.** Tap to share the page via email or text messaging, social networking, Bluetooth, and, depending on what software you have installed, potentially several other ways as well. You don't actually share the page itself; instead, you send a link to it. Selecting this option copies the URL to an email message or a text message. You can then select an address and add explanatory text to the message as well.

- **Find on page.** Looking for text on a page? Tap this option, and a search box appears, along with the keyboard. Type the text or phrase you're searching for, and the Galaxy S5 finds the text, sends you to its location on the page, and highlights it in blue. To find the next time the text or phrase is mentioned, tap the down arrow. To find a previous mention of it on the page, tap the up arrow.

- **Incognito mode.** There are times when you want to browse the Web in privacy—you don't want anyone else to know you've visited. Not to imply that you have anything to hide, but no matter the reason, select this option. The site won't be saved in your History list, and there'll be no trace you've ever visited.

- **Desktop view.** When you browse the Web with your S5, you'll often come to versions of sites optimized for its small screen. But there may be times when you want to see the full-blown site. If that happens, tap the checkbox in this option, and you'll see the whole shebang of the website. To switch back, get back to the menu and uncheck the box. When you select this option, it doesn't affect any other website, only the one you're visiting.

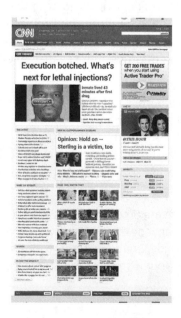

Some sites don't have versions optimized for smartphone screens. When you're visiting one of those, you see the page just as you see it on a larger computer, and the Desktop view option is grayed out.

- **Brightness.** Lets you select the screen brightness. A screen with a slider appears, which lets you set the brightness level. You can also leave the checkbox next to "Automatic brightness," and the S5 will adjust the light level for you based on ambient light.

Selecting and Copying Text

AS YOU BROWSE THE Web, you may also come across text on a website that you want to use elsewhere, say in an email or a document. It's easy. First, hold your finger on the text you want to copy. A magnifying glass appears. This tool makes it easy to maneuver to the exact text you want to copy. Move it by moving your finger, and then release it on the word you want to copy. If you want to copy more than one word (and you likely will), don't worry—just release your finger when it's on one of the words you want to copy.

He was 71.

His passing comes nearly two years after he retired from acting following a diagnosis of Parkinson's disease.

Hoskins was perhaps best known for 1988's live-action and animation hybrid "Who Framed Roger Rabbit." In the comedy, he played detective Eddie Valiant, who hates "toons" – cartoon figures who live in a separate showbiz world bordering Valiant's 1940s Los Angeles – and takes up the task of

He followed the turn with performances in a variety of films, including 1991's "Hook," which he played Smee, the pirate assistant of Captain Hook; 1995's "Nixon" as FBI Director J. Edgar Hoover; and 2001's "Last Orders" as the gambler friend of protagonist Michael Caine, whose pals gather to spread his ashes after his death.

Hoskins was nominated for an Oscar for 1986's "Mona Lisa" as a cabdriver who establishes a relationship with a high-priced call girl. Caine was also in the film. Hoskins won both a BAFTA and Golden Globe for his performance.

Robert Hoskins was born on October 26, 1942, in Bury St. Edmunds, England, the only child of a bookkeeper and a cook. He dropped out of school at 15 and took jobs as a truck driver and window cleaner, among others, before falling into acting by

When you release your finger, brackets appear around the word, and a tool-bar appears with six icons: Select all, Copy, Share via, Dictionary, Find, and Web search. Move the brackets until they surround the all the text you want to copy. Tap "Select all" to select all the text on the page. Select Copy to copy the highlighted text to the Clipboard. You get a notification that the text was copied. You can now paste it into an email, a document, and so on. Tap "Share via," and you'll be able to share your selection either as text or as an image file. You'll be able to share it via Bluetooth, email, text message, and more, depending on what you've got installed on your S5. Tap Dictionary to look up the text in an online dictionary. Tap Find to find other mentions of text on the page. And tap "Web search" to launch a Google search for the text on the Web.

Online Privacy and Security

WHETHER YOU BROWSE THE Web with a computer or with the Galaxy S5, there are potential security and privacy dangers out there—cookies, pop-ups, and malicious websites. So the S5 browser, just like its big-brother browsers on computers, includes the tools you need to keep you safe and protect your privacy when you browse the Web.

Pop-up Blocker

What's top on your list of web annoyances? Most likely at the pinnacle are pop-ups and pop-unders—ugly little windows and ads that either take an in-your-face stance by popping up over your browser so that you have to pay attention, or pop under your browser so that you don't notice they're there until you close a browser window, and then they demand your attention.

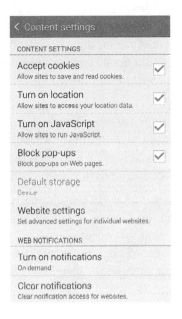

Sometimes these pop-ups and pop-unders are malicious, and if you tap them they attempt to install dangerous software or send you to a malicious website. Sometimes they're merely annoying ads. Sometimes, though, they may actually be useful, like a pop-up that shows a seating chart when you're visiting a ticket-buying site. The browser includes a pop-up blocker, and like all pop-up blockers, it can't necessarily distinguish between bad pop-ups and pop-unders and good ones, so it blocks them all.

However, if you're on a website that uses pop-ups that you want to see, you can turn off the pop-up blocker. From the Apps screen select Settings, scroll down to the Applications area, and tap Internet→"Content settings," and then uncheck the box next to "Block pop-ups." When you leave the site and want pop-ups blocked again, go back to the setting and tap it to turn it on. A green checkmark appears next to the setting, and you are protected.

NOTE When you turn off the pop-up blocker, it stops blocking pop-ups in *all* your browser windows, not just on one site. So be careful when you browse other places on the Web when the pop-up blocker is turned off.

Cookies

Cookies are tiny bits of information that some websites store on the Galaxy S5 for future use. When you register for a website and create a user name and password, the website can store that information in a cookie so you don't have to retype it every time. Cookies can also remember your habits and preferences when you use a website—your favorite shipping method, or what kinds of news articles you're likely to read. But not all cookies are innocuous, since they can also track your web browsing from multiple sites and potentially invade your privacy.

The browser gives you control over how you handle cookies—you can either accept them or tell the browser to reject them. Keep in mind that if you don't allow cookies, you may not be able to take advantage of cookie-based features on many sites—like remembering items in your cart on a shopping site.

To bar websites from putting cookies on your S5, from the Apps screen select Settings, scroll down to the Applications area, tap Internet→"Content settings," and then uncheck the box next to "Accept cookies." The checkmark disappears and, from now on, no cookies will be put on your Galaxy S5. You can always turn this setting back on again, if it causes problems with web browsing.

Privacy Settings

If you're worried about privacy, there are a number of browser settings you can change. From the Apps screen select Settings, scroll down to the Applications area, and tap Internet→Privacy. From here there are a number of things you can do to make sure your privacy isn't invaded. For example, you can clear your browsing history so that others who use the browser can't see where you've been.

At many websites, you log in by typing a user name and password, and other information such as your address. The browser remembers those user names, passwords, and other details, and fills them in for you automatically when you next visit. That's convenient, but it also presents a privacy risk, because someone else using your Galaxy S5 can log in as you. So in the Privacy settings, turn off the checkbox next to "Remember passwords."

If you turn off "Suggest search terms and Web sites," you won't be sending what you search to Google, but you won't get suggestions, either. Also, normally when you type information into web forms, your browser remembers it so that it can put that information in other forms automatically. But if that worries you, uncheck the box next to "Remember form data."

< Privacy

Suggest search terms and We..
Predict related queries and popular sites in
the Navigation bar as you type.
☑

Preload available links
Improve performance when loading pages.
☑

Remember form data
Remember data typed in forms for later use.
☑

Remember passwords
Save usernames and passwords for
websites.
☑

Delete personal data

You can also clear out website information your browser has stored on your S5. Tap "Delete personal data," and then select the kinds of data you want deleted from your phone, such as your browsing history, cookies, passwords, and so on. You also have a chance to clean out your *cache*. The cache is information the browser stored on your phone so it won't have to get that information from the Web the next time you visit that site. The cache speeds up browsing, since it's faster to grab the information—a website image, for example—from your phone than from the Web. Delete the cache if you want to clear all that information out, if you worry that the information there poses a privacy risk.

< Privacy

Suggest search terms and We..
Predict related queries and popular sites in
☑

Delete personal data

Browsing history ☐

Cache ☐

Cookies and site data ☐

Passwords ☐

Auto fill data ☐

Location access ☐

Cancel   Done

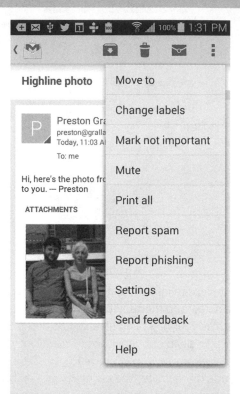

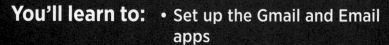

You'll learn to:

- Set up the Gmail and Email apps
- Compose and send mail
- Receive email
- Organize Gmail using labels
- Handle photos and attachments

Email and Gmail

YOU WANT EMAIL? YOU'VE got email. The Galaxy S5 does a great job of handling whatever email task you throw at it. Want to send and receive attachments like pictures; Word, Excel, and PowerPoint files; and PDFs? The S5 can do that. How about working with just about any email service out there? It can do that, too. You can also manage your mail, sync your mail, and plenty more right on your phone. It's a great way to have your email always in your pocket.

Understanding Email on the Galaxy S5

THE GALAXY S5 RUNS on Google's Android operating system (described in the box on page 26), so it comes as no surprise that it includes Gmail built into it. You don't have to use Gmail if you don't want to, though; you can use your current email service instead. Or you can use both. Gmail on the S5 works a bit differently from other email services, so this chapter covers Gmail as well as regular email.

NOTE The Email icon on your Home screen is Android's app for handling *other* email accounts, not Gmail. Gmail has its own app, which you can find in the Apps screen, as described in the next section. If you'd like to get started with a different email account (your work or home account, for example), flip to page 245.

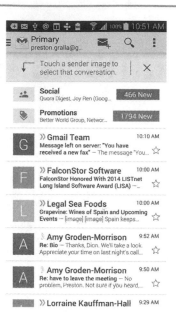

Setting Up Gmail

ANDROID IS BUILT FROM the ground up to integrate with Google services—search, Google Maps, and Gmail. If you already have a Gmail account, then when you set up your Galaxy S5, you tie into that account. If you don't have a Gmail account, you first need to set one up.

> **NOTE** When you first bring your S5 home, you may already be set up to use Gmail. Your wireless company's sales staff may have set up your Gmail account right in the store for you.

When you use the Gmail app on your S5, it synchronizes with your web-based Gmail. So when you delete an email on the phone, for example, it deletes it on the web-based Gmail; when you create and send an email on your phone, it shows up in your Sent folder on the Web; and so on.

Signing up for a Gmail account is free and takes only a few minutes. You can create it on the Web or on the S5. To do it on the Web, head to *www.gmail.com*. Fill in the usual information, such as first and last name, login name, and password. The login name you choose becomes your email address. So if you use the login name *petey.bigtoes*, then your email address will be *petey.bigtoes@gmail.com*. So make your login name something pleasant and easy to remember.

When you create a Gmail account, you're actually setting up an account for all of Google's services, not just Gmail. You use the same account to access Google Calendar, Google+, Google Drive, Google Play, and so on. In other words, if you have a Google Calendar account, then you already have a Gmail account. Use that information when setting up Gmail on your Galaxy S5.

Now that you have a Gmail account, you're ready to set up Gmail on your S5. When you set up your Gmail account, you'll also be setting up your Calendar account and importing your Gmail contacts into your Galaxy S5. On the Apps screen, tap the Gmail icon. After a brief welcome screen, Gmail asks whether you have a Google account. If you haven't already set one up, tap New, and then fill in the information required. Make sure to leave the box next to "Automatically configure account" turned on. That way, the S5 will do all the heavy lifting of properly configuring your new account.

TIP If you plan to use Gmail a lot, drag its icon from the Apps screen to your Home screen.

If you already have a Gmail account, tap Existing. Enter your Gmail address and the other basic information. If you have a Google Contact list, the S5 automatically starts downloading it in the background, and also syncs your mail.

NOTE What if you have multiple Gmail accounts? You can have the Galaxy S5 handle more than one. To set up a second account, go to the Apps screen and tap Settings→ Accounts→Add Account→Google and follow the directions for setting up an account. If you prefer, you can also use the S5's browser (Chapter 9) to visit Gmail and access your other accounts that way.

Reading Mail in Gmail

ONCE YOU'VE GOT YOUR Gmail account set up, it's time to start reading mail. Launch the Gmail app by tapping it on the Apps screen. You see a list of emails, but the list you see depends on what you were doing the last time you were using Gmail. For example, if the last time you used Gmail you were in your inbox, you see all the mail in your inbox. If you were viewing mail in a different *label* (the term Gmail uses for a folder), you see just the mail in that label.

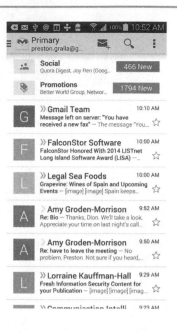

While most email programs use *folders* to let you organize your email, Google uses *labels* in its web-based email, and that's what you use on the Galaxy S5.

Most of the time, of course, you'll land in your inbox, which lists all your mail. Mail you haven't read is boldfaced and has a white background; the rest of your mail is in a normal font and has a gray background. At the top of the list of mail, you'll see a couple of buttons, labeled Social and Promotions, followed by a number indicating how many messages fall into that category. Social refers to all mail related to your social media accounts; Promotions refers to newsletters and advertising. Tap either to see all the mail in that category.

The S5 regularly checks your Gmail account for new mail, and if it finds any, it displays an email icon in the status bar. Pull down the Notification panel, and then tap the Gmail notification to launch Gmail.

When you're viewing mail in a list like this, each piece of mail shows the following:

- The sender

If the sender is one of your contacts and you have a photo for him (or if he's a friend on Facebook with a photo), you'll see a photo of him at the far left of each email. If he's not a contact, or is but you don't have a photo of him, you see a big letter—that's the first letter of his name.

- The subject line

- The date it was sent or, if it was sent today, the time it was sent

- Whether it has an attachment

- Whether it has images

To open a message, tap it. Scroll up, down, and sideways in the message using the normal Galaxy S5 gestures of dragging and flicking.

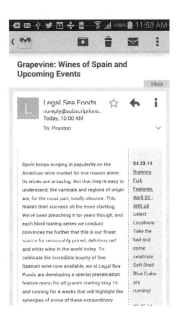

All the links you see in the email message are live—tap them, and you go to the linked web page in the Galaxy S5's web browser. Tap an email address, and a new email message opens to that address. Tap a YouTube video, and the video plays.

In fact, in many instances, the text in the email message doesn't even need to be a link for the phone to take some kind of action on it. If there's a phone number in an email, tap it to call that number. Just tap the phone button to dial. If you tap a street address, the S5 shows you that location in Google Maps.

NOTE Gmail, Google Calendar, and your Gmail contacts are all set up to sync between your S5 and your various Google accounts on the Web. All of this happens automatically, in the background, without you having to take any action. You can turn syncing off or choose to sync manually. For details, see page 382.

Handling Graphics in Gmail

There are two basic kinds of graphics you may get in Gmail. Some are embedded in the content of the message itself—for example, a company logo. Other times, the sender attaches the image to the message, like a family member sending you Thanksgiving photos.

If the graphics are embedded in the content of the message, you'll see the graphics themselves, right where the sender put them.

If someone has attached a graphic, you see the graphic displayed in the email message, a thumbnail of the image being sent.

To save the picture to your Galaxy S5, first tap the thumbnail to display it. Tap the screen, and you see information about the picture, including its filename. Tap the Menu button at top right, and you can save the picture to the Gallery and share it with others via email, Bluetooth, cloud storage, and perhaps other ways, depending on what apps you have installed on your S5. (For details about the Gallery, turn to page 115.)

Attachments in Gmail

Gmail lets you download graphics attachments, including those in the .jpg, .png, and .gif formats as well as Word, Excel, and PowerPoint files. It lets you preview those files and other file types as well.

If you get an attachment that you can preview, you see a paper clip icon near the bottom of the message. The attachment's name appears next to the paper clip icon. Tap the paper clip to download it. If it's a Word, Excel, or PowerPoint file, it opens in any of a number of apps that can open or read the file, depending on what you have installed on your S5: Google's Quickoffice, Microsoft's Office Mobile, POLARIS Office, or others. If you have more than one of these apps installed, you'll get a screen asking which you want to use, and whether to use it just this one time or always. When you're done reading the file, you can save it (via the app) to whatever location you want.

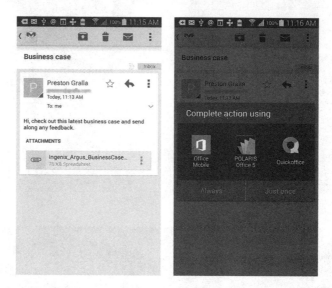

If you want to save the attachment without first reading it, tap the three dots next to it and select Save. It will be saved in the Gallery's Downloads album.

Information about the Sender

If you want to get information about the sender of the message, tap the person's picture or icon. If that person is in your Contacts, the Contact information screen (page 79) opens up. (If the person isn't in your Contacts, nothing happens.)

Replying and Forwarding in Gmail

NEAR THE TOP OF the screen in Gmail, next to the sender's name, you'll find a small toolbar of icons for replying to and forwarding mail:

- **Star.** Adds a star to the message in the email list to call your attention to it later. You can use stars to flag messages that contain important information, say, or those that require further research. If the message already displays a star, tap it to remove it.

- **Reply.** Replies to the message's sender only. A new email window opens, addressed to the sender, with the original email text quoted in it. (If there's an attachment in the original email, it won't be included.)

- **More options.** This launches a menu that lets you reply to all recipients of the message (not just the sender), forward the message to someone else, or print it.

- **Expand header.** Tap the small down arrow just beneath the toolbar, and the message header expands—you'll see the full email addresses of all message recipients, as well as the date and time that the message was sent.

Understanding Gmail's Organization

GMAIL HAS ITS OWN terminology and worldview when it comes to handling email, so you have some new terms and ideas to get used to. Here are the most common Gmail concepts:

- **Labels.** Think of these as email folders. Your regular email program has a folder called Inbox, for example, and lets you create other folders, such as Family, Work, and so on. Gmail calls these email containers *labels*.

  That said, there's a slight underlying difference between the way you work with Gmail's labels and how you work with another email program's folders. In your typical email program, you might move mail between folders by dragging them. Not so in Gmail. In Gmail, you affix a label to an email message. When you do that, that email automatically appears when you sort for that label.

If you use Google Hangouts, either on a computer or on your Galaxy S5, the conversations you have will show up in your Chats label.

Labels actually give you more flexibility than folders, since you can attach multiple labels to a single email message to have it show up in multiple labels. For example, if you get an email from your brother about advice for your upcoming trip to France, you can add the labels Family and France to the email. That email then shows up in both your Family label and your France label.

The Gmail app on the S5 is designed to work in concert with Gmail on the Web. So you can't do everything in the Gmail app that you can do on the Web. The Gmail app can't create labels, for example, so to create new ones, you must visit your Gmail account on the Web, using either the S5 browser or a computer.

- **Overall mail organization.** Because Gmail uses labels rather than folders, you may find mail in more than one location. Also, unlike some email software, Gmail gives you the option of viewing all mail in one single area titled "All mail," including mail you've archived and all other mail.

- **Archive.** In some instances, you'll get mail that you want to keep around but don't want showing up in your inbox, because your inbox would otherwise get too cluttered. So Gmail lets you *archive* messages. Archiving a message doesn't delete it, but it removes it from your inbox. You can still find the message listed in your "All mail" folder. You can also find it by searching.

Managing Incoming Mail in Gmail

ONCE YOU'VE READ A Gmail message, it's time to decide what to do with it. At the top of your screen when you're reading email, you'll find three buttons that can help:

- **Archive.** This button appears if you haven't given the email a label. Tap the button to archive the message. It vanishes from your inbox but still appears in "All mail."

- **Delete.** Deletes the message. What if you tap this button accidentally? No problem. For the next few moments, an Undo button appears at the bottom of the screen. Tap it to undelete the message. What if you delete the message, don't undo it, but later on decide you wished you hadn't done it? Google still has your back. The message still actually exists—in your Trash folder. Go to the folder (page 244), and you can read it there or undelete it by moving it to a new folder. However, it stays there for only 30 days. After that, it's gone forever.

- **Inbox.** This doesn't help in managing your mail. It just scoots you straight to your inbox.

But wait, as they say in late night commercials, there's more! Tap the Menu button and you get these options as well:

- **Move to.** Even if you haven't applied a label to a piece of mail in your inbox, it already has a label preapplied to it—Inbox. Tap this button to change the message's label. When you tap the button, a screen appears with all your labels on it. The labels for the mail you're reading have green checkmarks next to them. Add checkmarks for all the labels you want to add, and remove checks for labels you want to remove.

- **Change labels.** What gives? This sounds a lot like the "Move to" option—and it is. But there's a minor difference. With "Move to," you can move the mail to more labels than you can with "Change labels."

- **Mark important/Mark not important.** Google watches your mail usage and marks some mail as important. If you're reading a message considered important, you can change it to "not important." And if you're reading a message considered not important, you can change it to important.

- **Mute.** Tap this button, and the email and all conversations related to it bypass your inbox and are automatically archived. When you mute a piece of mail, you're not just archiving that one piece of mail, but the entire "conversation" of which it's a part. Let's say, for example, you subscribe to a mailing list, and there is a long, ongoing series of back-and-forth emails about a topic in which you have no interest. (Justin Bieber, anyone?) You're tired of seeing emails in that conversation pop up in your inbox. Tap the Mute button, and you won't see it in your inbox anymore. It will, however, still appear in "All mail."

- **Print all.** Prints the entire message.

- **Report spam.** Tap the "Report spam" button, and a note goes to Google, saying you believe the email is spam. Google uses that information to determine which mail should be considered spam and be automatically rerouted into people's Spam label.

- **Report phishing.** Tap this, and a note goes to Google saying you believe the email is a nasty piece of work known as a *phishing attack*. In this kind of scam, you receive an email that *looks* legitimate—from your bank, for example—but in fact it's from someone who's trying to trick you into revealing personal information such as your bank login information. When you click a link in the email, you're sent to a site that looks like the real site, but in fact is one set up only to grab your information.

- **Settings.** Sends you to a screen that lets you change your Gmail settings, including adding a new account.

- **Send feedback.** Tell Google what you think of Gmail.

- **Help.** Get technical help with Gmail.

Managing Multiple Email Messages

You can also handle *groups* of messages rather than individual ones. To do that, first you need to group them all. Hold your finger in turn on each message that you want to take action on in a group. Each message gets a check put next to it, and the top of your screen shows how many you've put in the group. Now use the icons at the top of the screen for managing them all, such as moving them, archiving them, deleting them, changing their labels, and so on. To get to the full list of actions, tap the three stacked squares on the far right of the screen.

Writing Messages in Gmail

WHEN YOU WANT TO create a new Gmail message, start from the inbox and then press the Compose button at the top of the screen—it's a plus sign on an envelope. A new, blank message form opens, and the keyboard appears so you can start typing.

NOTE If you want a larger keyboard, turn your Galaxy S5 90 degrees.

Write your message this way:

1. **Type the recipient's address in the To field.** As you type, Gmail looks through your Contacts list, as well as the list of people you've sent email to in the past, and displays any matches. (Gmail matches the first few letters of first names as well as last names as you type.) If you find a match, tap it instead of typing the rest of the address. You can add as many addresses as you wish.

2. **Send copies to other recipients.** Press the Menu button, and tap Add Cc/Bcc from the menu that appears. Two new lines appear beneath the To field—Cc and Bcc.

   Anyone whose email address you put in the Cc and Bcc boxes gets a copy of the email message. The difference is that while everyone can see all the Cc recipients, the Bcc copy is sent in private. None of the other recipients can see the email addresses you enter in the Bcc field.

NOTE The term *carbon copy* comes from those long-gone days in the previous century when people typed mail, documents, and memos on an ancient device called a type-writer. To make multiple copies, typists added a sheet of carbon paper and another sheet of typing paper. The force of the keys striking the paper would imprint ink on the second sheet, using the ink in the carbon paper.

3. **Type the topic of the message into the Subject field.** A clear, concise sub-ject line is a good thing for both you and your recipient, so you can immedi-ately see what the message is about when you scan your inbox.

4. **Type your message into the Compose email box.** Type as you would in any other text field. You can also use copy and paste.

5. **Add an attachment.** To add an attachment, tap the Menu button and then tap "Attach file." You'll come to a list of locations where you have files, including the Gallery, your Documents folder, Google Drive, and more. Tap the location, and then select the file to attach. You'll see a thumbnail of your attachment right in the message. Tap the X button if you want to remove the attachment. You can keep adding attachments, if you want.

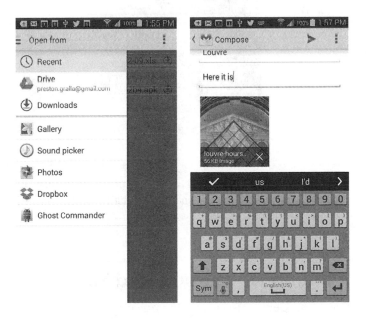

6. **Tap the send icon at the top right of the screen, and the message gets sent immediately.** If you instead want to save the message as a draft, tap the Menu button and select "Save draft." If you'd prefer to call the whole thing off and get rid of the draft, tap the Menu key and select Discard, which gets rid of the message for good.

Adding a Signature

The Gmail app can automatically add a signature—your contact information, for example—at the bottom of every outgoing message. To create a signature of your own, from the inbox, tap the Menu button and then select Settings, tap the name of your account, and then tap Signature. Type a signature, tap OK, and the signature will be appended to the bottom of all messages you send.

NOTE The signature will be appended to the bottom of outgoing Gmail, but not your other email accounts. You need to set up signatures separately for each email account.

Working with Labels and Search

LABELS ARE AN EXCELLENT way to organize your email in Gmail, because they're far more flexible than folders. A single message can appear in as many or as few labels as you want.

To go to a different label from the one you're currently in, tap the icon next to the label at the top left. You see a listing of every one of your labels. Scroll to see all of them. Gmail automatically creates the following labels for you:

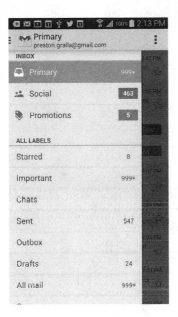

- **Inbox** contains all your incoming messages. There may be categories within it, such as Social and Promotions (page 230).

- **Starred** shows all the messages you've starred.

- **Important** shows all the messages you've tagged as being important.

- **Chats** contains the contents of all chats done via Google Hangouts.

- **Sent** lists all messages you've sent.

- **Outbox** shows mail you've created and asked Gmail to send, but that has not yet been sent.

- **Drafts** contains mail you've created but not completed.

- **All mail** contains all mail and chats, except for Spam and Trash. It also includes mail that you've archived.

- **Spam** contains all mail marked as spam, either by you or by Google.

> **NOTE** You can remove mail from Spam by going into the Spam label, reading a message, and tapping "Remove label" from the bottom of the screen.

- **Trash** contains mail you've deleted but that hasn't been removed from the trash yet. Email is removed from the trash when it's more than 30 days old.

NOTE If you use Gmail's Priority Inbox on the Web, you'll also see a label here called Important, which shows all the messages that Gmail has flagged as being important to you. For details about how Priority Inbox works, and to set it up on the Web, go to *http://bit.ly/14GiCXL*.

If you've created any labels other than these, using Gmail on the Web, then you see them here as well. You can't create new labels in Gmail on the Galaxy S5. To create a new label, visit Gmail on the Web, using your phone's browser or a computer.

To see your labels, when you're in the inbox, swipe in from the left.

Searching Gmail

GOOGLE MAKES WHAT MANY consider the best search engine on the planet, so it's no surprise that it builds Google Search into Gmail on the Galaxy S5. Searching is straightforward. To search, tap the Search button. As you type, Gmail displays previous searches you've done that match those letters and narrows the search as you type. If you see a search term you want to use, tap it. If not, type the entire search term, and then tap Search.

After you enter your search terms, you see a display of all matching email. Gmail searches through the To, From, and Subject fields, as well as the messages' text. In the upper-left corner, you see the search term you entered.

Advanced Gmail Searching

Gmail lets you do some pretty fancy searching—after all, Google is the search king. So you can search by To, From, Subject, specific labels, and a lot more. Say you want to search for all email with the word "Halloween" in the subject line. Type the following in the search box:

```
Subject:Halloween
```

You can search other Gmail fields, as shown in the following list (head to *http://tinyurl.com/gmail-search* for a more complete list):

- **From.** Searches for mail from a specific sender.
- **To.** Searches mail for a specific recipient.

CHAPTER 10

- **Subject.** Searches the subject lines.

- **In <label>.** Searches in a specific label.

You can combine these search terms with one another, and with a search of the text of the message. So to search for all email in your Work label with the word "budget" in it, you'd do this search:

```
In:Work Budget
```

Setting Up Email Accounts

YOU'RE NOT CONFINED TO using Gmail on the Galaxy S5—you can use your other email accounts as well. How you set one up depends upon what kind of email account you want to add.

To get started, tap the Email icon. Fill in your email address and password, and then tap Next. If you're setting up a web-based mail account like Yahoo Mail or Microsoft's web-based mail (find it at Outlook.com or Hotmail.com), the S5 is smart enough to do all your setup for you, including your incoming and outgoing mail servers. After a moment or two, it makes sure everything is working properly and then sends you to a page with your various account options, such as how you want to sync emails between the Web and your S5, whether to notify you when mail arrives, and so on. Most of the time, your best bet is to stick with the options the S5 picks for you—it's plenty smart about making the right choices.

POP3 and IMAP Accounts

If you instead want to set up a general email account, such as from your Internet service provider (ISP), after you fill in your email address and password and tap Next, you'll come to a screen that asks what type of account you want to add—a POP account, an IMAP account, or a Microsoft Exchange ActiveSync account.

> **TIP** If it's a Microsoft Exchange ActiveSync account, it's likely a work account. For details on how to set up ActiveSync and other corporate options, see Chapter 14.

As for POP and IMAP, that's techie talk for two different kinds of email services. Here's what you need to know about each before making your choice:

- With a **POP (Post Office Protocol)** account, the POP server delivers email to your inbox. From then on, the messages live on your Galaxy S5—or your home computer, or whichever machine you used to check email. You can't download another copy of that email, because POP servers let you download a message only once. So if you use your account on both a computer and your S5, you must be careful to set up the account properly, as described in the box on page 248, so you won't accidentally delete email. Despite this caveat, POP accounts remain the most popular type of email accounts and are generally the easiest to set up and use.

- With an **IMAP (Internet Message Access Protocol)** account, the server doesn't send you the mail and force you to store it on your computer or phone. Instead, it keeps all your mail on the server, so you can access the exact same mail from your S5 and your computer—or even from multiple devices. The IMAP server always remembers what you've done with your mail—what messages you've read and sent, your folder organization, and so on. So if you read mail, send mail, and reorganize your folders on your S5, when you then check your mail on a computer, you'll see all those changes, and vice versa.

  That's the good news. The bad news is that if you don't remember to regularly clean out your mail, your mailbox can overflow if your account doesn't have enough storage to hold it all. If your IMAP account gets full, then when people send you email, their messages bounce back to them.

> **NOTE** With the exception of a Gmail account, only accounts that have been previously set up can be added to your Galaxy S5. If you get a new email account at work or home, get it all set up before you add it to your phone.

Choose which type of account you want to use. In some cases, your ISP will let you use either IMAP or POP, but in other cases, it will require you to use one or the other. So check with your ISP. After you choose your account type, the S5 attempts to automatically configure your email account for you. Most of the time it will be able to figure out your settings, but sometimes it fails. In that case, it shows you a screen where you need to fill in techie details, such as server names for the outgoing mail server (SMTP), whether you use POP3 or IMAP, the incoming mail server name, and so on. If you don't have the information at hand (and face it, who does?), check with your ISP or your corporate tech support staff.

Depending on the kind of account you set up, you may come to a screen with options like whether you want to be notified when email arrives, for how long to sync your email, and so on. You may find that the S5's choices work just fine for you, but if not, make whatever changes you want and tap Next. You'll be asked to give it an account name or leave it as is. Tap Done.

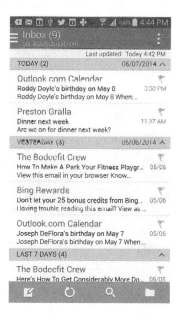

TIP If you're already using an email program on your computer, that means you've set up the account there, and its settings are in the email program. So go to the account settings on your computer, and grab the information from there.

Keeping Your POP Mailboxes in Sync

The difference between POP and IMAP accounts is that POP email lives only on whatever machine you download it to. With IMAP, a copy automatically remains on the server so you can download it again on another device. Say you read incoming email on your Galaxy S5, delete some of it, keep some of it, and write some new messages. Later that day, you go to your desktop computer and log into the same email account. You won't see those incoming messages you read on your phone, nor the ones you sent from it.

When you're using both your phone and home computer to work with the same POP account, how do you keep them in sync? By making your POP account act more like an IMAP account, so it leaves a copy of all messages on the server when you download them to your home computer. That way, you can delete messages on the Galaxy S5 and still see them in your inbox at home.

In Outlook 2013, choose File→Account Settings→Account Settings and then double-click the account name. Select More Settings→Advanced. Turn on "Leave a copy of each message on the server." Also turn on "Remove from server when deleted from "Deleted items" so you won't fill up the server space allocated to your account. (In Outlook 2010, this setting is called "Delete messages from server after they are deleted from this computer.")

In Outlook 2011 for Mac, choose Tools→ Accounts, choose the POP account in the left column, and then click Advanced at lower right. Turn on "Leave a copy of each message on the server," and also turn on "Delete copies from the server after deleting from this computer."

To get to these settings in earlier versions of Outlook, choose Tools→ E-mail Accounts→E-Mail→"View or Change Email Accounts"→*your account name*→Change→More Settings→Advanced.

Reading Mail

ON THE GALAXY S5, reading email on a non-Gmail account is much like reading Gmail. In the Apps menu, tap Email to launch the Email app, and it sends you to your inbox immediately and downloads any waiting mail. As with Gmail, the Email app displays the subject line, time and date of delivery, and the sender of each message.

NOTE This section covers a Microsoft Outlook.com account. If you use a different ISP, the screens and options may vary somewhat from what you see here, but generally things work the same.

NOTE If you're using a POP 3 account and you've organized your mail into folders on your computer, that organization won't be reflected on the Galaxy S5. You won't be able to see or use the folders from your computer's email software.

To read a message, tap it. At the bottom of the screen are icons that take you to the next and previous messages, for deleting mail and for replying to or forwarding mail. If the sender is a contact for whom you have a picture, his picture will show up next to his name in the From area.

But there's a whole lot more you can do with your mail message than that. Tap the Menu button next to the sender's name, and you'll get the following choices, which will vary according to whether you're checking mail from an ISP or web-based mail, and according to the web-based mail program you're using:

- **Mark as unread.** When you look in your inbox, the mail will appear bold-faced, as if you hadn't yet read it.

- **Move.** Lets you move the message to another folder.

- **Save email.** Lets you save the mail locally on your S5. It's saved in a file that ends in .eml. You'll be able to read the mail by using a file manager and browsing to the My Files folder (page 324).

- **Register as spam.** Considers the mail as spam. The sender also will be sent to your spam list, so all new mail coming from him will be considered spam.

- **Add to priority senders/Remove from priority senders.** When you add someone to your priority senders, whenever mail shows up in your inbox from the person, an orange icon appears next to his name, indicating that his mail is important. If someone is already a priority sender, select "Remove from priority senders," and his mail will instead be treated like everyone else's in the world.

- **Print.** Prints the mail to a wirelessly available printer.

There's still more you can do. There's another Menu button, just above this one, at the top of the screen, with these three settings:

- **Font size.** Lets you choose a larger or smaller font size for easier reading.

- **Settings.** Brings you to the general setting screen for the mail account. From here, you can make many changes to things such as whether you want a confirmation screen flashed before you can delete an email, and so on.

- **Help.** Gets you help.

Handling Attachments and Pictures in Email

MORE AND MORE EMAIL messages contain pictures. Sometimes, the picture is in the content of the message itself, such as a company logo. Other times, the picture is an attachment, like a family photo. Email handles the two types of graphics differently.

If the graphics are embedded in the content of the message, you'll see a "Show images" button at the top of the mail, and where the photos would normally be, you'll see text. Tap "Show images," and the photos appear right in the mail, where they were placed.

If someone has sent an email and attached a picture, you'll see an icon that looks like a paper clip, and next to it the size of the file. Tap it and two buttons appear—Preview and Save. Tap the Preview button, and the image gets downloaded so you can preview it. Depending on the size of the photo, it might take some time. You'll see the progress as it downloads. After it downloads, the photo opens in the Gallery, as any photo normally does, or if you have multiple photo apps, you get a choice of which to use. If it's a wide photo, you can rotate the phone 90 degrees and see the full picture as the phone switches to its wider orientation.

Attachments in Email

When you receive an email attachment in Word, Excel, PowerPoint, or some other file types, you can preview and download it. You handle these attachments in the same way you handle pictures. The attachment button shows up in the email, and when you tap it you can preview it or save it in the same way you can a photo. If it's a Word, Excel, or PowerPoint file, the preview opens in an app called Polaris Office that's built into the Galaxy S5.

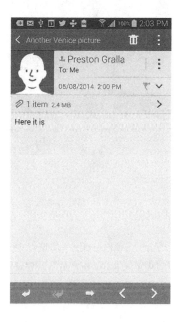

Adding the Sender to Your Contacts

If you get a message from someone and would like to add her to your Contacts list, open the email and then tap the picture of the sender's name. A screen appears that lets you create a new contact with the sender's name and email address, or send email to that contact. If you tap the name of someone who is already a contact, you'll see a button that lets you view that contact's information and take action on it, such as sending an email, making a phone call, and so on.

Managing Mail

WHEN YOU'RE IN YOUR inbox, you've got more options for managing your mail. Tap the Menu button, and a menu appears with these options:

- **Select.** Displays your inbox with checks next to your mail. Turn on the checkboxes next to mail you want to select, and then perform an action on them, such as deleting them.

- **Filter by.** Lets you sort your email in several different ways: unread mail, read mail, flagged mail, and so on.

NOTE The options that appear here vary according to whether you're reading mail from an ISP or web-based mail, and according to what web-based mail service you use.

- **View mode.** Lets you choose the traditional way of viewing mail (sorted by date and such) or by "Conversation view," which groups entire conversations together. Conversation view takes some getting used to, but it's the best way to track a message trail.

- **Compose event invitation.** If you use a mail service like Hotmail.com or Outlook.com that also includes a calendar, you can create meeting invitations by choosing this.

- **Documents.** If you use Hotmail.com or Outlook.com, this lets you view documents from a Microsoft file service such as SharePoint Services. If you don't know what that is, you don't need to use this option.

- **Font size.** Changes the font size of your messages.

- **Delete.** As with Select, this displays your inbox with checks next to your mail. Check the boxes next to messages you want to delete and then delete them.

- **Delete all.** Think of this as a nuclear option. It deletes all your email. Don't do it.

- **Settings.** Brings you to a settings screen for the email account.

- **Help.** Need help with your email service? Here's where to get it.

You've got even more options than that. Look down at the bottom of the screen. You'll see a bar with four icons. The leftmost one lets you create a new mail message; the one to its right checks for new mail. The one in the shape of a magnifying glass lets you search mail. And the one on the far right that looks like a folder displays all your folders for the mail service you're currently using. Tap any folder to go to it.

Creating and Sending Mail

TO CREATE A NEW email message, when you're in the inbox or any folder, tap the pencil-and-paper icon in the lower left of the screen. If you want to create a new message when you're reading an email, tap the Menu key and then tap Compose.

You create a new email message in nearly the identical way in the Email app as you do in the Gmail app, so go to page 240 for details about filling in the To, Subject, and other fields.

Adding a Signature

When you send an email, the Galaxy S5 appends text to the bottom of it but will read something like: "Sent from my T-Mobile 4G LTE Device." That text is visible as you type, and you can delete it if you want. In fact, you may want to delete it from every message and use some text of your own there instead—your email signature.

To add a signature to all your outgoing mail or to delete the built-in text at the bottom of the screen from all outgoing mail from any email service, in the inbox tap the Menu button, select Settings→Manage Accounts, and then tap the name of the account. Tap the Signature setting. To stop the built-in signature from being sent on all messages, from the screen that appears, switch the setting from On to Off. To create a new signature, tap "Edit Signature," type the text you wish to use, and then tap Done.

The changes will affect all the email messages you send with the Email app. (The signature you make in Email doesn't apply to your Gmail account. For details about handling signatures in Gmail, see page 242.)

Using Web-Based Mail Programs

OUTLOOK.COM (AKA HOTMAIL) AND Yahoo Mail are both web-based mail programs, but the Galaxy S5 lets you read them using its built-in email software. Just create new accounts for them, and you'll be able to use its email software to read them.

But if you'd like, you can read email from Hotmail and Yahoo, or any other web-based mail program. Simply visit the site with your phone's web browser and use the email site just as if you were using it on a computer. In some cases, when you visit the site, you're automatically routed to a site specifically built for smartphones, so all the features are formatted nicely for your phone.

In some instances, there might even be an app you can download from the Google Play store, or from the Web, that you can use instead of a web browser. Search the Google Play store to see.

NOTE In some cases the downloadable app may not be built by the company that owns the web-based email service, but instead by a third party. It's generally better to find an app built by the original developer.

You'll learn to:
- Use Facebook on the S5
- Use Twitter on the S5
- Use Google+ on the S5
- Chat and videochat on the S5

CHAPTER 11

Facebook, Twitter, Google+, Chat, and Videochat

THE GALAXY S5 HAS everything you need to keep in touch with friends, family, and associates throughout the world via social networking apps like Facebook, Twitter, Google+, and more. It connects to the Internet, has GPS capabilities (so you can let others know where you are), a big beautiful screen for displaying updates, and a camera so you can take photos and videos and share them. Because it's also got a front-facing camera, it's great for videochat as well. If you're a social butterfly, you've landed on the right phone.

In this chapter you'll find out how to get the most out of your S5 and social networking services, chat, and videochat.

NOTE At this writing, the S5 doesn't have social networking apps built into it. You have to download those apps from the Play store. But that may change, so check your Apps screen to see if any social networking ones are included. See Chapter 12 for the full details on installing and using apps.

Facebook

FACEBOOK IS NOT JUST popular; it's ubiquitous. Millions of people around the globe use it to keep in touch with friends, play games, and publicize their favorite causes. In fact, millions of businesses now have Facebook pages, showing how much social media has become integral to marketing and public relations.

To use Facebook on the S5, you can go to *www.facebook.com* in the Browser, but most Facebookers use an app that's specially designed for the phone. As mentioned earlier, the app doesn't come preinstalled on your S5, so you have to download it and install it yourself. Search for Facebook on Google Play, and then download the app. After a few minutes, when it completes downloading, tap the Open button to run the app.

TIP Make sure that you download Facebook, not Facebook Home. Facebook Home nearly takes over your entire S5. Many people have complained long and loud about Facebook Home—at this writing half the people who rated it gave it only one out of a possible five stars.

After you launch the app, sign in. If you don't yet have a Facebook account, tap "Sign up for Facebook" at the bottom of the screen and follow the directions. You'll be asked to enter a bunch of personal information to create your account.

Once you sign in, you get a chance to sync your Facebook pictures, contact information, and status updates with your existing contacts. You can choose to sync with your existing contacts, not to sync, or else to have Facebook add its contacts to your own Contacts. The suggested choice is to sync with existing contacts, which ensures that you can interact with all your Facebook friends on your S5 without creating duplicates.

Tap Sync. In the background, your contacts sync. Meanwhile, you're taken to your Facebook News Feed so you can start using Facebook right away.

TIP When you use Facebook and look at your contacts in the S5's Contacts app, any of them who are also Facebook friends will have a small Facebook icon next to them.

The first screen you come to is the main Facebook page—your News Feed page. You'll see updates from all your Facebook friends, including their pictures, how long ago the update was posted...pretty much the same thing you see when you visit Facebook on the Web.

Scroll through the feed the same way you scroll through any other screen on your S5, by flicking and dragging. Keep scrolling as long as you want. If you've got a lot of friends, there may seem to be no end to the eternity of postings.

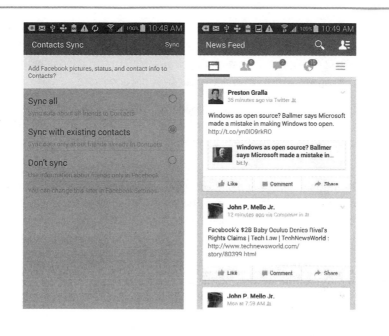

NOTE This chapter assumes that you already know the basics of using Facebook. If you don't, check out the Facebook website at *www.facebook.com*. Click the Help link at the top of the page. On the Help Center page, click the "Get Started on Facebook" link. And if you want to become a real pro, check out *Facebook: The Missing Manual* by E. A. Vander Veer.

The Facebook app regularly checks for updates on its own. If you're like most Facebook denizens, though, you likely can't wait. To make sure you're seeing up-to-the-minute postings from every single one of your friends, tell the Facebook app to check Facebook for any new postings. The S5 gives you a quick way to do that: drag the top of your News Feed down a bit and then release it. The Facebook page appears to bounce and then refreshes itself. Use Facebook for a few minutes, and this gesture will become second nature.

As you scroll down the News Feed, look at the bottom of each update. There are three buttons there: Like, Comment, and Share. Tap the appropriate button for what you want to do.

Tapping Like sends your friend a notification of your approval and adds your name to the list of people who also gave the post a thumbs-up. Tap Comment, and you'll see a list of all comments to the post and a box where you can add your own. Tap in the box, and the S5's keyboard appears. Type your comment, tap Comment, and off it goes. You can also add a picture to your comment by tapping the photo icon and choosing a photo from the Gallery (page 115). Tap Share and you can share the post on Facebook. You get to choose with whom to share it—to the general public, just to your friends, and more.

When you're on the screen for making a comment or adding a Like, you can view the profile of the person whose update you're reading. Tap the Menu key at the bottom of the page and select View Profile.

NOTE The official Facebook app that you use may look and work a bit differently than what you see pictured here. That's because the app gets updated, so you may be using a different version of the app from the one in use when this book was published.

Writing Posts, Uploading Photos, and Using Check In

Now that you've got Facebook on your S5, what should you do? Start posting, of course. What's the point of Facebook if you can't share your innermost secrets with the world?

To post an update, tap the Status button at the Facebook screen's lower left; the keyboard appears. Type what you want, tap Post at upper right, and you'll share with the world the all-important news about your cat's recently changing sleep patterns.

Ah, but what if you want to not just talk about his sleeping patterns, but also show a picture of him sleeping as part of the post? What if you want to share the post only with specific friends? What if you want people to know the exact location of your cat while he continues with his frustrating sleep habits?

That's where the icons just above the keyboard come in. Tap the leftmost one (the picture of a person), to send the post to a specific friend. Tap the location button just next to it to choose a location. Tap the camera icon to go to the Gallery to choose a photo to include in the post. If you want to instead take a photo, after you tap the camera icon, tap it again from the screen that appears to launch the camera, take a picture, and then embed it in your post. If you're a fan of emoticons and smiley faces, tap the icon of the smiley face to bring up a gallery of them. And tap the icon all the way on the right to choose how private the post will be: for anyone to see, for friends only, friends of friends, and so on.

You can also just post a photo without tying it to a post: back on the News Feed page, tap the photo icon in the middle bottom part of the screen, and then choose a photo from your Gallery to post. And if you want to choose a location for your postings, tap the Check In icon just to the right of the icon of the camera.

Navigating Facebook's World

Look just below the very top of the Facebook app's screen—there are five icons there. They're there so that you can navigate Facebook's gigantic, ever-changing world. Here's what they do, from left to right:

- **The leftmost icon** brings you back to your News Feed, no matter where you are.

- **The second-from-left icon (two people)** shows you all the requests for people to friend you. Respond to any right on the screen.

- **The middle icon (a message balloon)** lets you see any messages sent to you. Tap any message to respond to it, Like it, and so on.

- **The second-from-right icon (a globe)** shows notifications left to you, likes and comments to your posts, messages from games you play, and so on.

- **The rightmost icon** gives you quick access to your Facebook friends, events, groups, apps, and so on.

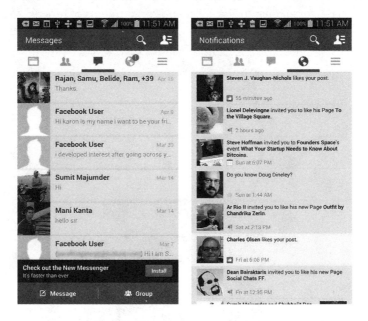

Interacting with Friends and Finding New Ones

Facebook is all about keeping in touch with friends and making new ones. To do that, you'll use two icons at the top right of the screen, just above the row of icons described in the previous section. Tap the rightmost top icon—a person with three horizontal lines—and a screen appears with a list of your current Facebook friends. Tap the person with whom you want to chat and a chat screen opens so you can chat with her.

To find a friend, tap the Search icon, type the name of the friend you're looking for, and you'll get a list of matches. For example, if you search for *ly*, you'll find people with the first name of Lydia, Lynn, and Lysa, people with the last name Lyons, and so on. Scroll through the list and tap the one you want to chat with.

What if you want to see a list of all of your friends? Don't use the very top row of two icons. Instead, tap the rightmost one in the group of five just below it. That brings you to a menu of many Facebook features. Tap Friends from that screen to see the whole list.

How about if you want to add new friends? It's a snap. When you tap the Find Friends button, a screen appears with a list of people you might know. How is that list compiled? It's Facebook magic. But part of it comes down to mutual friends—if there's someone with whom you've got a lot of friends in common, he'll show up here.

Viewing Your Friends' Walls, Info, and More

Whenever you see a friend in a list, tap the name, and you'll get sent to his Timeline, where you can see his most recent updates and much more. Scroll down to see all his updates; tap the Message button to send a message; tap the Photos button to see photos; tap the Friends buttons to see his friends. You can comment on any post...well, you get the idea. You can do anything with the Android app that you can do on the Web.

Facebook Notifications

Facebook uses your S5's Notification panel to let you know when something important has happened—someone responded to a friend request, wants to chat, and so on. You'll get a notification via the Notification panel. Tap it to open it and take any action needed.

Add a Facebook Widget

If you want to interact with Facebook updates at a glance, you don't need to run the Facebook app. Instead, add a Facebook widget on one of your Home screen panes. Adding a widget is a great way to use Facebook on your S5, because that way you can get updates and interact with Facebook without having to run the app.

To add a widget, when you're on a pane, hold your finger on the Recent Apps button. Tap the Widget icon that appears at the bottom of the screen. Flick through the list of available widgets until you find the ones for Facebook. Widgets are in alphabetical order, so it shouldn't take you too long to get to the Facebook ones.

When you find the one you want, hold it and drag it to the highlighted area of the screen that appears above. There may be several widgets, so drag as many as you want. Facebook Status is a good one, since it shows you all your friends' updates at a glance. The widget constantly refreshes itself. Tap it to go straight to Facebook. You can post right from the widget—tap "What's on your mind?" and go crazy.

NOTE If you try to put a widget on a pane that's already full, the widget will refuse to be put there. For more details about handling widgets, see page 28.

Twitter

ARE YOU ONE OF the vast army of tweeters? Celebrities, politicians, pundits, and even the pope communicate with the world in 140-character tweets. With the help of an app, you can tweet right from your S5. Make sure it's the official one from Twitter; Twitter will be listed as the author on the app's description page.

NOTE This section assumes that you already know how to use Twitter on the Web (or have at least heard of it). If you're just getting started, go to *www.twitter.com* and click the Help link at the upper right of the page. The Help Center features a "Welcome to Twitter" link where you can learn more.

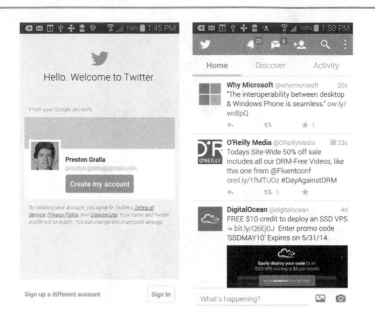

Once you install it, log into your existing Twitter account or click the Sign Up button to create a new one. After a screen or two asking things such as if you want to authorize your S5 to use Twitter, you'll be logged in. Tap Finish. Voilà—you're there! You'll see updates of all the people you're following. Scroll through to read them.

NOTE When you sign in, you'll be asked whether Twitter can use your location. If you're worried about your privacy, just say no.

When you come to the main Twitter screen, look across the top—that navigation bar is Twitter central for your interactions. Here's what each of the buttons do, from left to right:

* **The bird button** takes you to Twitter's main screen.
* **The bell button shows notifications**—like when people have retweeted or favorited tweets of yours.
* **The envelope button** shows direct messages that people have sent to you.

A retweet is when you forward someone's tweet to your own Twitter stream. Sort of like saying, "You've gotta see this tweet!" Your Twitter followers can also retweet you (more on that in a moment).

- **The button with an icon of a person with a + sign** helps you find people to follow and interact with.

- **The search button** lets you search Twitter for people and topics of interest.

- **The Menu button** gives you access to other features, like viewing drafts of tweets you haven't yet sent, changing account settings, and adding a new account.

Just below those buttons are three tabs:

- **The Home tab** brings you to your main Twitter page.

- **The Discover tab** shows you trending hashtags and tweets that people you follow have favorited.

- **The Activity tab** shows you the activity of people you follow, such as who they're following and which tweets they've favorited.

Creating a tweet is simple. At the bottom of Twitter's main screen is a text input box with "What's happening" in it. Tap the box and a new screen appears, where you type in your tweet. As you type, you'll see an indication at the top of the screen about how many characters you have left to help you stay within Twitter's 140-character limit. Tap Tweet when you're done to send your message out to the Twitterverse.

At the bottom of the screen for creating tweets are three buttons that let you enhance your tweet in the following ways (they're listed from left to right):

- **The picture button** launches the Gallery, where you can take an existing photo and attach it to the tweet.

- **The camera button** lets you take and send a photo as part of the tweet. It launches the Camera app (page 129), where you can snap a photo; that photo is then included in the tweet.

- **The location button** turns on location services, so that your location is shared along with your tweet.

Taking Action on Tweets

The Twitter home screen shows you all the tweets, retweets, and direct messages from the folks you follow. You see a list of tweets, along with the person's Twitter ID and photo, as well as how long ago the tweet was made. Small icons give more information about the tweet—for example, whether it's a retweet, a direct message between people, or if the tweet has a photo attached.

Press and hold any tweet, and a bar appears with four icons on it that let you reply to a tweet, retweet it, add it to your favorites, or share it.

Twitter Notifications

Twitter uses your S5's Notification panel to let you know when something important has happened—you have a message sent to you, you've been retweeted, and so on. Tap the notification to open it, and take any action needed.

Google+

GOOGLE'S SOCIAL NETWORKING SERVICE, Google+, isn't as popular as Facebook or Twitter, but those in the know will tell you that it's a winner and a great way to extend your social circle. Google+ also has some capabilities that competing social networking services don't have, like the ability to organize your friends and family into *circles*, which lets you better manage how you interact with them. Circles also integrate with Google Hangouts, YouTube, and Gmail. So when someone comments on a post on Google+, for example, it also shows up in Gmail.

Circles form the core of Google+, which makes it very different from Facebook and other social networks. When you add friends, family, and so on, you add them to a specific circle or circles, which you create according to your needs. That way, you can fine-tune posts so that only certain circles see them—for example, sending a post about your upcoming 35th birthday party to your Family circle, or about next year's soccer league schedule to your Soccer circle. Similarly, you can more easily follow posts based on interests as well, by looking at posts from specific circles.

No need to download it; it's built right into your S5. Tap the Google+ icon in the Apps Screen, and you're ready to go. You may already have a Google+ account without knowing it, because it's tied to your regular Google account. That's another advantage of Google+ over other social networks: connecting to all your Gmail contacts in Google+ is a breeze.

NOTE This chapter assumes that you've already tried your hand at Google+ on the Web. If you need to learn more, check out the Google+ information page at *http://bit.ly/1a6DdXx*. And if you want to become a real pro, check out *Google+: The Missing Manual* by Kevin Purdy.

When you first launch the app, it asks whether to add your Google+ connections to the contacts on your phone. (It's nice to have it all in one place, no matter where you are.) Tap Next and you'll be asked whether to back up your photos from your phone to Google+, and if so, how to back them up—in other words, only when you're connected to a WiFi network, or when you're connected to a

WiFi network or your mobile network. (If you've got a lot of photos uploaded to your Google+ account, it's better to back up only when you're connected to WiFi, to cut down on any potential charges for using too much data on the network.)

After that, you're logged into Google+ and ready to go. When you first launch it, you'll see the feed from all the people in your Google+ circles.

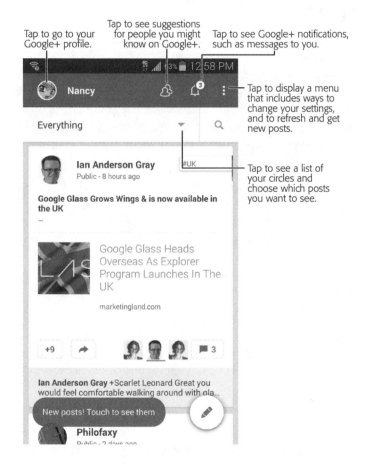

Tap to go to your Google+ profile.

Tap to see suggestions for people you might know on Google+.

Tap to see Google+ notifications, such as messages to you.

Tap to display a menu that includes ways to change your settings, and to refresh and get new posts.

Tap to see a list of your circles and choose which posts you want to see.

Scroll through the list to read them, and tap any to read the full post if it's too long to display on the initial screen. Beneath each post there are buttons for adding your +1 to it (the equivalent of a Like on Facebook), adding a comment to it, or sharing it. At the very bottom, you can see a live feed of comments people are adding.

The red bar at the top of the screen has all your Google+ tools. Tap your name or picture at the top left to go to your own profile page. The two-person icon reveals a list of people you may know and want to add to your circles. To see any notifications, tap the icon that looks like a bell. (If there are any new notifications, you'll see a number on the bell.)

Below the red bar, you see the word "Everything" with a triangle beside it. A drop-down list appears, letting you see only a subset of all the Google+ posts from your circles. Some subsets are auto-created, like "What's hot." But most of them let you see just posts from the various Google+ circles that you've created. The Search icon lets you search your circles for posts from a particular person or about a certain topic. For example, searching for "car" brings up results like a person named "Carlisle" as well as photos of automobiles.

To write a new post, tap the icon of the red pen on the lower right. Type the text in the text area, and tap the word "Public" at the top of the screen to select with whom you want to share the post.

When you post to Google+, you can do more than just write. At the bottom of the text screen, tap the camera to choose a photo from the Gallery to include in the post, tap the chain link to include a link to a web page, and tap the smiley face to choose an emoticon to indicate your mood. And if you want to let people know where you're posting from, tap "Add your location." When you're done, tap the paper plane, and off your message goes.

Back on the Google+ main screen, you'll notice a few other icons down at the bottom of the screen. They mirror the icons at the bottom of the screen when you're creating a post. With them, you can upload a photo, share your location, and choose an emoticon to indicate your mood.

Chat and Videochat with Google Hangouts

SOCIAL NETWORKING APPS ARE great for keeping in touch with people by posting comments, reading people's posts, commenting on their posts, and so on. But if you want direct, live communication, there's something better—chat and videochat. With them, you establish a direct connection with one or more people simultaneously, and then communicate via the keyboard or video.

Galaxy S5 phones come with a feature called Hangouts. Hangouts replace a previous Google program called Google Talk, and they do much more than talk—like make it easier to videochat in groups. In that respect, they're similar to the Hangouts feature built into Google+ on the Web.

If you don't see the Hangouts app on your S5, download it from the Play Store.

To run it, tap the Hangouts icon in the Apps screen. You'll come to the main screen, which shows you previous Hangout sessions, and lets you create new ones.

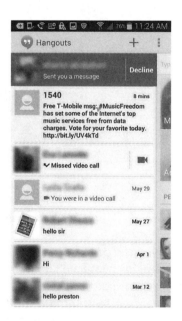

The app name "Hangouts" is a broad term that describes any interaction in it between you and other people. So a Hangout can be as simple as a one-on-one text chat or as complex as a group videochat.

NOTE
Hangouts are often used by websites to broadcast video discussions. They set up a Hangout, invite specific people to participate, and then do a bit of magic to broadcast it from a website. For example, The Huffington Post has a site called HuffPostLive (*www.huffpostlive.com*) that frequently uses Google Hangouts to broadcast. This author has appeared on it for a panel discussion about Apple, Microsoft, and the power of branding.

On the screen with a list of your previous Hangouts, tap any previous Hangout to initiate a chat with the person listed. You can also add additional people to a Hangout by tapping the "Anyone else" button next to the person's name, and then adding that person.

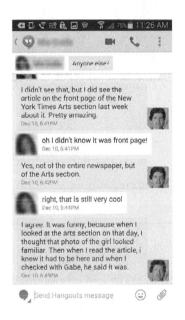

To start a new Hangout with someone else, tap the + sign, or else swipe in from the right side of the screen. Whichever you do, you come to a screen with lists of people, gathered from several places—Google+ and your normal contacts list. At the very top are big icons representing people with whom you communicate most frequently, not necessarily via Hangouts, but via email as well.

Either scroll through the list to find someone you want to chat with, or at the top of the screen, type a name, email address, or even a Google circle that you've created. When you find someone you want to chat with, tap her name.

At this point, one of two things will happen. If the person uses Google+ or Hangouts already, you'll be able to initiate a Hangout with her. If not, you'll come to a screen that lets you contact the person via phone, email, SMS, or in another way in order to invite her to a Hangout. In practical terms, this means she'll get a message but will have to download Hangouts to her phone or head to it on the Web if she wants to communicate with you.

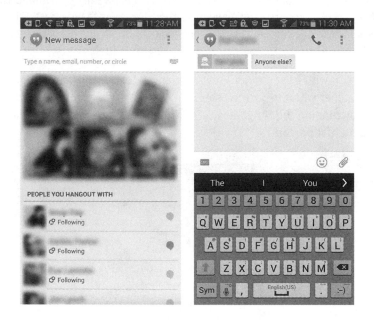

You can create a Hangout and chat with a single person or multiple people. To create one with multiple people, tap "Anyone else?" and keep adding people until you've added everyone you want. Here's also where Google+'s Circles feature helps. You can initiate a Hangout with an entire Circle. In fact, if there are people you frequently videochat with—for example, a group of people at work with offices in different locations—you can create a Circle for just that purpose.

The next step is simple. To chat via the keyboard, tap "Send a message" at the bottom of the screen. Type in your message, tap the little airplane icon to the right of the message, and off it goes.

You'll then see your message onscreen, next to your picture, or an icon representing your face. The person responds, and you see the reply onscreen. Keep chatting this way as long as you like.

You can send a photo as well. Tap the icon of the paper clip to the right of the text input box, and a screen appears that lets you take a photo and send it, or grab the photo from your Gallery. To browse the Gallery, tap "Other photos" and select the one you want to send. You can also send location information by tapping Location.

If you want to switch to a videochat, tap the video camera icon at the top of the screen. The next section gives you the lowdown on how to videochat with Hangouts.

Videochat with Hangouts

When you videochat, your S5 uses the front-facing camera as a videocam. When you speak, its microphone sends what you're saying, and when the other person speaks, the S5's speakers play his words.

The main part of the screen shows the person with whom you're videochatting, and you'll see a picture of yourself down toward the bottom. Normally during the chat the screen around all that is black. But if you tap the screen, one icon appears at the top of the screen, and a row of icons appears at the bottom. At the top of the screen, tap the + icon to add someone else to the videochat.

Here's what the bottom icons do, from left to right:

- **The microphone icon** turns off your microphone. If it's already off, it turns it back on.

- **The speaker icon** lets you turn off the speaker, or else switch to wired headphones, a handset earpiece, or Bluetooth headphones.

- **The video camera icon** turns off the video camera and sends your Google+ picture or, if you don't have one, a generic icon representing a person.

- **The video camera with arrow icon** switches your camera from the one facing you to the one facing away from you. If you're using the one facing away from you, tapping the icon switches to the camera facing you.

The big red bar with the telephone icon at the bottom of the screen shows how long the videochat has been going on. Tap the bar to end the call.

Retrieving Archived Hangouts and More

If you tap the Menu button on a main Hangouts screen, you'll get these options:

- **Set mood** lets you choose from a number of icons that represent the way you currently feel. People will see it when they see your online presence.

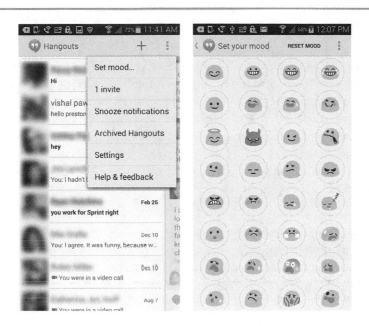

- **Invites** shows you the Hangout requests you've gotten but have not yet responded to.

- **Snooze notifications** stop any notification requests for Hangouts. Tap this and you can turn them off for a variety of intervals ranging from an hour to 72 hours.

- **Archived Hangouts** lists all the Hangouts you've archived. Tap any to review it. If it was a text Hangout, you'll see the text. If it was a video Hangout, you'll see a summary of who was on the call and her pictures, but not the video itself.

- **Settings** gives you control over a variety of Hangout settings, such as changing your Google+ profile picture, whether to be alerted via sounds and vibrations when you get requests for Hangouts, and so on.

- **Help & feedback** lets you find help for using Hangouts, and give feedback to Google about it.

Responding to a Hangouts Invitation

When you receive a message via Hangouts, it will appear in the status bar. Pull down the Notification panel, and then tap the message. You'll be sent to Hangouts, where you can chat or participate in a video call as outlined earlier in this section.

Chat and Videochat with ChatON

THERE'S ANOTHER WAY TO chat or videochat on your S5—Samsung's ChatON app. So far, very few people use the app, so it might be a lonely place to be until it catches on. Launch the app by tapping the ChatON icon in the Apps screen. The first time you launch it, it may take a few minutes to set itself up. When the registration screen appears, tap in your phone number and then tap Next. (Your number may already be filled in for you.) After you tap Next, you'll be asked whether you want to verify the phone number via text (SMS) or a voice call. Make your choice, get verified via either voice or phone, and you're ready to go.

NOTE In order to use ChatON, you'll first have to have a Samsung account. To find out how to set one up, turn to page 22.

After verification, contacts from your phone will be imported into ChatON. That means that you'll be able to contact them directly from the app, and they'll be able to contact you as well—as long as they use ChatON, that is. Not all your contacts will be imported, only those who also use ChatON. So you may only have a friend or two, or you may have many available for videochats.

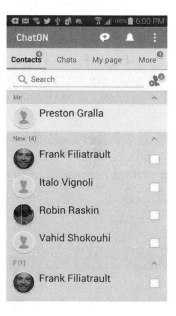

On the ChatON main screen, you see all your contacts. The screen has four tabs across the top: Contacts, Chats, My Page, and More. Contacts lists your ChatON contacts. Chats shows your chat history. My Page contains personal information you can add, such as your mood, current status, and more. More has a variety of other features, including other services and things you can buy.

Chatting is simple: Tap the person with whom you want to chat, and on the screen that appears select the way you want to contact him. Tap the balloon to chat with him, the phone to call him, and the icon of the video camera for a videochat.

Other Social Networking Apps

Facebook, Google+, and Twitter are just three of the most popular social networking apps—there are plenty more out there, many of which have nifty Android apps for your S5. To find many of them, head to the Play store and go to the Social category

Here are just a few you might want to try:

- **WhatsApp.** This service, bought by Facebook for an astonishing $19 billion, is a cross-platform messaging app that lets you chat and exchange messages on any type of phone without having to pay text-messaging charges.

- **Snapchat.** This clever app lets you quickly take a photo and share it with others. But there's a catch—the photo vanishes after the amount of time you specify. After that, it's as if it never existed. This app has become extremely popular.

- **Vine.** Create short, looping videos with your camera, and share them with friends, family, and anyone else you want.

- **Instagram.** This popular app lets you customize photos by adding filter effects and then share them with others.

- **Foursquare.** This app is designed for mobility from the ground up. Share your location information, share pictures, get discounts, and so on.

- **Seesmic.** Technically, this isn't a social networking site. Instead, it's a piece of software that works as a kind of front end to Facebook and Twitter, so you can use both from the same interface.

- **Hootsuite.** A front end to multiple social networks, including Facebook, Twitter, LinkedIn, and others.

- **LinkedIn.** Think of LinkedIn as Facebook for business. It's buttoned-down, and mainly for work, although it has begun expanding beyond that as well.

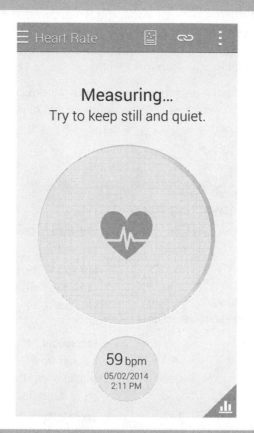

Measuring...
Try to keep still and quiet.

59 bpm
05/02/2014
2:11 PM

You'll learn to:
- Find and download apps
- Use Google Play to download apps
- Download apps from the Web and using a barcode scanner
- Update, manage, and uninstall apps
- Get 13 great apps

CHAPTER 12

Downloading and Using Apps

WHY DO YOU HAVE the Samsung Galaxy S5 rather than a plain-Jane cell-phone? If you're like most people, it's for the phone's apps, which let you do remarkable things like using your phone as a bar code reader or guitar tuner.

The S5 features plenty of great built-in apps, which are covered throughout this book. In fact, you've been using apps and may not even know it. When you check your email on the S5, that's an app. When you shop at Google's Play store, it's courtesy of an app. One of the phone's great features, though, is that it lets you download and use new apps as well—and those new apps do just about everything under the sun (and sometimes things that seem beyond the range of the solar system).

In this chapter, you'll find out how to get and use those apps, as well as how to uninstall and troubleshoot them. It'll also show you a few of the more amazing Android apps available online.

The Galaxy S5's Free and Easy Approach to Apps

THE SAMSUNG GALAXY S5 takes a different approach to the use of apps than some other devices in that there's absolutely no limitation on what you can download. Android's developer, Google, doesn't step in to say what you can and can't download, and neither do the phone's manufacturer, Samsung, or its carriers. If the app runs on Android, you can run it on your S5.

You're free to choose from hundreds of thousands of apps, with thousands more being written every month. There are apps for tracking expenses, playing music, chatting with people, playing games, using social networks like Facebook and Twitter, finding new friends, making your S5 work better, viewing maps of the night sky, and much more.

> **TIP** Some Android apps cost money, but many more are free. So whenever you find a for-pay app, do a bit of searching to see if you can find a free one that does the same thing.

These apps tie into the Galaxy S5's unique hardware and software. One even automatically detects potholes as you drive, using the S5's various sensors to measure sudden movements. The app then uses the phone's positioning software to locate exactly where the pothole is and creates a text file with all the relevant information so you can send it to your local Department of Public Works. (Unfortunately, no app has yet been developed that will get your local Department of Public Works to actually fix the pothole.)

Running apps is simple. Tap their icons on any Home screen or pane, or on the Apps screen.

Apps and Multitasking

THE GALAXY S5 IS great at multitasking—running more than one app at a time. For example, you can browse the Web while you listen to music, receive email, and have Facebook updates delivered to you, all without breaking a sweat.

You usually don't notice that Android is multitasking, because unlike in an operating system like Windows or Mac OS X, you typically don't see all running apps simultaneously in their own separate windows at once. However, if you turn on the S5's Multi Window feature, you'll be able to run multiple apps on the same screen at once. For details, see page 38.

When you're in an app and want to do something else on the S5, you typically press the Home key. From there, you can tap to run an app such as the web browser, or open the Apps screen to run more apps. When you do that, though, that first app is still running in the background. If it's a music-playing app or a radio app, it keeps playing until you close it. With many other apps, though, at some point the phone will notice that you haven't used it in a while and close it down. You won't even notice that the S5 has closed it.

NOTE You can find apps called *task killers* that claim to speed up your Galaxy S5 by automatically closing apps when they're no longer needed, or by letting you manually close those apps. However, the era of task killers is drawing to a close, since the S5 has built-in features that do the same thing. For details, see page 300.

There is a way to make sure that an app closes when you switch away from it, though. Rather than pressing the Home key to run another app, press the Menu button and look for a menu choice that closes the app. Not all apps offer this choice, but that's OK; the S5 will close the app when it's no longer needed. If for some reason, though, you want to close an app and it doesn't have a menu choice for that, you can still do it—use the Task Manager (page 300).

Seeing Your Most Recently Run Apps

There's a quick way to see the most recent apps you've run or that are still running. Tap the Recent apps button on the lower-left part of the phone, and you'll see them all in a scrollable list. Tap any app in the list to run it. You can also swipe away apps you're no longer using to close them, thus shortening the list.

Where to Get Apps

THE GALAXY S5 OFFERS you not just one, not just two, but three different ways to download and install apps:

- **Google Play store.** Here's the primary way that most people download and find apps. It's right on your Home screen. Tap the Play Store button, and it launches. From here you can search for apps, find information about apps, and pay for them.

- **The Web.** You can download and install apps from websites. Visit the site on your phone's browser and download from there.

NOTE In a few cases, you can download an app to your PC or Mac, and it will then be installed on your Galaxy S5 when you connect your computer. Generally, this happens if you've downloaded an app that works with your PC or Mac as well as with Android.

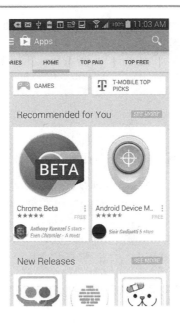

- **Using a bar code scanner.** Of all the amazing tricks the Galaxy S5 can do, this one may just be the coolest. A free app gives your S5 the ability to scan bar codes and QR codes. (*QR codes* are a special kind of bar code used by smartphones, cameras, and other devices.) After you've installed this app, you can scan a QR code to download other apps. When you're browsing the Web with your PC or Mac, and you come across a bar code or QR code for downloading, just point your phone at it, click a button, and the magic begins. The phone grabs and installs the software from the website. For more on bar code scanning, see page 296.

Using Google's Play Store

TAP THE PLAY STORE icon, and you get sent to Google Play, which has not just apps, but also movies, music, books, and more. Tap the Apps icon to be sent to the Apps area, which has hundreds of thousands of apps you can download, with more added every month. The apps are either free or very low cost—typically under $4, although some business-related apps can cost up to $30:

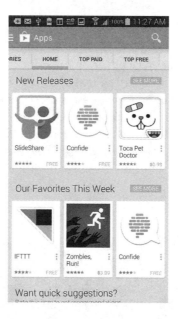

- **Tap the Categories tab** at the top to see categories of apps, including Games, Business, Entertainment, and many more.

- **Featured apps, games, movies, and more** take up most of the screen and scroll off the bottom. Flick to see them; tap any one for more details.

At the very top of the screen, at upper right, is a search button. Tap it to search for an app.

Browsing by Category

Tap one of the categories, and you come to a screen that lists the apps in it. Notice across the top of the screen that there are buttons for Top Paid, Top Free, and others. You can't see them all onscreen, so swipe to the right to see them in turn. Tap any category or list, and you come to a list of all the apps in that category. Each listing shows the name of the app, its maker, its price, and an average user rating.

Searching Google Play for Apps

Browsing is all well and good when you've got the time and want to scroll leisurely through lists looking for an app. But sometimes you're on a mission: You know the type of app you want, and you want to find it fast.

In that case, you want to search. You can search by the type of app, the name of the program, or the name of the software company that created it. Tap the Search button, and a keyboard and search box appear. Type your search term or select a term from the list that appears when you begin typing. You'll see a list of apps that match what you're looking for, sorted into their categories.

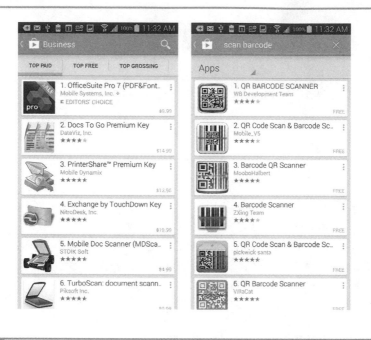

When you view a list of apps, you may notice that some of them, instead of showing a price, will show the word "Installed." Yup, it means what you think it means—you've already installed the app on your Galaxy S5.

Getting Info About an App

No matter what type of list you look through—whether as a result of a search or by browsing—you'll eventually want to get more details about an app and possibly download it. In that case, tap the name of the app, and you come to a page with a great deal of information about it, including the number of downloads, the total number of ratings on which the star rating is based, the price, a description of the app, screenshots, and individual reviews.

Be careful when using the star ratings as a guide to download and pay for an app. In some instances, that star rating may be based on just a rating or two. Any star rating based on a few ratings may not be particularly accurate, especially because the ratings may come from the developer and the developer's friends. If there are a dozen or more ratings, they're more trustworthy. So read the actual reviews, and see how *many* ratings each app has gotten.

Scroll down, and you'll find a load of information about the app, including any videos showing it in action, individual reviews, and a particularly useful section that's often overlooked—information about the developer. It lists other apps the developer has written, links to the developer's homepage, and lets you send email to the developer.

> **NOTE** If you come across an app that you believe has inappropriate content, such as pornography or gratuitous violence, scroll to the bottom of the page and tap "Flag as inappropriate."

Downloading and Installing Apps

So you've read all about an app, and you've decided to take the plunge. You're ready to download. What's next? Depending on whether the app is free or paid, you do things slightly differently.

If the app is free, you see an Install button. Tap it. A screen appears, telling you what kind of information and features the application has access to, such as your location, your phone's storage, and so on. Typically, the application needs this kind of access—a GPS app can't do its job without access to your phone's GPS features, after all. Still, it's a good idea to take a look, and if you're concerned about anything, don't download. (See the box on page 293 for more information.)

To download it, tap Accept. The app immediately starts downloading in the background. You'll see the progress of the download onscreen. While the download goes on, you can use your phone in any way you want; the download won't interfere. Soon a checkbox appears, indicating that the download is complete. Pull down the Notification panel, and you see that the app has downloaded and been installed. Tap the notification to run the app. You can also run the app by heading to the Apps screen and tapping the icon there. Or you can stay in the app page, on the Play Store, and wait for the download to complete. If it's not a big file and you're on WiFi, it can happen in a snap.

If the app is free, it will install by itself, and you'll see an Open button. Tap it to run the software. Tap the Uninstall button beneath it if you want to uninstall it.

If the app is a for-pay one, you need a Google Checkout account, so set one up ahead of time on the Web at *https://checkout.google.com*. It's simple and free. With that done, you can buy the app. Instead of an Install button, a Buy button appears. Tap it. As when you're downloading a free app, a screen tells you what kind of features and information the app will use. Tap Accept. Now it's time to pay. On the next screen, you see how much the app costs. Tap Buy, and follow any onscreen instructions that appear. After you've paid, the download proceeds in the exact same way as for free apps.

UP TO SPEED

Download with Caution

Your Galaxy S5 is a computer, and just like any computer, it can be targeted by malware or by hackers trying to steal personal data or track your online behavior. There's software—like Lookout Security (*www.lookout.com*)—that you can use to keep yourself safe. But software by itself isn't enough—you also need to be smart about what to download.

One of the biggest dangers comes from apps that invade your privacy by sending out information about you, or that dial your phone without your knowledge to call for-pay services, or send text messages to for-pay services. There's a way to see what kind of information apps will grab, and what kinds of access they have to your computer—and you can see that before you download. When you tap to download, you see a list of the features and information the app can access.

Look closely at that information. If an app is asking for access to information or features that don't seem related to the app, it could spell trouble. For example, if you're downloading a simple, single-player game and it says that it uses your GPS to determine your location, that might be a red flag, because there's generally no need for a game of that kind to have that information. The app may attempt to track your location and send information about it to advertisers.

On the other hand, a social networking app that connects you to friends nearby will certainly need access to your GPS location. So the key is to see whether the information and features seem to match the purpose of the app.

For more details and more advice, see this Computerworld article on privacy with smartphone apps: *http://bit.ly/q4bRyG*.

Downloading from the Web

YOU'RE NOT LIMITED TO getting apps from the Google Play store—you can download them from the Web as well. You can either visit the app developer's website to download the app, or instead head to one of the many web libraries that house thousands of apps.

NOTE Be aware that when you install apps from the Web, they don't go through the same kind of vetting procedure that they do in Google Play. So be careful about what you download. It's a good idea to download apps only from well-known developers or well-known, trusted download libraries.

Downloading from the Web takes a bit more work than from Google Play. It's a several-step process, rather than a simple all-in-one:

1. Go to a website using your phone's browser and search for an app, or go directly to a developer's site.

2. Download a file to your S5.

3. Install the app using the downloaded file.

NOTE You can also download the file to your PC or Mac and then transfer it to your S5. For details about transferring files between computers and your phone, see page 319.

Unless you know a specific app you want to download and the URL of the developer's website, your best place to start is one of the many Android download libraries. The Android Freeware site—*www.freewarelovers.com/android*—is one good place. The download library *www.download.com* also has an Android area, and *www.appbrain.com* is good, too.

Once you find a file you want to download, tap the link to download it. A file will then be downloaded, and you'll see the progress on a download screen. You'll notice an odd filename—*Ghost_Commander_1.52b4.apk*, for example. (Android apps end in the extension *.apk*.)

NOTE In some instances when you go to a website to download the file, when you click to download, you'll be sent to Google Play and can then download it from there in the usual way.

After the file downloads, tap the notification. Either the file will install, or else you'll come to a screen asking you whether you first want to scan the file with an anti-malware program, if you've got one on your S5. (Your S5 may come with the anti-malware program Lookout.) It's a good idea to scan first, so go ahead and do that for safety's sake. If it passes muster, then continue the installation. If it doesn't pass, then don't install the software.

NOTE Don't worry if for some reason you miss the notification after the download. You can still easily find the file. In the Apps screen, tap Downloads, and you'll see it.

Depending on how your S5 is set up, you may next come to a screen saying that, for security purposes, you can't install any software outside the Google Play store. On the Apps screen, tap Settings. From the screen that appears, scroll down to the System section and tap Security. Scroll down and turn on the checkbox next to "Unknown sources." A screen appears warning you that if you do this, you may be vulnerable to attack. Tap OK.

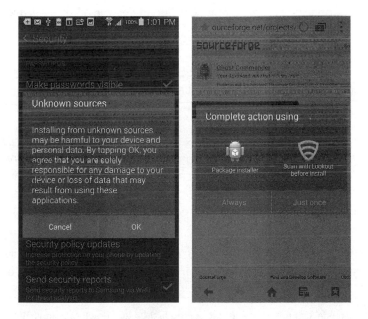

A screen similar to the one you've seen in the Google Play store appears, which tells you what kinds of features and information the app will need access to. Tap Install to install the app, or Cancel to cancel the installation. When the app is installed, you can immediately run it by tapping Open, or tap Done and run it later. You'll be able to run the app anytime from the Apps screen.

When you're done installing the app, you won't need the original download file any longer, so you can delete it.

Downloading and Using a Bar Code Scanner

HERE'S AN EVEN COOLER way to download apps—using a bar code scanner. You browse the Web by using your PC or Mac, and when you come across a file you want to download, point your S5's camera at the onscreen bar code, and the app downloads to your PC. In fact, you don't even need to browse the Web to download apps in this way. The bar code can be somewhere in the physical world—like in a magazine.

First you need to get one of the many bar code scanner apps. One highly rated, popular app is called Barcode Scanner, from ZXing Team. And it's free, as well.

NOTE Barcode Scanner does a lot more than just let you download apps. It can also scan a bar code on a product, identify the product, and send you to web pages with more information about it, including reviews and places to buy.

After you install the scanner app on your Galaxy S5, you're ready to go. Many web-based Android libraries and developer websites have bar codes next to the app descriptions, so you can easily download them.

Place a barcode inside the viewfinder rectangle to scan it.

When you come across a bar code for downloading an app, run Barcode Scanner, and then point the phone's camera at the bar code just as if you were snapping a photo, centering it in the window in the middle of the viewfinder. The app quickly recognizes the bar code and shows you information about it, including the web page's URL. At the bottom of the screen, tap "Open browser," and the file downloads just as if you had tapped a download link. You can then install the app in the usual way. For details, see page 291.

NOTE You can also share the link to the app with others by tapping either "Share via email," or "Share via SMS." If you do that, you won't send the app or the bar code, but instead a link to the page, using either email or text messaging.

Updating Apps

APPS ARE OFTEN UPDATED, and the nice thing about the Galaxy S5 is that it tells you when any of your apps are ready for updating—and then lets you update them with a single tap. When an update is available, you get a notification in the Status bar. Drag down the bar, tap the notification, and you see a list of all the apps that have updates available, as well as all your downloaded apps. Even better, many apps automatically update themselves, so you don't need to do anything.

Tap any update you want to download, and you see the description page you normally see before downloading an app, except that the buttons at the bottom have changed. Tap Update to update the app or Uninstall to remove it from your phone. You can also update all your out-of-date apps in a single swoop by tapping "Update all." When you tap Update, you'll get the same note about the features and information the app will use. Tap to install it, and the S5 downloads the app in the background. You see its progress as it downloads, but you don't have to watch it unless you really want to.

TIP If you want the app to update itself automatically, instead of you having to update it, turn on the checkbox next to "Allow automatic updating" on the Update screen.

Managing, Sharing, and Uninstalling Apps

AFTER A WHILE, YOU MAY suffer from app overload: You've downloaded so many apps you don't know what to do with them. It's time to get them under control.

There's a single app for doing that, the Application Manager. Tap Settings from the Apps screen, scroll down to the Applications section, and tap Application Manager.

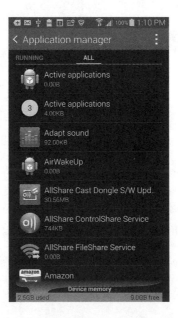

You'll see a list of your apps, including their names and file sizes, categorized in four tabs. It's tough to tell at first that there are four of them, because there's not enough screen real estate to show them all, but they're there. To see each tab, swipe to the right. Here's what each tab shows:

- **Downloaded.** These are apps that weren't on the Galaxy S5 when you started using it but that you've downloaded and installed.

NOTE Some apps show up on the Downloaded tab even if they were preinstalled, such as those you've updated. But even some you didn't update show up there...go figure!

- **All.** This is the mega-list of your apps—every single one on the phone, including those built into it and those you've downloaded.

- **On SD card.** Normally, apps install to your Galaxy S5's main memory, not to its SD card. But as you'll see in a bit, there's a way to move some of them from the phone's memory to its SD card.

- **Running.** These are apps that are currently running on your S5.

TIP The list of apps is arranged alphabetically. You can instead view them by their size (biggest first). Tap the Menu button, and then choose "Sort by size" to list them by size order.

Tap any app, and you come to a screen chock-full of information about it—its version number, its total size, the size of any data associated with it, the size of the program itself, and, toward the bottom of the screen, information about what kinds of features and data the app uses.

You can uninstall the app—tap the Uninstall button. If you see that an app is running and you want to close it, tap the "Force stop" button. That button is grayed out if the app isn't currently running.

TIP It's easy to uninstall an app from the Apps screen or any other screen it's on. Hold your finger on the app you want to uninstall, and then drag it to the trash can icon at the top of the screen.

From this screen, you can also move an app from the Galaxy S5's main memory to its SD card—simply tap "Move to SD card." If an app is already on the SD card, tap the button to move it back. (Not all apps can be moved to the SD card—its developer must have programmed that capability into it.)

Using the Task Manager for Managing Apps

The Galaxy S5 also has a handy built-in task manager that shows information about your apps and lets you control them in some very useful ways. To launch it, tap the Recent apps button on the lower left of the S5 and tap the far-left button—it looks like a pie graph. You'll see a screen that looks a little bit like the one covered in the previous section. There are some big differences, though. The Task Manager is designed for closing down apps and managing memory and storage, and more as well. It's a great app that shows all the applications that are currently running. It also shows how much RAM (memory) each uses, and how much of your smartphone's CPU it uses. (The CPU is your phone's brain.) If any app is problematic (for example, using too much battery, too much RAM, or too much CPU), it shows up red. This information is helpful if you find your S5 running sluggishly, because it may be that your apps are taking up too much memory or too much of your CPU. To free up memory or the CPU, you can force some apps to close. Tap the End button next to any you want to close. It also shows how much storage you have on your main system and SD card, and how much you've got left.

Putting an App on the Home Screen or Panes

THERE MAY BE AN app you use so frequently that you get tired of the constant dance of having to open the Apps screen, scroll down to the app's icon, and then tap it. There's a much easier way: You can put its icon right on your Home screen or any screen, so it's always there at your command:

1. **Go to the Apps screen.**

2. **Hold your finger on the app you want to put on the Home screen or other screen.**

3. **The last screen you were on before going to the Apps screen appears at the top of the screen, but smaller than normal.** Below it you'll see representations of each of your screens, including the Home screen.

4. **Drag the app's icon to the Home screen or pane where you want it to appear.**

5. **The icon is added to the Home screen or a pane.**

NOTE The Home screen or pane may have too many app icons on it to have any new ones added. In that instance, you'll have to first remove an icon from the screen or pane before you can add a new app.

What if you want to delete the icon but still keep the app? Put your finger on the app and hold it there until a trash can appears at the top of the screen. Drag the icon to the Trash. The icon disappears, but the app remains and is accessible from the Apps screen.

Troubleshooting Apps

IN A PERFECT WORLD, apps would never misbehave. Unfortunately, it's not a perfect world. So an app may quit the moment you launch it, or cause your Galaxy S5 to restart, or do any number of odd things. If that happens, try these steps:

- **Launch the app again.** There's no particular reason why this should work, but it often does.

- **Uninstall and reinstall.** There may have been an oddball installation problem. So uninstall the app and then reinstall it. That sometimes fixes the problem.

- **Restart your Galaxy S5.** Just as restarting a computer sometimes fixes problems for no known reason, restarting the S5 may have the same effect. Power it down by pressing and holding the Power/Lock key, and then press and hold the Power/Lock key again to restart.

- **Reset the Galaxy S5.** If an app causes the phone to stop responding, you'll have to reset the phone. See page 384 for details.

If none of this works, it's time to uninstall the app. Don't fret; there are plenty more where it came from.

Thirteen Great Apps

THERE ARE TENS OF thousands of great apps, and a whole world of them to discover. To give you a head start, here are 13 favorites—and they're all free. You can find each of them in the Google Play store, although in the instance of S Health, it's already right on your S5.

S Health

This very useful Samsung app helps you manage your health, including setting and keeping fitness goals, and keeping track of your health in general. To run it, tap S Health in the Apps screen.

After you agree to the terms of use, you fill out a basic profile about yourself, including your name, age, gender, height, weight, and activity level. Based on that, S Health calculates how many calories you should consume a day, and how many calories you likely burn a day. When you're done, tap the Start button.

Keep in mind one thing about S Health: It can be a guilt-inducing little app, tracking every part of your health. The truth is, though, that it's unlikely you'll use every part of it. So pick and choose what you want to use, and it'll be your friend instead of a nag.

The S Health's main screen shows you the current state of your health, including the calories you've burned today and how many calories you've eaten. But it can do this and keep track of other parts of your health only if you tell the program to start tracking you.

To do that, tap the icon of three horizontal lines at the top left of your screen. You'll come to a screen with various modules for tracking your health, including for walking, exercise, weight, sleep, and others.

Tap the module you want to use, set a goal if you wish, and then press Start. For example, if you choose Running, press Start and start pounding the pavement. There's even a button that lets you play music on your S5 as you work out. When you're done running (or ready for a break), tap Pause, and when you're ready to see your final results, tap Stop. S Health shows you how long you ran, how much distance you covered, how many calories you burned, and (if you have GPS turned on) the route you ran.

The Sleep module is designed to work with the Samsung Gear Fit activity monitor. It detects your sleep pattern as you wear it on your wrist and then syncs it to your phone. If you already have an activity monitor, like a Fitbit, it may sync with the S5. Give it a try!

There are still more features that take advantage of the S5's built-in magic:

- **Pedometer** uses the S5's sensors to track how much you've walked in a day. Just turn it on and carry your S5 with you. At the end of the day, it tells you how many steps you've walked and how many calories you've burned. It tracks this over time, so you can see graphs.

- **Heart rate** does exactly what it says—it measures your current heart rate. Hold your finger on the sensor at the back of the S5 (it's just underneath the camera), tap the Start button, and keep still. The S5 then does its magic and measures your heart rate. To test it out, try it in multiple circumstances— after heavy exercise, when you wake from sleep, after sitting still, and so on.

The Stress module works in a similar manner, but you have to hold your finger on the heart rate sensor longer. As far as anyone can tell, this feature works by looking for variations in your heart rate over time.

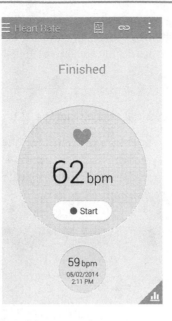

Make sure to check in regularly to S Health to see how you're doing, and adjust your meals, exercise level, and so on to keep on track. To get an overview, tap the small chart icon at the bottom right of the screen to see graphs that display how you're doing over time.

Endomondo Sports Tracker

If you're serious about running, cycling, hiking, mountain biking, or other sports, you should give Endomondo Sports Tracker a try. It's a combination training tracker and analyzer combined with social media and networking. The app uses the S5's sensors, notably its GPS, to automatically track your workout. So you can use it while running, for example, to see your progress—running distance, time elapsed, and current and average speeds. After your run or workout, you upload the information results so that friends can see them—and either sneer at your measly results or go green with envy over your athletic prowess. There's plenty more here as well, such as automatically created maps of your workouts, and linking to music apps so you can listen to music while you jog and sweat.

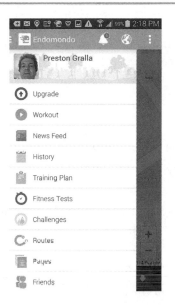

TuneIn Radio

There are thousands of Internet radio stations all over the world, just waiting for you to listen to them. Most are streams of traditional stations, but there are many Internet-only stations as well. No matter the kind of music, news, entertainment, talk, or more, you'll be able to find it on this great free app. It lets you browse and search for anything you want. You may even find it useful for learning foreign languages, because you can tune in to radio stations from all over the world.

Google Play Newsstand

Here's another excellent free app for news and information junkies. It grabs stories from many resources, publications, and sites, ranging from print news-papers and magazines to blogs, websites, television channels, and more. You can follow constantly changing sections, such as Business, Science & Tech, Entertainment, Sports, and so on, or you can instead follow just a single publica-tion, such as The Daily Beast. It's also easy to share stories with other people. And a particularly useful feature is Save, which lets you download articles to your S5 in a single location for later reading.

NOTE   Even though the app is called Google Play Newsstand, it may show up on your S5 with the name of its predecessor, Currents, or Google Currents. Go figure.

Evernote

If you suffer from information overload, here's your remedy. Evernote does a great job of capturing information from multiple sources, putting them in one location and then letting you easily find them—whether you're using your com-puter, your tablet, or another Android device.

Not only that, it's free.

You organize all your information into separate notebooks, and can then browse each notebook, search through it, search through all notebooks, and so on. No matter where you capture or input information, it's available on every device on which you install Evernote. So if you grab a web page from your PC and put it into a notebook, that information is available on your S5, and vice versa.

You can capture information from the Web, by taking photos, by speaking, and by pasting in existing documents. And you can also type notes.

The upshot of all this? Evernote is the best app you'll find for capturing information and making sense of it all.

Aldiko Book Reader

That big 5.1-inch, high-resolution S5 screen is crying out for you to use it for something other than making phone calls or sending and receiving texts. And with this free app, you can do just that—read books, and plenty of them. It's a very good ereader that gives you access to reading (for free or pay, depending on the book) thousands of books. There are plenty of nice options, like changing the reading settings between Day mode and Night mode (black text on white background for day; white text on black background for night). There are also bookmarking features, a good search feature, and plenty more. (Full disclosure: There's also an excellent selection of O'Reilly books for download.)

> **TIP** If you own a Kindle or a NOOK, you should also download the appropriate app for your S5. You'll be able to read any of your Kindle or NOOK books right on your phone. And when you leave off reading on the S5 and start reading again on your Kindle or NOOK, you'll be able to start in right where you left off—and vice versa.

Candy Crush Saga

This free puzzle adventure game is so addicting that you should start playing only when you know you won't have something that needs doing for the next 20 minutes...or hour...or two. You touch and swipe candies on a grid in order to put three of them in a row. When you do, they're crushed, and more candies slide in. Match even more candies, and you create special candies that can be used for more power. They can also be combined for even more power.

Simple, yes? Well, not so much, as you'll find out as you make your way through this increasingly complicated game. The game has been popular for a long time and shows no sign of slowing down.

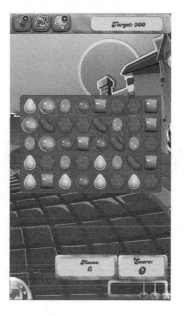

Google Goggles

This may well be the most amazing app you'll ever see. Run Google Goggles, and then point it at an object, a sign, a piece of artwork, a logo, the label on a bottle of wine, and so on. It will identify what you're looking at (or translate the sign if it's in a foreign language), and provide more information about it. Point it at a menu in a foreign country to translate the menu, identify landmarks... there's a lot more here as well. It doesn't always work, but when it does, it's mind-boggling.

WhatsApp Messenger

Facebook paid $19 billion for this multi-messenger app, but you won't have to pay a penny. It's a cross-platform messenger program that lets you send and receive SMS text messages without having to pay your cellphone carrier. You'll be able to send the messages and chat with those who use WhatsApp on other phone platforms.

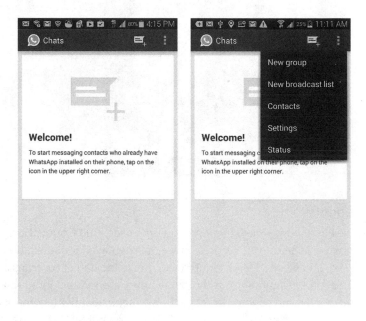

Vine

This Twitter-created app does for videos what Instagram does for photos—it lets you create simple, 6-second looping videos, and then post them and share them with others. And it lets you check out looping videos that others create as well.

Creating a looping video is simple. Launch the app, tell it to create a video, and it switches to your camera. Hold your finger on the screen to record; lift your finger from the screen to stop recording. A bar across the top shows you how much you've already recorded of your 6 seconds of fame, and how many seconds are left. After you've created a video, it's ready to go and can be shared via Twitter and Facebook. There's also a Vine feed, so that people can subscribe to your feed, and you to theirs. That means you'll be able to see a constantly changing feed of these little videos. Vine has all the usual social media features, such as comments.

Revined by Editor's Pick

Paulette Griswold   04 Apr
Enjoying the sun 🌸 #hulaloops
#AllNaturalVines /All Natural Vines
#theblackkeys

158.9k people like this

Instagram

This popular app combines excellent photo filtering tools with photo sharing, and is a great way to play with photos and share them with friends and family, especially via Facebook. And it's also great for seeing photos that others take, and not just friends and family, but the famous as well, many of whom seem to be Instagram junkies.

baifernbah   33m

♥ 12,497 likes
baifernbah ขอบคุณที่แวะมาเยี่ยมเยียนอุดหนุนนะครัช
พรุ่งนี้เจอกับเฟินได้ที่บูธ B85 ย่ายโมงครัช ส่วน @cheerny
ก็อยู่ใกล้ๆกัน @inspired_you #inspiredyou

Load Instagram, use its tools to snap a photo, and then use its magic. You can add a frame and select a specific focus point, but that's just the beginning. It's the filters that you'll care about, well over a dozen. Retro, black and white, Nashville, Hefe, Kelvin...you'll find anything you need to indulge your inner photographer.

After you're done, it's time to share, and Instagram makes it easy. You can share via Twitter, Facebook, Flickr, Tumblr, or Foursquare without any heavy lifting, because they're all built into the app. And you can use the app to follow others' photos as well.

New to Instagram is a Vine-like capability for creating and sharing videos as well. Oh, and by the way, if you're looking to take a selfie, this is a great app to do it with.

Snapchat

This app is a great mash-up of chat, social media, and photos. You take a photo or video, add text and drawings, and then send it to a friend or friends. Those friends can be ones gathered from your social networks, your contacts, and so on, or new ones you make on Snapchat. When you send a snap to a friend, it ends up in her Snapchat mailbox.

Sounds straightforward, and it is. But here's the twist: The photo or video is perishable, and lasts between 1 and 10 seconds after it's opened. After that, it gets deleted from your friend's phone and the Snapchat servers. It's a great app for taking selfies and annotating them so your friends can see exactly what you're up to at exactly that instant.

Duolingo

Parlez-vous francais? Parli italiano? ¿Habla usted español? If you don't, you soon will if you use this excellent free language tutor. Through games and repetition and learning your strengths and weaknesses, it makes learning a new language or brushing up on your existing skills fun.

NOTE From the author: I've used Duolingo for French and Italian, and while I can't begin to pretend to be even close to fluent in either, I can at least order a decent meal in each language.

Advanced Features

CHAPTER 13:

Transferring Music, Videos, Pictures, and Other Files, and Using Group Play

CHAPTER 14:

Taking the Galaxy S5 to Work

CHAPTER 15:

My Magazine, Google Now and Voice Search and Control

CHAPTER 16:

Settings

You'll learn to:
- Transfer files to your PC or Mac
- Use the S5's My Files app
- Beam files and use WiFi to transfer them
- Use Group Play to share screens and files, and to play games

CHAPTER 13

Transferring Music, Videos, Pictures, and Other Files, and Using Group Play

YOUR GALAXY S5 IS not an island—it's built to work with your computer as well. So if you've got a music collection on your PC, for example, you can copy that collection to your phone and listen to music there. You can also transfer pictures and videos between your S5 and PC or Mac. In fact, you can transfer any file between your S5 and your computer.

When you transfer files between your Galaxy S5 and your computer, the S5 looks to your computer just like a USB storage device, and in many ways you transfer files the same way as you do between your computer and any USB device. In fact, you have a few more options, including WiFi and some nifty sharing features built into the S5. This chapter covers them all. You can even *beam* files back and forth with other S5 owners—like magic!

Another sharing option on the S5 is Group Play—a Samsung innovation that lets you share files by WiFi with nearby Galaxy phone fans. You can even use Group Play to...well, play group games by WiFi.

Connecting Your Galaxy S5 to Your Computer

TO TRANSFER FILES BETWEEN your Galaxy S5 and your computer, first connect your S5 to your Mac or PC by using the phone's data cable. Connect the microUSB plug into your S5 and the normal-sized USB plug into your computer's USB port.

A USB icon (⚡) appears in the status bar. That means that your S5 is ready to start transferring or receiving files.

NOTE When you connect your Galaxy S5 to your Windows PC for the first time, the PC may not recognize it. It may need a special *driver*—a small piece of helper software—in order to see the S5 and communicate with it. Your PC will look for and install the drivers automatically, assuming it's connected to the Internet.

If you pull down the notification, you will see that the notification reads, "Connected as a media device." Tap the notification, and you come to a screen that tells you that you've connected your phone to your PC as a media device— in other words, you can transfer media files between it and a PC or Mac. To do so, make sure the "Media Device (MTP)" checkbox is turned on. Underneath that setting, there's another one, "Camera (PTP)." Turn on this box if you have a camera and want to transfer files between the camera and your phone.

TIP If you're having trouble transferring files between the phone and a PC or Mac, not a camera, it's a good idea to turn on the "Camera (PTP)" checkbox anyway, because it can sometimes make sure that files transfer smoothly.

Transferring Files by Using Your PC

AFTER THE DRIVERS HAVE been installed on your PC, when you connect your Galaxy S5 to it, the AutoPlay screen may appear, as it sometimes does when you connect a USB device to your PC. However, don't be concerned if it doesn't, because it doesn't show up on every PC; that depends on your operating system and computer setup (and maybe even the phase of the moon).

After you've connected it to your PC, launch File Explorer in Windows 8, or Windows Explorer in any other version of Windows. Your S5 now shows up as a removable disk, just like any USB drive.

You can now use your phone as if it were any USB flash device—copying files to and from it, creating folders, and so on. That's fine in theory, but in practice what can you actually do? You'll find a number of folders on the S5, some of which have names that are clear, and some of which have names that make no sense—like DCIM.

The exact folders you'll see may vary dramatically from what's listed here, depending on the apps you use and other factors.

There are several important folders that contain information you might want to transfer from your S5 to your PC, or vice versa. You'll see a lot more folders, but these are the important ones:

- **Documents.** If you've got Word files, PDF files, and similar files, here's where they'll likely be.

- **Download.** If you've downloaded content to your Galaxy S5 from the Internet, such as pictures or web pages, you see them in here.

- **DCIM.** Here's where the Galaxy S5 stores all the photos and videos you've taken. Drag photos from this folder to your PC to copy them, or drag photos from your PC here to put them into the Galaxy S5 Gallery (page 115).

- **Movies.** As the name says, here's where you'll find movies and videos you've watched or transferred to your S5.

- **Music.** The Galaxy S5 stores music here, although it might also store music in other places as well. If you download music files by using the Amazon music app, for example, there will be an Amazonmp3 folder where your music is stored.

- **Pictures.** Here's where your photos are stored. There may be subfolders underneath this as well.

- **Podcasts.** Yes, you guessed right. Here's where your podcasts are.

- **Ringtones.** Downloaded ringtones to your phone? Here's where to find them.

- **Samsung.** Samsung uses this folder for a variety of different reasons. For example, in addition to the primary music player built into the phone and other Android phones, Samsung has its own music player, and music for it is found in a subfolder underneath this folder.

TIP To be on the safe side, don't make any changes to the Samsung folder. Let Samsung handle it.

If you're transferring music from your PC to your Galaxy S5, first create a new folder on the phone using File Explorer or Windows Explorer, as you would create any other folder. Then transfer the music to that folder, using subfolders if you want. When you do this, your S5's music player will automatically recognize the music you've transferred. (For details about using the music player, see Chapter 4.)

Transferring Files by Using Your Mac

TO TRANSFER FILES BETWEEN your Mac and Galaxy S5, you must first download the free Android File Transfer tool. Go to *www.android.com/filetransfer/* and follow the instructions for downloading and installing it.

Once you do that, connect the S5 to your Mac with the USB cable. Then run the Android File Transfer app. After you run it for the first time, it should automatically start after that whenever you connect your S5 to your Mac.

Name	Last Modified	Size
▶ Alarms	--	--
▶ Android	--	--
▶ data	--	--
▶ DCIM		--
▶ Documents	--	--
▶ Download	--	--
▶ Movies	--	--
▶ Music	--	--
▶ Notifications	--	--
▶ Pictures	--	--
▶ Playlists	--	--
▶ Podcasts	--	--
▶ Ringtones	--	--
▶ Samsung	--	--

SM-G900T

14 items, 9.73 GB available

You can then transfer files back and forth between your Mac and your S5 using Android File Transfer. It works just like Finder or any other file management app.

If you specifically want to transfer photos between your Mac and your S5, first change the S5's USB mode to tell it you're going to transfer photos. Connect your S5 to your Mac via USB; the USB notification appears in the status bar. Pull down the Notification panel, tap the USB notification, and on the screen that appears, select "Camera (PTP)." You can then use iPhoto to transfer photos between the Mac and your S5.

Using the Galaxy S5 My Files App

TO BROWSE THROUGH THE files of your Galaxy S5, you don't need to rely on your PC or Mac—you can use the S5's My Files app. From the Apps screen, tap My Files to launch it.

If you've seen the My Files app on previous versions of the Galaxy phone, you'll be surprised, and pleasantly so, by what you find when you open it on the S5. It's been thoroughly revamped and makes finding and managing files a breeze.

The top of the screen is organized into various categories of files, such as Recent files, Images, Videos, Documents, Audio, and Downloaded apps.

Tap any category and you'll see a list of files, including thumbnails of images if the files are pictures. Tap any file to open it. In some instances, if there are multiple apps that can open a file, you'll be asked which app to use. Tap the app you want to open the file, and then select whether you want the app to be used for opening that file type just this once, or every time you open the file. If you tap Always, you won't see the screen again.

Whenever you want to get back to the My Files main screen, tap the icon of the home at the top of the screen.

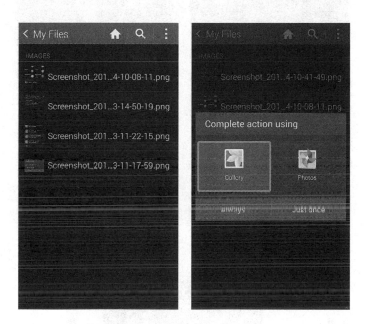

The My Files app also lets you manage files. Hold your finger on any file, and you'll come to a screen with all the files in the folder, with checkboxes next to each one. Check the boxes of the files you want to manage. Then tap one of the buttons at the top of the screen to accomplish the following:

- **Share (the button on the left).** Lets you share the files with others in a wide variety of ways, including email, Bluetooth, WiFi, and via many other apps. When you tap the button, icons representing the ways you can share appear. Tap the icon of the app or means you want to use, and follow the directions.

- **Delete (the trash can).** Lets you delete the files.

- **More options (the button on the far right).** Brings up a menu for managing files, including moving them, deleting them, renaming them, and getting more details about them, including their sizes, the last time they were modified, and so on.

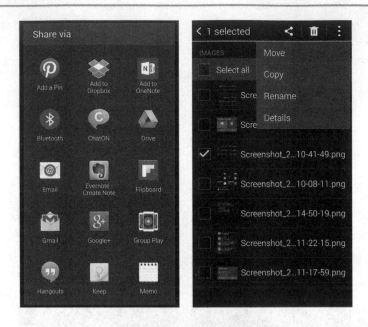

You can also browse through all of your folders and files, not just the ones at the top of the screen. Toward the bottom of the screen, tap Device Storage to see a list of all folders. Tap any to browse through it, and tap the back arrow at the top left of the screen to move back up the folder list. Select a folder or folders in the same way you select individual files. Tap the trash icon to delete it. Tap the Menu button on the far right for these options:

- **Move, Copy,** and **Rename,** which do just what you think they do.

- **Add shortcut,** which adds a shortcut to the folder on the S5's Home screen.

- **Zip,** which compresses the folder and its contents into a .ZIP file.

- **Details,** which gives you details about the folder or folders, including its name size, the last time it was modified, and its exact path (such as */storage/emulated/0/ringtones.*

To create a new folder, when you're viewing a list of folders, tap the Menu key, select "Create folder," type its name, and then tap OK. To select multiple folders and move or delete them all, tap the Menu key; checkboxes appear next to all folders. Tap any folders you want to select for moving or deleting, and then tap Move or Delete from the menu.

To search for files or folders, tap the Search button at the top of the screen. And if you'd like to see how much storage you've used, and what it's devoted to—how much is in images, videos, audio files, documents, and others—back at the top of the main screen, tap the icon of a pie chart.

> **NOTE** You can navigate to other specific locations from the main screen, including directly to your downloaded files, and to some cloud-based storage services, such as Dropbox.

Sharing Files by NFC and Beaming

THE GALAXY S5 CAN share files with other phones without the help of cable or WiFi or even Bluetooth. These awesome powers are not always obvious. So here's your secret decoder ring.

NOTE Beaming files works only between your S5 and other mobile devices, not Macs or PCs.

Beaming is made possible by a relatively new technology called NFC, which stands for near field communciation. Depending on your point of view, NFC is either the future of mobile computing, or else a dead end that few people will ever use. At the moment it's somewhere in between, but who knows what the future holds? The point is, you've got it baked right into the guts of your S5, so there's no reason not to give it a try.

NFC is a way to get mobile devices to talk or to transfer files by touching the devices to each other. You may have seen it in Samsung's ads.

You can use the S5's NFC only with another device that uses NFC. At this point not many do. But S5s do, so you can always start there. To turn on NFC, tap Settings from the Apps screen, scroll down to the "Connect and share" section, tap the NFC icon, and switch NFC on. Then, on the NFC screen, tap S Beam and switch it on.

You can then transfer files to another device using NFC and S Beam, just by tapping the devices together. First open the file you want to transfer, such as a photo, video, song, or other file. Then tap the phones together. Screens appear on both devices with the words "Touch to beam" on them. Touch the screen, and the file gets transferred.

You can also use NFC with NFC card readers to get information, and even make payments—that is, if you actually ever see any NFC card readers. With NFC turned on, tap the back of the S5 to the reader, and you'll see the information from the reader, or else make a payment by tapping "Tap and pay."

Quick Connect

THE S5 HAS A new feature called Quick Connect that lets you easily connect to nearby devices without going through the multiple steps normally required. You can then do a variety of things, like transferring files and printing them. But you can do more as well, including connecting to a TV and using the S5 as a remote control.

Quick Connect works only with other devices that also have the Quick Connect feature, and at this point there aren't many of them.

Quick Connect makes the connection to other devices according to the device's specific capabilities, which means sometimes WiFi and sometimes Bluetooth. But you don't need to know the means of connection—Quick Connect takes care of that for you, behind the scenes.

To use it, open the notification panel and tap "Quick connect." Your S5 scans for devices to which it can connect and displays icons for them. Tap the one you want to connect to. What happens next varies according to the device you're connecting to. For example, if you select a printer, you'll come to a screen with a list of files you recently used. Select the ones you want to print. Then you'll confirm your printer settings and print the files.

Checking Space on Your Galaxy S5

IF YOU TRANSFER LOTS of music and files from your PC or Mac to your Galaxy S5, you may eventually run out of storage space. It's a good idea to regularly check how much space you've got left on it. To do so, from the Apps screen, tap Settings, scroll down to the System area, and then tap Storage. You see the total amount of capacity on your SD card and the phone's USB storage.

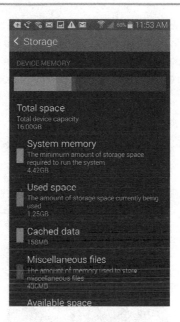

If you're running out of space, you can delete files (page 324).

WARNING If you're deleting music, use the Music app rather than the Files app, because if you delete the files using the Files app, the Music app may still show the music as being present, even after the files are gone.

Using Group Play

GROUP PLAY—A SHARING FEATURE introduced on the Galaxy S III—lets you share documents and photos with others nearby and also lets you participate in multiplayer games.

With Group Play, a leader sets up a group, and then others join it via WiFi. At that point, they can share files, play games, and so on.

TIP Group Play should already be installed on your S5. If it's not, download it from Samsung. Look for the Samsung Apps icon on the Apps screen.

Say you're the leader. To set up a group, first tap the Group Play icon on the Apps screen. From the screen that appears, tap "Create group." If you want to make sure the group is password protected, turn on the "Set group password" checkbox at the bottom of the screen. Give that password to other group members.

At that point, you've set up Group Play. Now other people can join the group. They tap the Group Play icons in their Apps screen, and when they come to the main screen, tap "Join group." They'll see the name of your device and can connect to it by using the password you've provided.

Once you're all connected, tap what you want to do: share music, pictures, or documents; or play games. Choose what you want to share by tapping the category. You're then prompted to choose what you want to share—for example, a specific photo or song. After you do that, if others in the group want to have it shared with them, they also tap that category. So, for example, if you want to share music, you'll tap "Share music," and then browse to the music you want to share. Everyone else then taps "Share music," and the music plays on all your devices—in surround sound.

Depending on what you choose to share, you may have sharing options. With music, for example, you can set which device plays which stereo channel. To set the sharing options, tap the Settings button (it looks like a gear).

You can do the same thing with pictures and documents, and whatever is on your screen will be visible to everyone in the group. If you use this feature, make sure to explore the various sharing options for each category you're sharing. For example, with pictures, there's a drawing mode so you can draw on the slide, and everyone can see what you're doing.

Dropbox

If you've ever have had to transfer work files or family pictures that were a *little* too big for email, you've probably already heard of Dropbox. It's a website that lets you easily drag files into an online storage unit. Anyone can then download them onto any computer as long as you share the link.

You can access this service from your S5 as well—just get the Dropbox for Android app from *www.dropbox.com/android* or Google Play.

When you choose games, you can play head to head. Note that you'll be able to play only games that have been specifically designed to be multiplayer games. Several come preinstalled on the S5; head to Google Play.

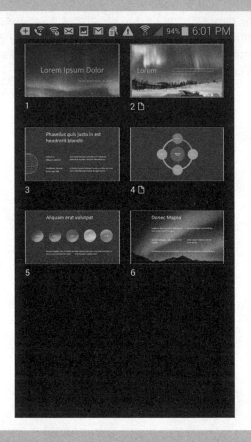

You'll learn to:

- Set the S5 to work with your company email account
- Connect to your company's virtual private network (VPN)
- Use Microsoft's Mobile Office for Android
- Use Google Docs

CHAPTER 14

Taking the Galaxy S5 to Work

YOUR GALAXY S5 MAY not wear a pinstriped suit and a rep tie, but that doesn't mean it can't be a good corporate citizen. In fact, the S5 can easily hook into enterprise-wide resources like your corporate email account and calendar.

A big reason is the Galaxy S5's ability to work with Microsoft Exchange ActiveSync servers. These systems are the backbone of many corporations, and they can automatically and wirelessly keep smartphones updated with email, calendar information, and contacts. So when you're hundreds or thousands of miles from the office, you can still be in touch as if you were there in person.

Setting Up Your Galaxy S5 with Your Company Account

FIRST, LET THE IT department know that you'd like to use your Galaxy S5 to work with the company's network and computers. They'll set up the network to let your phone connect. Then all you have to do is add the company account to your phone, which works much the same way as adding any other new email account.

To get started, on the Home screen, tap Apps→Email. If you haven't set up an email account yet, you'll come to the usual screen for setting one up (page 245). If you've already set up an email account, you'll go to the email account you've already set up, so you'll need to set up a new account. On the Home screen, tap Settings, and in the "User and Backup" area, tap Accounts→Add account.

What happens next depends on what kind of work email account you have. Check with your IT gods to find out which kind yours is. There's a good chance you're using a Microsoft Exchange ActiveSync, so that's what this chapter covers. Tap Microsoft Exchange ActiveSync. Then type the user name and password you use to log into your work email, and then tap "Manual setup" at the bottom of the screen.

On the screen that appears, enter all the information that your IT folks supplied you—the domain name, Exchange server, user name, and so on. You'll see that the user name and password you supplied on the first screen are already filled in.

TIP Make sure to enter the information in exactly the same way the IT staff gave it to you, including whether letters are capitalized. If you make even a single mistake, you may not be able to connect.

Ask the IT department exactly what you should use as your user name. If no one is around, here are some things you can try:

- The first part of your work email address. If your email address is *goodguy@ bighonkingcompany.com*, your user name may be *goodguy*.

- The first part of your work email address, plus the company's *Windows domain*—for example, *honkingserver\goodguy*. If this looks familiar, it may be what you use to log into the company network.

After you input all the information, there's a chance that you won't be able to connect, and you'll get an error message that the Galaxy S5 was unable to find the right server. If that happens, another screen appears, asking you to input all the previous information, plus the server name. You should then be able to connect. If not, check with your IT folks.

TIP When you type your domain name and user name together, make sure you use the *backslash* key, not the regular slash. On the Galaxy S5, it's not easy to get to. Tap the Sym key at lower left, and on the screen that appears, tap the 1/2 key. The backslash is in the second row from the top.

When you're done, tap Next, and you're set up and ready to go. If you run into any problems, check with the IT staff.

As with your Gmail account, you can choose whether to have your Galaxy S5 sync your mail, calendar, and contacts. When your new corporate account shows up in My Accounts, tap it and you'll be able to turn each of those on or off. You may now use your corporate account the same way you use your other accounts for email, contacts, and your calendar.

Virtual Private Networking (VPN)

IF YOUR COMPANY HAS a VPN, you may need to connect to it in order to do things like check your email. Check with the IT staff. If your company has a VPN, and if you're permitted to use it, they'll give you the information that lets your Galaxy S5 connect to the corporate network over the VPN. They'll also set up an account for you.

Here's what you'll need to set up your S5 to access the VPN:

- **The type of technology it uses.** The S5 can work with pretty much any kind of VPN technology out there. Ask whether yours uses PPTP (Point-to-Point Tunneling Protocol), L2TP (Layer 2 Tunneling Protocol), L2TP/IPSec PSK (pre-shared, key-based Layer 2 Tunneling Protocol over the IP Security Protocol), or L2TP/IPSec CRT (certificate-based Layer 2 Tunneling Protocol over the IP Security Protocol). (You don't have to memorize these terms. There's no quiz later.)

- **Address of the VPN server.** The Internet address of the server to which you need to connect, such as vpn.bigsecurehoncho.com.

- **Name of the VPN server.** The name isn't always needed, but check, just in case.

- **Account name and password.** The IT folks will supply you with this.

- **Secret.** When it comes to VPNs, there are secrets within secrets. If you use an L2TP connection, you'll need a password called a Shared Secret in addition to your own password in order to connect.

- **Other special keys.** Depending on which VPN protocol you use, you may require additional *keys*, which are essentially passwords. Again, the IT folks will know this.

- **DNS search domains.** These servers essentially do the magic of letting you browse the Internet and do searches.

Once you've got all that, you're ready to set up the VPN. On the Home screen, tap Apps→Settings, and in the Network Connections area, tap More networks→VPN. You'll have a choice between a Basic VPN and an Advanced IPsec VPN. Check with your IT folks about which to choose.

After you've chosen, before you can set up the VPN, you must first create a screen unlock pattern, PIN, or password (page 376). After you've done that, tap the + sign at the top of the screen that appears. Name the VPN, add the server address, choose the type of VPN by tapping the small triangle at the bottom right of the Type area, and then tap Save. (If you chose an advanced VPN option, you'll have more to type in.) A reminder: You'll need to get all these settings, including the server address and VPN type, from your IT folks.

The VPN connection you just set up appears on your VPN screen. To connect to it, tap it, and then type your VPN user name and password.

From now on, when you want to connect to the VPN, go to Settings and in the Network Connections area, choose "More networks"→VPN. Tap the VPN network to which you want to connect, enter your user name and password as described in this chapter, and then tap Connect. The Status bar shows you that you've got a VPN connection—or displays a notification if you've been disconnected, so you can reconnect.

To disconnect, open the Notification panel, touch the notification for the VPN, and then touch it again to disconnect.

Using Microsoft's Office Mobile for Android

THE GOLD STANDARD FOR creating and editing documents is Microsoft Office, and although your Galaxy S5 can't rival a computer when it comes to editing, it does give you several ways to work with Microsoft Office documents, notably Microsoft's Mobile Office for Android. It's the mobile version of Microsoft's best-selling Office suite, although it's not nearly as powerful or as useful as the big-boy version of the software.

Mobile Office for Android is free, which is a big deal, because once upon a time you had to pay for it.

> **NOTE** There's a chance that as you read this, Microsoft has changed its mind and once again is starting to charge to use Mobile Office for Android. If so, it will be part of an annual Office 365 subscription, which charges you every year to use Office on multiple devices, including computers, smartphones, and tablets.

To install the software, download it from Google Play. You'll be prompted to enter an email address and a password. If you're already an Office 365 subscriber, make sure to enter that address and password, because when you do that, it ties into your Microsoft account, which gives you access to OneDrive and all its files.

The app is designed to work with your OneDrive account. So when you run the app, if you're an Office 365 subscriber, it opens to a list of your most recently used OneDrive files. Tap any to open it. The file downloads from OneDrive, and you'll then be able to view it or edit it on your S5. The app does a great job of keeping fonts, graphics, and so on intact, although it may look somewhat different than it does on your computer, because Office Mobile reformats it for the smaller screen of the S5.

To view all the files on your entire OneDrive, tap the folder icon at the top of the screen, and then tap your OneDrive. From there you can browse all of your files, not just the newest. And from there you can also add new locations for browsing files, such as Team Site and SharePoint.

Viewing and Editing Files

When you open a file, you'll see it with all of its fonts and graphics in place. But you can do more than scroll through it. Tap the screen, and a row of icons appears across the top. The leftmost brings you to your file list, and the one to its right lets you see what is essentially an auto-generated table of contents of the document, which lets you jump to any section. The next one to the right lets you search for text in the document. The next to the right, which looks like a pencil, opens the document for editing. The one on the far right lets you share and save files. You can't edit files created for older versions of Office, such as .doc files. You will, however, be able to read them.

Office

OLDER

Windows 8 Cheat Sheet vp.doc
On OneDrive

Surface 2 review.docx
On OneDrive

Hacks sample.doc
On OneDrive

Windows 8 tablets.docx
On OneDrive

Windows 8 Digital Classroom...
On OneDrive

Office 15 review.doc
On OneDrive

Captions.doc
On OneDrive

Word 2013 Cheat Sheet.doc

10:54 AM

fx Lorem

	B	C	D	E	F
1	orem				
2	Aliquam Dapibus	Etiam	Cursus	Suscipit	
3	In Porttitor	$4,850	$4,600	$250	
4	Suspendisse Dui	$3,175	$3,340	$165	
5	UT NONUMMY	$1,675	$1,260	$415	
6					
7	orem Ipsum Dolor				
8					
9					
10	ellentesque				
11					
12					
13					
14					
15	Tincidunt				
16					
17		$0 $500 $1,000 $1,500 $2,000 $2,500 $3,000 $3,500 $4,000 $4,500 $5,000			
18					
19					
20	usce Est				
21	Vestibulum	Etiam	Cursus	Suscipit	
22	Vestibulum 1	$2,900	$2,800	$100	
23	Vestibulum 2	$1,800	$1,800	$0	

10:54 AM

Office

OPEN

Preston Gralla's OneDrive

+ Add a place

10:54 AM

Preston Gralla's OneDrive

Blog

Documents

Kaspersky

Music

Office 15 review

Office Live Documents

OneNote

Touch

Windows 8 Digital Classroom

NOTE The capabilities for browsing, searching, editing, and so on vary from app to app, so they'll be slightly different for Word, Excel, and PowerPoint.

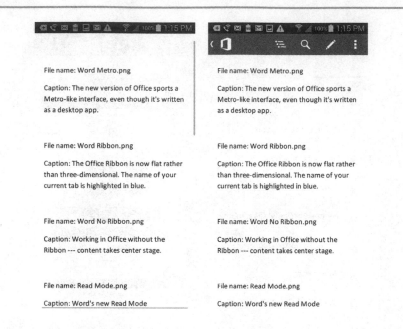

File name: Word Metro.png

Caption: The new version of Office sports a Metro-like interface, even though it's written as a desktop app.

File name: Word Ribbon.png

Caption: The Office Ribbon is now flat rather than three-dimensional. The name of your current tab is highlighted in blue.

File name: Word No Ribbon.png

Caption: Working in Office without the Ribbon --- content takes center stage.

File name: Read Mode.png

Caption: Word's new Read Mode

Tap the pencil to edit your document, and document editing tools appear. Don't expect full-blown Office editing tools, because you won't find them. They vary from app to app, and some are quite rudimentary. In Word, for example, you can't choose a specific font or font size, but you can change font attributes like bold and italic and make text larger or smaller. Excel lets you add formulas, and it's easy to navigate to different pages of a spreadsheet, but otherwise you'll find limited tools. And PowerPoint is the least powerful of all. You can rearrange slides and do basic things such as edit text, but not much else.

NOTE   Office Mobile lets you edit only files in the newest Office formats—.docx, .xlsx, and .pptx—not older ones. So you can't edit files in the .doc, .xls, or .ppt formats.

To create new files, head back to the main Office Mobile page, tap the icon at top right, tap the kind of document you want to create, and get to work. Especially useful is that there are pre-created templates for you—for example, a budget or mileage tracker for Excel, or an outline or report for Word.

Although Office Mobile is far from a powerhouse for editing files, you'll find its tools somewhat useful. But its ability to display Office files is superb, and particularly useful for reading Office files sent to you via email.

Google used to have a free app called Quickoffice that let you read and create new Office files. But Google has decided to kill it. It may be on your S5 because it came pre-installed, or because you downloaded it. But as I write this, Google is in the process of pulling Quickoffice from the Google Play Store so you won't be able to download it.

Using Polaris Office

THERE ARE OTHER WAYS to create and edit Office documents. A very good app that does that is Polaris Office. It lets you read, create, and edit Word files, Excel files, PowerPoint files, and PDF files.

To create a new document from the main screen, tap + and select the type of file you want to create. From there, you can create a text document, spreadsheet, or presentation in the usual way; the screen and keyboard are just a little smaller than what you're used to.

Depending on your carrier, Polaris Office may already be on your S5. Check your Apps screen!

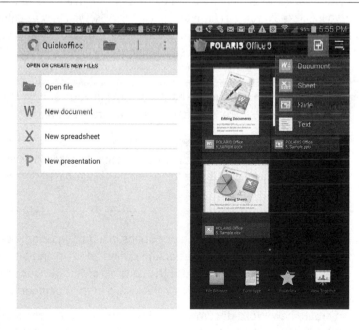

Using Google Docs

AN INCREASING NUMBER OF companies and government agencies use Google Docs for creating and sharing documents, including word processing files, spreadsheets, presentations, and more. Google Docs works much like Microsoft Office, but the software and all the documents live on the Web, where you can share them with others. The basic service is free for individuals, although companies of all sizes can pay for pumped-up corporate features.

NOTE Google also has an app called Google Docs that you can download. So if you prefer using an app to the Web, download it from the Google Play Store and start working.

With the Galaxy S5's browser, you can view all the documents you have access to on Google Docs. You can't edit them in the browser, but you can create new documents. Launch your browser and visit Google Docs on the Web at *http:// docs.google.com*. (If that doesn't get you to the right location, check with your IT department.)

NOTE If your Google Docs account is associated with a different account from the main one on your Galaxy S5, you may have to sign in. Otherwise, you may be automatically signed in when you visit Google Docs. For example, some people maintain separate Google accounts for their personal and work email addresses.

You come to a page that shows you all the documents in your Google Drive, which is the cloud-based storage where Google Docs stores its files.

NOTE When you first use Google Docs on the Web, you may be asked to download the Google Drive app—an app that makes it easy to use Google's cloud-based storage service and easier to use Google Docs as well.

To view any document, tap it. The document opens in a built-in Google document viewer. You can scroll through the document and zoom in and out using the usual finger gestures. You can also use the controls in Google Docs for zooming in and out, and moving forward or backward in the document.

You can also create new Word documents and spreadsheets. Tap the icon just below the "more" icon, and select the type of document you want to create.

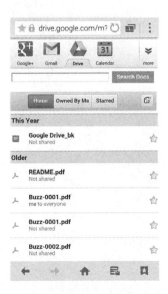

NOTE If you have PDF files in Google Docs, you'll be able to read those as well.

When you log into Google Docs, across the top of the screen you'll see navigation buttons for other Google services, such as Gmail, your calendar, and more. When you tap, you'll go to those services on the Web, not in any app you may have downloaded to your Galaxy S5. To see even more services than those shown, tap the "more" down-arrow at upper right.

Google Drive

There's another way to use Google Docs on the Web—the Google Drive app. Download it from Google Play. When you launch it, you see all your Google Doc files and any other files you've stored on your Google Drive. Simply navigate to a file and tap it to open it.

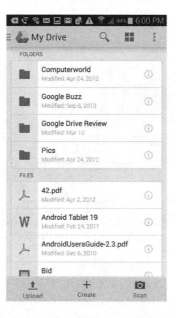

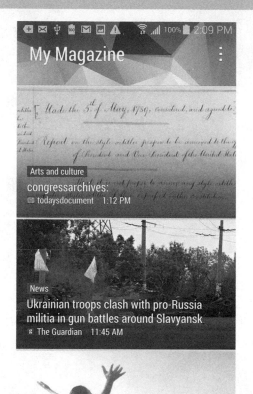

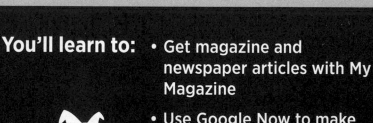

You'll learn to:

- Get magazine and newspaper articles with My Magazine

- Use Google Now to make your life easier

- Search your S5 by speaking

- Control your S5 with the magic of your voice

CHAPTER 15

My Magazine, Google Now, and Voice Search and Control

YOUR GALAXY S5 HAS a lot more tricks up its sleeve than you can imagine. Any smartphone will do what it's supposed to do if you press the right buttons and use the right screen gestures—but the S5 is a whole lot smarter than you think. It doesn't just respond to your commands, it can learn from your behavior and adjust itself to what you want. For example, it knows that you're headed out on vacation, and so suggests a faster way to get to the airport to bypass a traffic jam. It does this with a feature called Google Now.

The S5 can do more as well, with a new feature called My Magazine that scours the Web for interesting articles and brings them straight to you, complete with graphics. With just a few taps, you can have your own personalized magazine right on your phone.

You spend a lot of time talking into your phone when you make phone calls; that much is obvious. But you can do a lot more with your voice as well. Want to send a text message, get directions to a city or street address, or visit a website? Rather than let your fingers do the walking, let your voice do the talking, and you can do all that and more.

In this chapter, you'll learn to use My Magazine, Google Now, voice search, and voice control, all of which are built right into the S5.

Using My Magazine

MY MAGAZINE IS A seemingly clairvoyant app that automatically grabs articles it thinks you'll be interested in, based on your activities. It's a news junkie's dream, because it gleans articles from newspapers, magazines, and websites, and displays them complete with photos and graphics. You customize exactly what kinds of stories and publications you want to show. It's easy to use, beautiful to look at, and keeps you up to the minute on everything.

To set it up, on the Home screen, swipe from the left, agree to the terms of use, and get started.

Tap any story to read it. To share the story, tap the Share button at the bottom of the screen, and you'll be able to share via Facebook, Twitter, LinkedIn, or Google+. You can also share via other apps by tapping the "Share to other apps" button. At the top right of the screen, tap the Settings icon for more features as well, like changing the text size, style, and brightness; opening the page in the browser; and more.

My Magazine is already set up to grab a variety of news feeds from around the Web, but it's easy to change that to your own selections. There's a lot more to it as well. It's free, and it gives you great sources of information, so if you're a news junkie, or even if you're not, give it a try.

Using it is simplicity itself—tap any article to read it. Down at the bottom of the page (or top, depending on your carrier), you can interact with it in various ways: Liking it on Facebook, giving it a +1 on Google+, and commenting on it. To go to the next article when you're reading one, simply flip up from the bottom.

NOTE If you've ever used the Flipboard app, My Magazine may look familiar to you. That's because My Magazine is a version of Flipboard updated for the S5.

You can easily customize what kinds of articles My Magazine shows you. Tap the Menu button at upper right, select Settings, and you'll see a list of various kinds of content My Magazine can grab for you. Turn on boxes next to those you're interested in, and uncheck the boxes next to those you're not. That's all it takes.

TIP Don't like My Magazine? You can disable it. Press down on an empty area of any of your home screens and tap "Home screen settings." Then turn off the checkbox next to My Magazine.

Using Google Now

IMAGINE HAVING A NEARLY omniscient invisible assistant at your side all day long, giving advice when you need it—"Avoid the Mass Pike driving home; there's been an accident"—telling you when packages you've ordered online have shipped, warning you that your flight has been delayed...pretty much helping you take care of the normal business of life.

That's what Google Now is like. Throughout the day, it displays helpful cards on your S5 that give you the information you need and want without your having to ask for it. When you wake up in the morning, it can pop up the current weather—or the weather at your destination, if you're headed on a trip. It can tell you about flight delays, traffic on your daily commute, birthday reminders, and a lot more. It does all this through the magic of knowing your patterns of behavior, such as buying airline tickets, using your S5 for mapping and navigation, and doing web searches for particular items.

NOTE Some people feel that Google Now has a built-in "creepiness factor"; that it's too intrusive and invades your privacy far too much. Fear not: Google Now springs into action only after you've told it to. So if you don't want it hanging around, it won't.

To turn on Google Now for the first time, hold down the S5's Home button. A screen pops up telling you that you're about to use Google Now. To learn more, tap Next. Keep tapping Next through a series of screen describing Google Now's capabilities. Finally, you get to a screen that asks whether you want to turn on Google Now. Tap "Yes, I'm in" to turn it on, or "No, maybe later" to keep it dormant.

TIP If you've turned Google Now on and want to turn it off, or if you declined to turn it on, don't worry—it's easy to switch. Tap the Google search box on the Home screen (or anywhere else), and then press the Menu key and select Settings. At the top of the screen, move the slider to On or Off.

To turn Google Now on at any time, hold down the Home button. Also, whenever you tap into the Google search box to do a search, Google Now appears at the bottom of the search. However you launch it, you may find that Google Now has already been thinking about you. For example, if you've searched for information about your favorite sports team—not just on the S5, but using Google on your computer or other devices—it shows you news about it. It displays the current weather where you live. It may even have recipes for you, news likely to interest you, and so on.

It knows all this because it uses your Google Search history, Google Maps history, and other services you've used to do things like make restaurant reservations, purchase items online, and so on. It then delivers information relevant to what you tend to do.

At this point, all you really need to do to use Google Now is to tap the Google search box or hold down the Home button. Read on to see how to use it.

Using Cards in Google Now

What's nifty about Google Now is that once you turn it on, you don't really need to do anything to have it display cards for you. Just go about daily life...and use a variety of services on your S5. To understand how Google Now works, you need to understand how it interacts with these services.

For example, Google Now typically displays cards that are related to various confirmation messages sent to your Gmail account. Say you use OpenTable to make a reservation at a restaurant. OpenTable sends a confirmation email to your Gmail account, and it includes the location of the restaurant and the time of the reservation. That means that before your restaurant reservation comes around, you'll see a card reminding you about it in Google Now. Similarly, if you use a package delivery service that sends email updates to your Gmail account, that information is displayed in a card as well. Have you searched online for a recipe recently? Expect there to be a card waiting for you with search results.

At times, Google also takes a more proactive approach. For example, say that you can't remember the date of Father's Day this year. Do a search asking

Google when it is. You'll find right at the top of the search results a link that reads "Remind me on Google Now." Click it to get a reminder card.

Depending on your searches, online habits, map navigation, and other activities—who knows, maybe even the phase of the moon—the exact cards you see may vary. The following are a sample of some common types of cards you'll come across:

- **Commuting.** Probably at the top of the list of new cards will be one with a map, and with text about the kind of traffic on the map. Google asks whether it's the place you normally commute to every day. How does it do this? By tracking your location as you go about the day, as you drive, and as you use Google Maps. (Yes, it's creepy.) If it's the place you normally commute to, tap "Set as work." Otherwise, tap Edit and type your workplace's location; tap OK. From then on, you get a commuting card showing you the traffic en route to work. You can also ask for navigational directions if you suddenly suffer from amnesia and can't remember how to get there.

- **Nearby events.** Want to know about many different types of events near where you are? Tap the "View nearby events" card. What you'll see is exceedingly varied. For one example, I found everything from a Portuguese festival to the "Early Risers Horticultural Club" to a UNICEF fundraiser to a dance club event to a Red Sox game. Tap any event for more information about it.

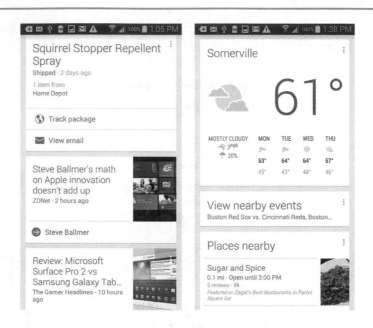

- **Weather.** Want to see the weather? This card grabs it for you.

- **Stocks.** Feel like gambling? Why go to Las Vegas when you can do it in the stock market? The Stock card shows you the current state of the market. To track specific stocks, tap the small information button (❶), and add the stocks you'd like to track.

- **Next appointment.** Tells you when and where your next appointment is. So you have no excuse to miss it (even if it's the dentist).

- **Flights.** Have you searched for a flight and looked at information about it? Then expect a Flight card in your future, showing you when it leaves, when it arrives, whether it's on time, what the traffic is like from your current location to the airport, and driving directions. With certain airlines, you'll even be able to get a boarding pass right on your S5.

- **Last transit home.** This card is for those who use public transportation and can't seem to drag themselves away from work. It detects whether you're still at work, and the last bus, train, subway, or other means of public transportation is going to leave soon. If you don't want to spend the night sleeping in your office, get a move on. (OK, like all of Google Now, this one is a bit creepy and intrusive, considering how much it knows about your life. But it sure is trying to be helpful.)

- **Movies.** Gives information about movies playing nearby.

Using the Magic of Voice Search and Voice Control

THE WHOLE WORLD, IT seems, knows about Siri, the iPhone's search assistant. But the S5 also includes voice-powered search and assistance, the one built into Android, and there are a lot of people who believe it beats Siri hands-down...or is that hands-off?

The best part of Galaxy S5's Voice Search feature is this: The only thing you really need to know is how to talk. Your voice is its command. Launching it is a breeze. Simply tap the microphone button to the far right of the Google search box. You can do this anywhere you find the Google search box on the S5.

NOTE The microphone icon shows up wherever the Google Search box does, either when you're visiting Google on the Web or in the Google search box, everywhere you find it on the S5.

One of the many amazing things about using voice search is that it seamlessly uses two different speech technologies to do what you tell it to: voice recognition and speech-to-text. With voice recognition, it recognizes the action you want to take and then accomplishes the action: "Send text" or "Navigate to," for example.

With speech-to-text, it translates your words into written text and, for example, embeds that text in an email or text message. Say you tell your Galaxy S5: "Send text to Ernest Hemingway. Consider using young woman and the sea as title because demographics are better." Your Galaxy S5 will find Ernest Hemingway's contact information and then send him the text message, "Consider using young woman and the sea as title because demographics are better."

When you tap the microphone button, all you need to do next is to tell the S5 what you want it to do, for example, "Find a Japanese restaurant near me." As you speak, the S5 displays onscreen what you've told it. Then it goes about and does what you've told it to do, sending the request to Google and displaying the results.

If the S5 can't connect to Google properly, after a few seconds you'll see a cryptic message—"Can't reach Google at the moment. Resend audio." It's actually asking, in its own confusing way, whether you want to send your request again to Google. To do it, tap "Resend audio." The odds are that, this time around, your request will get through.

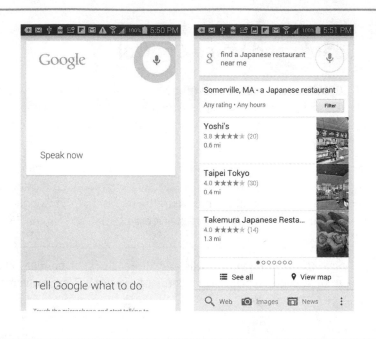

One thing to keep in mind is that you can use your voice to do much more than search the Web or find a nearby restaurant. You can also use it to control the S5 and its apps—compose an email or text message, for example.

What You Can Do with Voice Search

Here are the commands you can issue with Voice Search, along with how to use them:

- **Send text to [recipient] [message].** Composes a text message to the recipient with the message that you dictate. If there's confusion about the recipient, Voice Search displays potential matches. Choose the one you want.

- **Send email to [recipient] [subject] [message].** Composes an email message to the recipient with the subject and message that you dictate. As with sending a text message, if there's confusion about a recipient, Voice Search shows you possible matches, and you choose the one you want.

- **Navigate to [address/city/business name].** Launches the Galaxy S5 Navigation app to guide you with turn-by-turn directions to the address, city, or even a specific business.

- **Call [contact name] [phone type/phone number].** Calls the contact. If the contact has more than one phone number, say the type of phone number to call—for example, home, work, or mobile. Alternatively, you can dictate a phone number, and the Galaxy S5 will call that number.

NOTE In addition to looking through your contacts, the Galaxy S5 also searches contacts in social networking services such as Facebook that you have installed on your phone.

- **Map of [address] [city].** Launches Google Maps and opens it to the address or city you named.

- **Directions to [address] [city].** Launches Google Maps and shows directions for how to get to the address or city you named. If the S5 knows your location, it uses that as the starting point. If it doesn't know your location, you must type it when Google Maps launches.

- **Listen to [artist/song/album].** Don't expect this to launch the Music app and play music—that's not what it does. Instead, it links you to Google Play, where you can buy the track or album. It does this even if you have the album or track on your S5. However, as you'll see in the next entry, there is a way to tell the S5 to play music you own on your phone.

- **Play music [song name] [artist name].** Launches your usual music-playing app. If the S5 recognizes the artist or song you want to play, it will play them as well. If not, it simply launches the app, and you can then choose what music to play. Before it launches the Music app, the S5 shows you what it's going to play. Then it launches the Music app, which takes over from there.

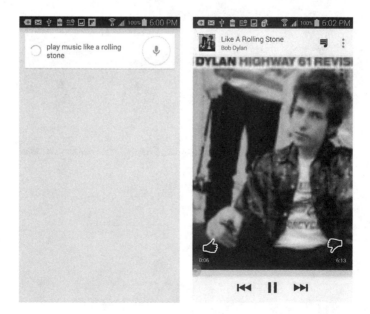

- **Call [business name] [location].** Calls the business you named. If there's more than one location, say the location. If the Galaxy S5 finds more than one phone number for the business, it lists all of them. Just tap the number you want to call. It will even list associated businesses. For example, if a café is located inside a bookstore, and you dictate the name of the bookstore, it may also list the café's phone number.

- **Go to [website].** Launches your browser to the website you dictated. Often, rather than going straight to the website, it displays a list of sites or searches that match what you dictated. Tap the one you want to visit.

- **[Search term].** Simply say your search term, and the S5 searches the Web, using Google.

- **[Contact name].** Say the name of a contact you want to open, and your Galaxy S5 displays it, along with a list of possible actions, like calling her by phone, sending her an email, sending her a text message, and so on. The list of actions will vary according to what information you have about that contact.

- **Open [App name] app.** Say this phrase, and the S5 cheerfully responds "opening app" before delivering you to the app's screen.

> **NOTE** If you say a search term that is also the name of a contact, the Galaxy S5 opens the contact, rather than searching the Web.

All this is just a start. In essence, just about anything you can do on the S5 with your fingers, you can do with your voice as well.

Editing Text Messages and Email with Voice Search

Voice Search does a great job of converting your speech into text when you dictate an email or text message. But it's not perfect. So you might be leery of using Voice Search to dictate a message, worrying that when you dictate, "I love you, too," the message sent will be, "I move YouTube."

Not to worry. Before you send a text message or email, you get a chance to edit the text. When you speak the text message or email, you see the text you're going to send. To send it, tap "Send message" or "Send email," respectively. But if you want to edit the text, simply tap the text itself, and from the screen that appears, edit the text. You'll come to the usual text app or Gmail or email program, depending on what you're sending.

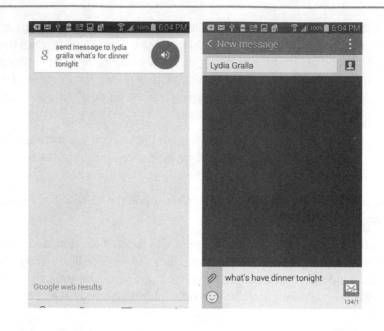

Sending Email with Voice Search

If you don't use the S5's voice capabilities carefully when you're sending an email or text, you may find that it's more trouble than it's worth because you end up spending so much time editing. So take these steps, and you'll find sending email with voice can be faster than a speeding bullet:

- **Speak slowly and distinctly.** Think of the S5 as someone who speaks English as a second language and still has some learning to do. Speak slowly and distinctly, pronouncing each word carefully. (But don't speak too slowly and take long pauses between words—if you do, Voice Search will think you're done and will compose the message before you've finished dictating it.)

- **Speak the words "subject" and "message"** to fill in those email fields. After you say the name of the person to whom you want to send an email, say the word "subject," and then say the subject of the email. Then say the word "message" and dictate the message you want sent. If you don't do that, your Galaxy S5 will become confused. It may interpret what you want to be the subject line as several email addresses, for example, and will put in addresses you don't want.

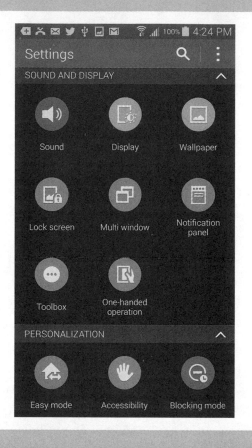

You'll learn to:

- Change your connection and wireless settings
- Change your device settings
- Change your keyboard settings
- Change your account settings
- Change your email and related settings

CHAPTER 16

Settings

RIGHT OUT OF THE box, the Samsung Galaxy S5 is set up for you and ready to go. But what if you want to change the way it notifies you when there's a call, fine-tune the way its location services work, or alter its music setup? You turn to this chapter, which describes all its settings and explains what they do for you. To get to the Settings screen, tap Settings on the Apps screen. You can also pull down the Notification panel and tap the Settings icon at the top right of the screen—it looks like a gear.

You'll find nine sections: Quick Settings, Network Connections, Connect and Share, Sound and Display, Personalization, Motion, User and Backup, System, and Applications. Scroll down to get to them all. Then head to the appropriate section of this chapter for the full description and advice.

Quick Settings

AS THE NAME SAYS, this section includes the settings you'll most commonly use, like turning on WiFi, locking the screen, controlling power savings, and more. Each of these settings is included in other sections in the Settings app—for example, WiFi in the Network Connections area, and Lock screen in Sound and Display. Rather than describe the same settings twice, this chapter covers them only once, under their home category where they can be logically found, such as WiFi in the Network Connections area.

Network Connections

THIS SECTION CONTROLS THE many various ways you can connect your S5 with other devices, including WiFi, Bluetooth, and beyond.

Wi-Fi

Tap On to turn on WiFi; if it's on, tap Off to turn it off. To connect to a WiFi network, tap the WiFi icon. For details on connecting to WiFi and other networks, turn to Chapter 8. You can also turn on WiFi by pulling down the Notification panel and using the WiFi widget there.

Download booster

Turn this setting on, and you'll combine the speed of WiFi with your data connection for a bigger download pipe. See page 190 for details.

Bluetooth

Tap On to turn on Bluetooth (page 91); if it's on, tap Off to turn it off. As with WiFi, there's a Bluetooth widget on the Notification panel.

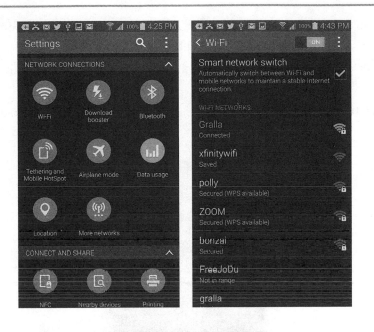

Tethering and Mobile HotSpot

This section covers settings related to using your Galaxy S5 to give Internet access to a computer or other device, either via WiFi or over a direct USB connection. Tap it for these settings:

- **Mobile HotSpot.** Turn this on to turn your phone into a mobile hotspot to which other devices can connect via WiFi. See page 192 for details.

- **Mobile HotSpot range.** Gives you your hotspot's range, based on current conditions.

- **USB tethering.** Lets you give a computer Internet access when it's plugged in via a USB cable.

NOTE You may need to pay an extra monthly fee if you want to use your Galaxy S5 as a mobile hotspot or to use USB tethering. Check with your wireless provider for details.

Airplane Mode

When Airplane mode is turned on, all your wireless radios are turned off, as airlines require during parts of the flight. But you can still use all your Galaxy S5 apps in this mode.

NOTE Increasingly, airplanes offer WiFi access, so you may not need to use Airplane mode during the entire flight. You can turn off all your radios by using Airplane mode, but then turn on only WiFi, so you can connect to the airplane's WiFi hotspot while you're in the air (usually at a price).

Data Usage

If your data plan charges you for data use above a certain limit, make this setting your friend. Tap it, and you'll come to a screen that shows your data use for the month. That way, you can see whether you're on track to stay under your limit. Tap "Set mobile data limit," and after a limit that you set, your data connection will be turned off.

TIP Your carrier may calculate data usage differently from your S5 does, so to be on the safe side, set the limit at less than your actual limit.

Location

Lets various Google apps access your location—or not. It's up to you. Tap it, then turn it on or off via the switch at top right. With Location turned on, you can use map apps and other location-based apps more accurately, but you'll also use up more of your battery. The screen also shows you which apps have requested to use your location.

More Networks

This setting is a bit of a misnomer, since it's not really about other networks. Instead, it's a grab bag of other wireless and network settings.

Default messaging app

Lets you change the app that your S5 uses for messaging. Out of the box, it uses the S5's built-in messaging app. If you have other messaging apps installed, though, you can use them instead. Tap this setting, and choose which app you want to use.

Mobile Networks

Here's where to configure a variety of options related to your wireless provider, such as whether to use the data network and how to handle roaming when you're outside the provider's network and can connect to another carrier. (Depending on your plan, you may be charged for roaming.)

VPN Settings

Here's where you can set up a virtual private network (VPN) connection (page 337) with your workplace and—once you've set it up—change settings like its URL, password, means of authentication, and so on. You'll need to get information from your company's IT gurus to make the connection, so check with them for details.

WiFi Calling

This feature is a godsend if you're ever out of range of your carrier's signal but within range of a WiFi network. When it's turned on, you can make phone calls via a WiFi network, even when you're not connected to your carrier's phone signal.

The availability of WiFi calling varies according to your carrier, so you may or may not see the setting, and if you see it, you may or may not be able to use it.

Connect and Share

THE NEXT SETTINGS ARE all related to ways you can connect to other devices and share files and other information. For details, see Chapter 13.

NFC

Tap this to turn on NFC (near field communication), which lets you share files with other nearby devices that use NFC. Not many other devices use NFC, so you may be waiting a long time to use this, unless you come across another S5 owner.

Nearby devices

Tap this, and you'll come to a page that lets you share files with other devices on a WiFi network. You can also configure the way you share by choosing which devices are allowed to share, which files you want to share, and so on.

Printing

Lets you configure a variety of wireless printing services so your S5 can use printers, like HP, Samsung, or a cloud-based printing service.

Screen Mirroring

Lets you share what's on your screen with nearby devices.

Sound and Display

HERE'S WHERE TO GO to change just about everything about the way the Galaxy S5 handles sounds, like playing music and your ringtone. It also controls all of your S5's display options.

Sound

Tap here for many sound options, including the following:

- **Volume.** Tap to set the volume for media, notifications, system sounds, and your ringtone. A slider appears that lets you set the volume for each individually. The Galaxy S5 plays the new volume level when you move the slider, so if you're not satisfied with what you hear, change it until you reach the level you want. Tap OK when you're done.

NOTE To set the *overall* sound volume for your Galaxy S5, use the volume buttons along its left-hand side, near the top.

- **Vibration Intensity.** Tap to control the intensity of vibration for calls, notifications, and feedback from the phone when you tap certain keys or take certain actions—for example, when you unlock the phone, press a key on the dialer or keyboard, or add a widget. (It's called *haptic feedback*.)

- **Ringtones.** Tap this to change your ringtone. When you tap it, a list of available ringtones appears, including the one you're currently using. Browse the list, tap the new one you're considering, and you hear a preview. Select the one you want, and then tap OK to make it your ringtone.

- **Vibrations.** Yes, you can even customize the type of vibration the phone makes when you get a call. Tap here to do it. Choose from Basic call, Heartbeat, Jinglebell, Ticktock, Waltz, and Zig-zig-zig.

- **Notifications.** Lets you choose the sound when you get a new notification.

- **Vibrate when ringing.** Want your phone to vibrate, too, when it rings? Turn on this box.

Display

Change your display options here. Tap this listing, and you get more options than you can imagine. This section focuses on the most important ones:

- **Brightness.** Normally, the Galaxy S5 chooses a screen brightness appropriate for the ambient lighting—less light in the dark, and more in sunlight, for example. If you'd prefer to set it at a specific brightness level, and have it stay at that level until you change it, tap this option. From the screen that appears, turn off the "Automatic brightness" checkbox. A slider appears that lets you manually set the brightness level.

- **Screen rotation.** Turn on this little bit of magic, and the S5 uses the front camera to automatically rotate the screen based on the orientation of your face.

- **Smart stay.** Keeps your screen on as long as you're looking at it, even if you don't touch the screen for beyond the time you've set for screen timeout, explained next.

- **Screen timeout.** In order to save battery life, the Galaxy S5's screen goes blank after a set amount of time. You can set that to as little as 15 seconds or as much as 10 minutes. Tap this option, and then choose the interval you want.

NOTE If you have "Smart stay" turned on, it will override screen timeout.

Here are a couple of other display settings to pay attention to:

- **Touch key light duration** When you press one of the buttons at the bottom of your Galaxy S5, the keys light up and stay lit for a few seconds. This setting lets you change the setting to 1.5 seconds, 6 seconds, always off, always on, or on only in the dark.

- **Auto adjust screen tone.** If you'd like to get every bit of use out of your battery, turn on this setting. It saves power by analyzing the image on your screen and adjusting the LCD brightness accordingly.

Wallpaper

You can change the wallpaper background of your Home screen and Lock screen (page 28). Tap here, select which you want to change, and follow the prompts.

Lock screen

Worried about someone unauthorized using your S5? No problem. Tap here, and you'll come to all the ways you can control how your device locks. The most important setting is "Screen lock." When your screen is locked, all you normally need to do is swipe the lock to the right to unlock it. Trouble is, that's all anyone needs to do to gain access to your phone. Select the "Screen lock" option, and you'll be able to set many different methods for unlocking your screen, including setting a PIN, using a pattern you draw on the screen, and even using the S5's fingerprint reader. Tap the method you wish to use and follow the directions for doing it.

To create a PIN, first tap "Screen lock." From here you can set several methods for securing your S5, including via a PIN or by a pattern lock. Select PIN, type in the PIN, confirm it, and you're ready to go. If you instead select a pattern lock, follow the instructions for drawing a pattern, and then confirm it. It's important that you remember the PIN or pattern to unlock your phone, because if you forget, you'll have to reset your phone to its factory settings to get into it (page 384).

Unlocking with your own fingerprint is the most secure. Tap Fingerprint, and follow the directions. You'll first "register" your fingerprint, in other words, have the S5 scan it so that it will recognize it in the future. You'll swipe your finger across the four-dot rows and over the home button eight times, each time waiting for a green circle to appear so you can do it again. After you're done, you'll be asked whether you want to use your fingerprint to unlock the screen, or to use a PIN or a swiping gesture. You can register more than one fingerprint if you want other people to be able to unlock your S5. Here are the most important settings:

Multi window

Do you want to be able to use more than one app at a time? Of course you do. So make sure this box is turned on. Page 38 has the full story on how it works.

Notification panel

Want to customize which widgets show up when you pull down the Notification panel? This does it. You get plenty to choose from. You can also choose whether you can adjust screen brightness from the panel.

Toolbox

This cool feature gives you super-quick access to your most-used apps. The Toolbox is a floating button that when tapped displays shortcuts to your apps, and lets you launch any by tapping its icon. Tap the Toolbox icon, and then move the switch from Off to On. By default there are a handful of popular apps on it, including the camera, web browser, notepad, and several others. But it's easy to delete what's already there or add new ones. After you've turned the Toolbox on, tap the Edit key and customize it however you'd like.

One-handed operation

The S5 is a big phone, and it can be hard to use with one hand. Turn on this setting to make it easier. It automatically adjusts your screen size and its layout for using with one hand. After you turn on the setting, hold the S5 in the hand you'll use it with, and then slide your thumb from the edge of the screen to the middle of the screen and back, in a single motion. The S5 will adjust the screen and layout just for you.

Personalization

THIS SECTION LETS YOU personalize the way your S5 looks and works.

Easy mode

Whether you're a smartphone pro or just getting started, you can choose the Home screen that works best for you. Tap here to use Easy mode. Easy mode strips down the standard Home screen and uses a much simpler layout and larger, easier-to-see icons. For details, see page 27. To switch back to Standard mode, tap here and choose it.

Accessibility

Here's where to go if you have vision, hearing, or dexterity issues and want to make the S5 more suited for you. For example, when you tap Vision, you have a number of settings to choose from, including choosing Talkback, in which the S5 reads the screen to you, changing the font size, using gestures to magnify the screen, and more.

> **TIP** The Accessibility section also includes a somewhat hidden feature that serves as a baby monitor. From this section, select Hearing→"Baby crying detector" and drag the "Baby crying detector" switch on. Then tap the big arrow in the middle of the screen and when the S5 hears a crying baby, it vibrates. Of course, as any parent will tell you, human beings are exquisitely attuned to their own babies' crying, so it's not clear what this feature really offers.

Blocking mode

Tired of getting so many notifications, phone calls, and alarms? Tap here, turn on "Blocking mode," and you can block incoming calls and decide which notifications and alarms to turn off.

Private mode

Tap and flip the switch to On, and you can hide files and other content that you don't want people to see. When you turn on Private mode, the files you want to hide remain hidden even from you. To see the files, turn Private mode off. Only people with the unlock code can turn Private mode on and off.

Finger scanner

Lets you use your fingerprint as a way to unlock the S5's Lock screen. For details, see the "Lock screen" section on page 375.

Motion

HERE'S WHERE YOU CONTROL all the Galaxy S5's motion features:

Motion and gestures

You'll find plenty of motion magic when you tap here:

- **Air browse.** With this turned on, you can scroll through lists and other content such as the body of emails just by moving your hand over the screen in the direction you want to scroll. Once you turn it on, you can customize which apps it works with, such as email, the Gallery, Browser, and Music.

- **Direct call.** With this on, you can call someone whose message or contact details are currently on the screen, simply by bringing the S5 close to your ear.

- **Smart alert.** With this turned on, the S5 will vibrate when you pick it up if you've missed any calls or messages.

- **Mute/pause.** Mutes or pauses music or a call when you cover the screen with your hand, or if you turn the device over. On the same screen you can turn on the "Smart pause" feature, which is a remarkable feature that detects when you're watching video and will pause it when you look away from the screen.

- **Palm swipe to capture.** Need to take a screenshot? Just swipe the bottom edge of your hand across the screen from one side to the other, making sure your hand touches the screen. If you want to take screenshots but don't want to use this gesture, you can always use the S5's built-in way to do it: Press the On/Off and Home screen button at the same time.

Air view

With "Air view" turned on, when you hover your finger above the screen, it will preview information or enlarge information or pictures. For example, hover over the event in the Calendar and you'll see more detailed information about it, or view pictures in the Gallery by hovering your finger over an album.

User and Backup

THIS SECTION HAS SETTINGS for controlling all your accounts, both on the phone and in the cloud, and for backing up and resetting your phone.

Accounts

Controls all the accounts you have on your S5. Depending on how you've set it up and what apps you've got installed, there may be many of them, or only a few. So what you see on your S5 may vary from what you see here. You'll find a listing for your Google account, for your Samsung account if you've created one, for the S Health account (see page 303) if you have one, and for accounts associated with other apps you've installed, such as Facebook, Twitter, Evernote, and more.

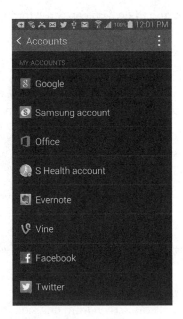

- **Google.** This section handles everything about your Google account, including how it syncs and your privacy settings. Tap Sync settings to customize how various Google services sync, such as the Calendar, Gmail, Google Drive, and others. Check the boxes next to any Google services you want to sync, and uncheck the boxes next to those you don't want to sync.

Cloud

Controls how Samsung stores, syncs, backs up, and restores data between your phone and Samsung's cloud services. Tap "Sync settings" to turn syncing on or off for various services such as the Samsung Calendar, your contacts, and more. Tap "Storage usage" to see how much data various services are using on your phone. Backup backs up your data; Restore does what it says—restores your data from the backup.

Backup and reset

Backs up your data and account. Also lets you choose the nuclear option of restoring your S5 to the way it was before you opened it—factory pristine with no data or accounts on it. These are the important settings you'll see here:

- **Back up my data.** Backs up your Galaxy S5 settings and data to Google's servers so if you later have a problem with your Galaxy S5, you can restore the settings and data. Obviously, if you don't feel safe with your data riding on an anonymous server somewhere, turn this option off.

- **Automatic restore.** With this turned on, if you uninstall an app and then later decide that you want to install it again, the Galaxy S5 automatically grabs the relevant data you've backed up using the "Back up my data" option and puts it back on your Galaxy S5.

- **Factory data reset.** When you're ready to get rid of your phone, you won't want anyone else to get all your data. Tap this button and then follow the onscreen instructions for setting the Galaxy S5 back to the way it was before you began using it. It deletes all your data, eliminates any changes you made to the phone, deletes any apps you've installed, and makes the phone look and work exactly the way it did when it was shipped from the factory.

System

HERE'S WHERE YOU'LL FIND a wide variety of settings having to do with every aspect of the S5's system.

Language and Input

This section lets you change the language you use, as well as other keyboard options and voice search customizations.

Language

Tap to choose your language.

Keyboards and input methods

You get to choose whether to use the Samsung keyboard, or another one, such as the Google keyboard, which lacks some of the Samsung keyboard's features, such as swiping to enter text. When you choose your keyboard, you can tap the Settings icon next to it to change that keyboard's settings, such as whether to use the predictive text feature, whether to auto-capitalize, and so on.

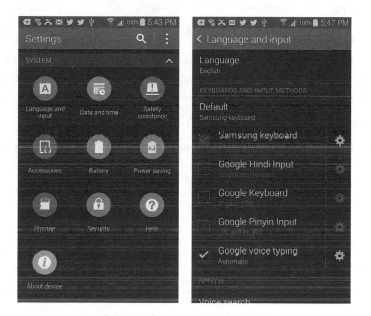

Voice search

Lets you choose a variety of options related to searching by voice, such as whether to hide offensive words in voice results.

Text-to-speech options

In this section you can customize various speech options, such as whether to block the results of a voice search using offensive words. Uncheck it if you don't want those results blocked. Choose the Google or Samsung search engine. You can tap the Settings icon to adjust how it works.

Read notifications aloud

With this on, your S5 will read new notifications to you, such as for incoming calls, text, and emails.

Pointer speed

Can you guess what this does? That's right, you win! It controls how fast your pointer responds to you. Tap it and move the slider to adjust the speed of the pointer.

Date and Time

Choose from these settings for the date and time.

Automatic date and time

As long as this checkbox is turned on, you won't have to worry about setting the date and time—the Galaxy S5 automatically gets it from your wireless provider's network, including your location (to set your time zone).

Set date

If you haven't turned on the Automatic setting and want to set the date yourself, tap here to do so.

Set time

If you're not on Automatic, tap here and choose your time.

Automatic time zone

With this turned on, your S5 automatically adjusts its time to the current time zone.

Select time zone

Use this to select your time zone if you're not on Automatic time zone.

Use 24-hour format

Tap if you prefer the 24-hour format—14:00 instead of 2 p.m., for example.

Select date format

You've got other options here if you don't like the U.S. standard (09/22/2014), including 22/09/2014, and 2014/09/22.

Safety Assistance

This emergency feature is designed to have the S5 automatically alert people if you need emergency assistance. Not only will it send texts, but it will also send your location information. Tap to turn it on, and then follow the directions for setting up to four emergency contacts. After that, if you run into an emergency and need assistance, you press the Power/Lock button three times quickly. That sends an emergency text message to your emergency contacts, along with location information, photos from your front- and back-facing cameras, and a short voice recording, if you want to create one.

Accessories

This section controls a grab bag of ways the S5 works with accessories like docks. It also lets you determine what audio output you want to use—stereo or surround sound.

Battery

Launches a screen that shows your current battery usage, whether to show the battery percentage on the Status bar, and most important, what has been using your battery. It's very useful if you want to figure out how to extend your battery life, because it tells you what's been drinking juice.

Power Saving

Galaxy S5 owners, like most people who use powerful smartphones, tend to be obsessive about battery life, and want to wring every last minute out of their batteries without giving up any of the phone's considerable power. This section helps you save battery life by controlling its power saving mode.

Power saving mode

With this setting turned on, your Galaxy S5 will switch to power saving mode when your battery gets low. Here are the features it uses when you turn it on:

- **Block background data.** This saves battery life by stopping apps from getting data in the background. When you turn on power saving mode, you have an additional choice of using this option or not by checking or unchecking the box next to it.

- **Grayscale mode.** Turns off color and displays everything in shades of gray.

Ultra power saving mode

Power saving mode isn't good enough for you? You want to save even more power? Then turn on this mode. It turns off WiFi and Bluetooth, turns off your data connection when the screen goes off, shows everything in shades of gray, and limits the apps you can use to the default ones (although you can add others if you want).

Storage

Here's where to get details about the storage on your phone and SD card (page 19). It shows you how much total space you have; how much has been used; and how much is used by various content types, such as applications, pictures, videos, and so on. For more information about your storage use, tap the appropriate section—for example, tap Used Space to see what is using up your storage space.

At the bottom of the screen, in the SD card section, tap "Mount SD card" if you haven't yet installed an SD card. Put the card in the phone, get here, and tap this so you can use the card. If you've already installed an SD card and need to remove your SD card for any reason, tap "Unmount SD Card" before removing the card. If you're installing a new SD card, or if your existing one gets corrupted for some reason, tap "Format SD card" to format it. Keep in mind that when you format an SD card, you erase all its contents.

If you've got an SD card installed, you'll get details about the storage on the SD card, including the total and available space.

Security

Worried about others getting access to your phone and all its data? This section lets you lock them out...or not, depending on how you like to balance security with ease of use.

Encrypt device

If you turn this on, your phone will be encrypted; that is, its contents will be scrambled so no one who happens to break into your information will be able to read it. To unscramble them, you'll need a password in addition to any screen lock.

Encrypt external SD card

Turning this on encrypts your SD card, so that a password will be required to access its data.

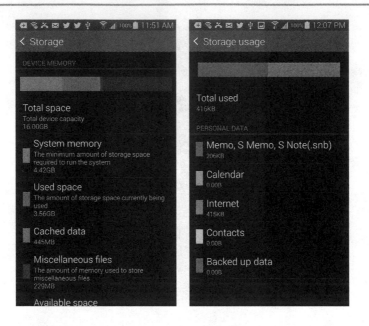

Set up SIM card lock

Select this option, and you can set a PIN that anyone who wants to use your phone has to type in. It applies only to the SIM card currently in the phone.

Make passwords visible

With this option turned on, you can see passwords as you type them. This setup makes it easier to ensure that you're typing in passwords correctly, but it could theoretically be a security risk if someone looks over your shoulder as you type.

Device administrators

Unless you're an IT god, you don't need to know all these settings. However, two are important. If you turn on "Unknown sources," you can download apps outside of Google Play. And if "Verify apps" is turned on, you'll get a warning if you try to install an app that the S5 thinks might be dangerous.

Unknown sources

Turn this setting on if you want to be able to download apps from places other than the Play store—for example, from the Web. Keep in mind that when you do this, you may be more vulnerable to attack, because Google tries to keep the Play store free from apps that are malicious.

Verify apps

Blocks or warns you about apps before you install them that might invade your privacy or do harm to the S5.

Security policy updates

Automatically downloads any new security policies to your S5 that can help keep it safe. Obviously, keep this one turned on.

Send security reports

With this setting turned on, if the S5 detects any potential security issues, it will send information about them to Samsung over WiFi.

Credential storage

Your IT gods need to know about this section, not you, so skip it and leave it as is.

Help

Here's where to go for help with your S5.

About Device

Go here for more information than you can ever imagine about your phone, including the version of the Android software you're running, your current signal strength, whether you're roaming, and much more. Much of what you find here is informational only.

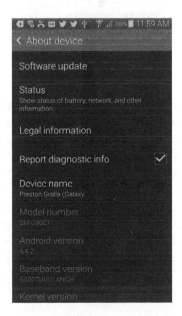

Software update

Tap here to check whether you need to update your S5's software. It checks to see if an update is needed. If it is, follow the instructions for installing it.

NOTE Technically, you don't need to update your phone's software manually by tapping "Check for updates." Updates are automatically delivered to you over your wireless provider's network, via what's called an over the air (OTA) update (see the Note on page 63).

Status

Tap for a mind-boggling amount of detail about your phone's status, including its signal strength, whether it's roaming, the battery level, your phone numbers, the phone's WiFi MAC address (a unique number that identifies your Galaxy S5), the network you're using, and a barrage of techie details that only a full-time geek could love.

Legal information

Here's where you can while away the hours reading Google's terms of service, and the licenses that govern the use of Android. If you're not a lawyer, you don't want to read this. In fact, even if you are a lawyer, you don't want to read this.

Device name

Shows you the name of your S5. Tap it to change it.

Model number

Gives you the official Samsung model number of your phone, like SGH-M919-SGH-I777.

Android version

Lists the current version number of your phone's Android operating system.

Other information

The rest of the screen gives you a variety of very technical information that you most likely will never need to know, such as the kernel version and the baseband version. However, if you ever need tech support, you may need to read the information to a techie.

Applications

HERE'S WHERE YOU GO to change the settings for the S5's built-in apps, such as for email, Contacts, the Gallery, and more.

Application Manager

Tap to launch the nifty Application Manager, which lets you control how your apps work. Page 298 has the details.

Default Applications

Lets you set which applications the S5 should use for different features, such as which app it should use for messaging. Out of the box, it uses the built-in Messages app, but you can use others you install, such as Google Hangouts.

Tap Home if you want to change how your Home screen works. Normally it's Samsung's TouchWiz, but you can change it to the TouchWiz Easy mode screen, that offers a simpler, stripped-down look. See page 379 for details.

Calendar

This section lets you change a variety of settings, including whether to show events that you've declined, whether to show week numbers, and more. This affects only the Samsung Calendar, not Google Calendar. For details about Google Calendar, see page 161.

Call

There are plenty of easy-to-use settings here. For example, tap "Answering and ending calls" to have the S5 let you answer calls by pressing the Home key, using voice control, or waving your hand over the screen. There are plenty of other settings as well, such as for turning on or off call notification pop-ups, and turning WiFi calling on or off. (See page 370 for details.)

Contacts

Here's where to change settings for the Contacts app. The most important entry is the Import/Export one, which lets you import or export contacts from a USB drive or SIM card. You can also choose to display contacts either by first name or last name, among other options. There's also a setting for adding an account that will import contacts, such as from Facebook or others.

Email

There are a handful of settings here. The "Manage accounts" one is useful if you want to create a new email account or delete an existing one. For information about setting up new email accounts, see page 245. Also pay attention to the Display setting, which lets you change options such as many lines to display in the message preview (out of the box, it's one, but your choice is between zero and three). And in the Display settings, you might want to turn on the "Auto fit content" feature, which will shrink email content so that it fits the screen. Finally, if you're prone to send off an email and then wish you hadn't, turn on the "Delay email sending" option, which delays emails before sending them, so you can cancel them before they're sent. Think of it as the "Don't insult the boss" option.

Gallery

You probably won't want to change any Gallery features, but there are some settings here that you might want to pay attention to. If you're worried about going over your data plan limits for the month, make sure the box is checked next to "Sync via Wi-Fi only." That way you won't use up gobs of bandwidth by sending photos over your data network. Out of the box, it's turned on, so it's a good idea to keep it that way. You can also turn on the "Face tag" feature, which will automatically tag the faces of people in photos. (See page 122 for details.) The "Filter by" setting is useful if you want to turn off the various ways that the Gallery lets you filter photos—by People, Scenery, Food, Pets, and so on.

Internet

Here's where to go for doing things such as setting your homepage and selecting the kind of Internet data you want to sync if you have a Samsung account, such as bookmarks and currently open web pages. If you get weary of filling out Web forms manually, tap "Auto fill forms" and then "Add profile," and you'll be able to pop information directly into web forms, such as your name and address, phone number, and email address.

The Privacy section is worth visiting, because it lets you turn off many features that you might worry affect your privacy. For example, normally the S5 suggests search terms and web pages when you do a search, which is a very useful feature. But in order for it to work, it means Google needs to remember your past searches. So you may want to turn off its checkbox. And if you want to clean out Internet data, such as your browsing history, cache, passwords, and more, tap "Delete personal data," turn on the boxes next to what you want deleted, and then tap Done.

There are also a variety of other miscellaneous settings on the Internet settings screen, such as for changing font and screen settings when viewing web pages.

Messages

There's plenty here, most of which you probably don't care about, but there are some notable settings you might want to check out. Tap Signature to create an email signature (see page 242), and tap Notifications if you want to turn notifications on or off. Tap "Spam filter" if you get messaging spam and want to cut down on it. There are several ways the S5 can block messaging spam. You can enter specific phone numbers that you want to be considered as spam and be blocked, you can add phrases that you want to be considered as spam (for example, any that ask if you want to enlarge certain private body parts), and you can block all unknown senders. And if you also send messages and then wish you hadn't, tap "Delay message sending" to turn it on. That way, your messages won't be sent immediately, and you can cancel them before sending.

S Voice

This Samsung app lets you perform tasks by speaking. Initially it's turned off, but tap this setting to turn it on. You can then take a quick tutorial on how to use it, or simply start using it right away. You'll then be able to do things like get the weather by saying "Today's weather," make phone calls or send texts by speaking the instructions, and performing voice searches. Once you turn it on, you can customize it by changing the language it understands, hiding offensive words, and more.

The S5 already includes Google's very good voice search and voice control features, so you may not see much of a need for using S Voice. But if you do, here's where to turn it on and customize it. For details about Google's voice search and voice control, see page 357.

Appendixes

APPENDIX A:

Setup and Signup

APPENDIX B:

Accessories

APPENDIX C:

Troubleshooting and Maintenance

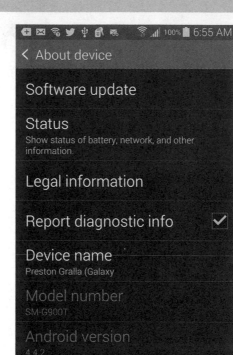

You'll learn to:
- Select a service plan
- Set up the S5
- Make service plan changes on the Web
- Upgrade the S5's software

Setup and Signup

SETTING UP YOUR SAMSUNG Galaxy S5 is easy, especially if you buy it at your wireless carrier's store. There, the sales folk will walk you through the process of activating your phone and signing up for a plan. If you buy your Galaxy S5 over the Web, you set everything up either on the Web or over the phone. This appendix tells you everything you need to know.

Choosing a Plan

WHEN YOU BUY A Samsung Galaxy S5, you'll usually get it in conjunction with a one- or two-year service plan in addition to the cost of the phone. When you buy a plan, your provider knocks a few hundred dollars off the list price that usually runs between $600 and $700. The cost of the plan varies according to how many minutes of talk you want each month, and whether you want text messaging as well. Your carrier offers enough permutations to meet almost any need imaginable.

For the most recent rates, visit your wireless carrier's website. You'll have to buy a data plan, and you may also have a data cap, which means that if you use more than a certain amount of data in any given month, you'll pay extra. You can buy texting on a per-text or unlimited basis. Heavy texters will find that the unlimited plan is cheaper in the long run, while occasional texters will do better paying on a per-text basis.

Your Phone Number

The phone number you use on your Galaxy S5 depends on whether you already have an account with your existing provider:

- **Keeping your old number.** If you already have an account with your provider, you can have an old cellphone number transferred to your new Galaxy S5. Transferring the number to your new phone usually takes an hour or less. During that transition time, you can make calls with your Galaxy S5, but you can't receive them.

- **Getting a new number.** If you don't already have an account with your provider, the company will assign you a new phone number. They'll try to give you one within your area code, and they may have several numbers you can choose from. Once you get the new phone number, you can start making and receiving calls.

> **TIP** If you already have an account with your provider, you may not be able to get the reduced price when you switch to a Galaxy S5. Providers usually require you to have your current phone for a certain amount of time—usually a year or more—before you can get a reduced price for buying a new phone. However, if you have a family phone plan, there may be a workaround. If one of your family members' lines is eligible, you may be able to get the reduced price. Just make sure that your provider connects your Galaxy S5 to your phone number and not the family member's.

Making Account Changes on the Web

YOU CAN CHANGE THE details of your plan anytime—for example, adding new services, or taking away old ones—via the Web. Sure, you can do the same thing by showing up at one of your carrier's stores, but it's much easier on the Web. Head to your provider's website.

Upgrading to the Newest Software

YOUR SAMSUNG GALAXY S5 uses the Android operating system, built by Google. The S5 also includes some tweaks and changes that Samsung made to Android, so your phone's software will look a bit different from other phones running Android.

Google regularly upgrades the Android operating system, but unlike with a computer, you won't need to buy the upgraded software, or even download it. Instead, it comes automatically to your phone, by an over the air (OTA) upgrade. You don't need to do anything about it; it happens automatically.

TIP Wondering which version of Android you're running? The Galaxy S5 will be happy to tell you. From the Home screen or any pane, press the Menu key and then select Settings→More→"About device." Look at the Android version number for the version of Android you've got on your phone.

To check whether your phone has the latest and greatest software from Google and Samsung, from the Home screen or any pane, from the Apps screen select Settings→"About device"→"Software update." The phone will let you know whether your system is up to date. If an upgrade is available, the phone will ask if you want to install the new software, and then do so over the air.

NOTE After Google releases a new version of Android, it takes at least a month—maybe even several months or more—before your Galaxy S5 gets its OTA update. That's because Samsung has to add its tweaks to the new version of Android and make sure everything works properly on the Galaxy S5.

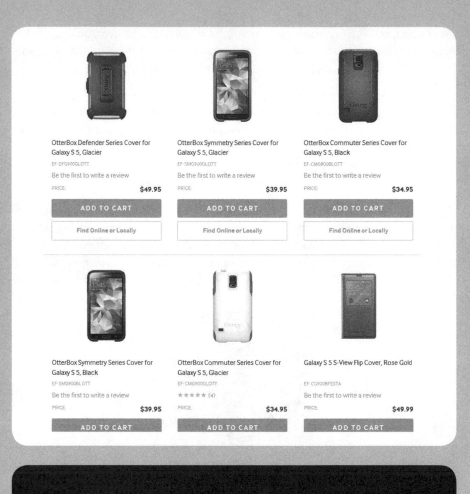

OtterBox Defender Series Cover for Galaxy S 5, Glacier
EF-DFG900GLOTT
Be the first to write a review
PRICE: **$49.95**

ADD TO CART

Find Online or Locally

OtterBox Symmetry Series Cover for Galaxy S 5, Glacier
EF-SMG900GLOTT
Be the first to write a review
PRICE: **$39.95**

ADD TO CART

Find Online or Locally

OtterBox Commuter Series Cover for Galaxy S 5, Black
EF-CMG900BLOTT
Be the first to write a review
PRICE: **$34.95**

ADD TO CART

Find Online or Locally

OtterBox Symmetry Series Cover for Galaxy S 5, Black
EF-SMG900BLOTT
Be the first to write a review
PRICE: **$39.95**

ADD TO CART

OtterBox Commuter Series Cover for Galaxy S 5, Glacier
EF-CMG900GLOTT
★★★★★ (4)
PRICE: **$34.95**

ADD TO CART

Galaxy S 5 S-View Flip Cover, Rose Gold
EF-CGR00BFESTA
Be the first to write a review
PRICE: **$49.99**

ADD TO CART

You'll learn to:

- Buy useful accessories
- Find the best places to get accessories

Accessories

THERE ARE PLENTY OF accessories you can buy to get more out of your Samsung Galaxy S5—for example, to protect its case or screen, connect it to a car charger, and more. In this appendix, you'll get the rundown on what types of accessories are available and a sampling of where to buy.

Useful Accessories

IF YOU ENJOY TRICKING out your car or accessorizing your outfits to the max, there's plenty of Galaxy S5 bling out there for you to find. If, however, you're in the market for something useful, consider the following:

- **Samsung Galaxy Gear watch.** It's Dick Tracy time. This smart watch teams with your Galaxy S5 to put amazing things on your wrist. Make phone calls, lock and unlock your phone, get notifications from your S5, and more.

- **Gear Fit.** This wearable wristband partners with your S5 to track your activity level and the progress of your workout. It also receives notifications from your S5.

- **Cases.** Cases protect the Galaxy S5 against damage—when you drop it, for example. You'll find plenty of kinds of cases to choose from, depending on your style preferences, budget, and needs. You'll find hard protective cases, rubberized protective cases, holsters with belt clips, and more.

- **Screen protectors.** These thin sheets of plastic safeguard your S5's glass screen, greatly reducing the risk of scratches. They're thin enough so that you won't notice they're there.

- **Car chargers.** Plug one end into your S5 and the other into your 12-volt power outlet, and you can charge your phone while you're on the go.

- **HDMI adapter.** This adapter lets you connect your S5 to a TV and watch HD video from your phone on the TV's big screen.

- **Multimedia docking station.** Put your S5 into the docking station, and you can watch video, use it as a digital picture frame, and so on. You can also connect an HDMI cable from it to a TV.

- **Chargers and cables.** There are plenty of battery chargers and USB cables you can buy to supplement or replace the ones that came with your Galaxy S5, including portable chargers.

- **Bluetooth headset.** With one of these, you can talk on your Galaxy S5 by speaking into the wireless headset.

- **Headphones.** You'll want these to listen to your music collection. Headphones can be as cheap as $30 or less for basic ones without great sound, or up to $300 or more for high-end noise-canceling ones. It's a good idea to try them out, or at least read reviews before buying.

- **External and Bluetooth speakers.** Want to share your music with others? Get external speakers to plug into the Galaxy S5. There are plenty made for portability, with surprisingly good sound. Increasingly popular are Bluetooth speakers, so that you don't need to physically connect your S5 to them. Merely make a Bluetooth connection.

- **MicroSD cards.** These cards give you plenty of extra storage. The S5 can handle ones with up to 128 GB of additional memory. The higher the storage capacity, the more you'll pay. For example, you can generally get a 128 GB card for between $70 and $120, and a 64 GB card for about $40 to $60.

Places to Shop

THERE ARE COUNTLESS PLACES online where you can buy Galaxy S5 accessories, but you want to make sure to order from someplace reputable, and where they know what works with your phone. Here are a few of the best:

- **Samsung** (*http://bit.ly/1nJVthp*). You can buy accessories straight from Samsung, which makes the Galaxy S5. Head here and shop to your heart's content. Prices here tend to be higher than elsewhere, and there's less of a selection. However, what you buy here is guaranteed to work with the Galaxy S5!

- **Shopandroid** (*http://www.shopandroid.com/*). Sells accessories for many types of Android phones, including the Galaxy S5.

- **Best Buy** (*www.bestbuy.com*). Both the physical stores and the website are well worth checking out for a wide range of products. You can even order online, choose a nearby store where you'll pick up what you're ordering, and it will be waiting for you when you get there.

- **Your carrier.** The place that sells the Galaxy S5 also sells accessories. As with Samsung, prices tend to be high and selection low. Go to your carrier's website and search for accessories. There may be some available at its brick-and-mortar store as well.

- **Amazon** (*www.amazon.com*). This shopping site has a good selection of accessories. Search for *Samsung Galaxy S5*.

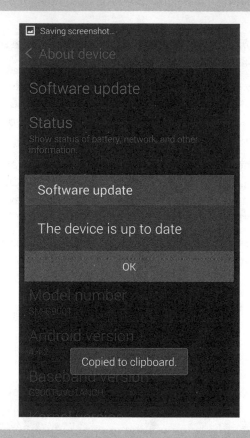

Saving screenshot...

< About device

Software update

Status
Show status of battery, network, and other information.

Software update

The device is up to date

OK

Model number
SM-G900T

Android version
4.4.2

Copied to clipboard.

Baseband version
G900TUVU1ANCH

You'll learn to:
- Make sure your software is up to date
- Fix a frozen phone
- Troubleshoot email settings
- Troubleshoot an SD card
- Reset your phone
- Find out where to go for free help

Troubleshooting and Maintenance

THE SAMSUNG GALAXY S5 runs on the Android operating system, so it's vulnerable to the same kinds of problems that can occur in any computer operating system. Like any electronic device, the Galaxy S5 can be temperamental at times. This appendix gives you the steps to follow when your phone is having... issues.

Make Sure Your Software Is Up to Date

NO COMPUTER OR PHONE is ever perfect; neither is any operating system. So phone makers and software companies constantly track down and fix bugs. They then send those fixes to you via software updates delivered wirelessly—called over the air (OTA) updates (page 63).

So if you have a bug or other nagging problem with your phone, there may already be a fix for it via one of these updates. You shouldn't have to do anything to install these updates, because they're delivered automatically. On the off chance that you didn't get your update, you can check and download it manually. To do it, from the Apps screen, tap Settings→"About device"→"Software update." The phone will let you know whether your system is up to date. If an upgrade is available, the phone will ask if you want to install the new software, and then do so over the air.

Fixing a Frozen Phone

IT'S EVERY PHONE OWNER'S nightmare: Your phone won't respond to any of your taps, or even when you press any of its hard keys. There's seemingly nothing you can do.

Often, your best bet is to try a quick reset by removing and replacing the battery, and then turning on your phone again. First turn off the phone. Then, to remove the battery, flip the Galaxy S5 over, put your fingernail underneath the small slot on the upper right, and remove the cover. You'll see the battery. Gently remove it.

After you've taken it out, put the battery back into place and put the cover back on. Now turn on the Galaxy S5. In many cases, this thaws your frozen phone.

Correcting Email Settings

THE GALAXY S5 EASILY syncs with your Gmail account, but when you add other email accounts—like your work email or home ISP account—you have to enter all the account and server information yourself. And that's where errors can creep in despite your best efforts. Even if you set the account up successfully at first, you may encounter problems later, like being unable to send email.

If Email Doesn't Work at All

If you're having trouble getting email to work for the first time, the most likely problem is that you've got a setting wrong, like your incoming or outgoing server. To check these settings, on the Apps screen tap Settings→Email and tap the name of the account you're having problems with. Then tap More Settings and scroll to the bottom of the screen. Check the Incoming settings and the Outgoing settings, and make sure you've entered everything correctly. Even a single misplaced letter or number will cause a problem. Check your ISP's website or call your ISP to confirm the settings. You may have copied down the settings wrong, or your ISP has different settings for accessing email on a mobile phone. If it's a work email account, call your company's IT department for assistance:

- Make sure you actually have a WiFi or cellular signal. You can't send or receive email if you don't have a connection.

- If you're connected via WiFi, try turning it off to see if that solves the problem—just make sure you have a cellular signal.

If You Can't Send Email

Any computer—including your Galaxy S5, which is, after all, a computer—uses *ports* to communicate with the Internet. They're not physical things; think of them as different channels. So one port is used for web traffic, another for sending email, another for receiving email, and so on. To cut down on spam-sending, some ISPs curtail the use of the standard port for sending mail—port 25. When you send mail using port 25 via these ISPs, they let your mail go to your ISP's mail servers but not get sent anywhere from there. So your message never gets delivered to the recipient. To get around the problem, you have a couple of alternatives.

Try using a different port

On the Home screen, tap the Menu key and select Settings. Go to your advanced settings for the account, as just outlined. On the Outgoing Server listing, in the Port box, delete 25 and type *587*.

Use Gmail's outgoing mail server

You can use Gmail's server to send email from another account. On the Outgoing Server screen, use the following settings:

- For SMTP, enter *smtp.gmail.com*.
- For Port, enter *465*.
- For username and password, use your Gmail user name (your full Gmail address) and password.
- Turn on the checkboxes next to "Use secure connection" and Verify Certificate.

Troubleshooting the SD Card

HAVING PROBLEMS WITH YOUR SD card? There's plenty that can go wrong, so try following this advice:

- First, make sure that the SD card is the right type. It has to be a microSD card, and can only be up to 128 GB.

- Make sure the card is *mounted*—that it's showing up in Windows Explorer or the Finder. If it's not mounted, the Galaxy S5 won't recognize it, and you can't access files from it or store files on it. To mount your SD card, on the Apps screen tap Settings→Storage, and then make sure that "Unmount SD card" is highlighted. If it isn't, that's your problem. Turn off your Galaxy S5 and restart it. If it's mounted and you're still having problems, turn off both your computer and your Galaxy S5 and restart them—that should remount the SD card.

- Try removing the SD card and putting it back in or replacing it with a new one. From the Apps screen tap Settings→Storage→"Unmount SD card." After several minutes, the card will be unmounted—the Galaxy S5 reports that you have no SD storage available.

- Next, turn off the phone's power and remove the battery cover, as described earlier in this chapter. Then slide out the microSD card. (It's located just above the battery. Make sure that you're not sliding out the SIM card, which is more prominent.) Examine it to make sure it's not damaged. If it's not damaged, slide it back into the empty space, replace the cover, and turn on your Galaxy S5. That may fix the problem. If the card is damaged, put in a new one.

- If all else fails, try reformatting your SD card. This option *erases all its data*, so do it as a last resort. From the Apps screen tap Settings→Storage→ "Format SD card," and then tap "Format SD card" from the screen that appears to confirm that's what you want to do. After the card is formatted, either turn off your Galaxy S5 and turn it on again, or connect it to a PC or Mac via the USB connection, and after the computer recognizes the phone, unplug the USB cord. In both cases, the Galaxy S5 should recognize the card.

Resetting the Galaxy S5

IF ALL ELSE FAILS, you may need to reset your Galaxy S5—that is, delete all its data, and return it to the state it was in before you bought it, with all the factory settings replacing your own. Your contacts, social networking accounts, email and Gmail accounts, and so on all get deleted, so save this step for a last resort.

NOTE A factory data reset doesn't delete files you have on your SD card, which means that your photos, videos, and any other files stored there will stay intact after the reset.

From the Apps screen select Settings→"Backup and Reset." Make sure that the boxes next to "Back up my data" and "Automatic Restore" are both turned on. That means your settings and other application data are backed up to Google's servers, and after you reset and log back in, the Galaxy S5 will automatically restore the data and settings. To perform a reset, tap "Factory data reset." That erases all the data on your phone. (Now you see why it was so important to back up first.)

Warranty and Repair

THE GALAXY S5 COMES with a one-year warranty from Samsung. If you bought your Galaxy S5 from someone else, or someone gave it to you, the warranty doesn't transfer to you; it covers only the person who originally bought it.

The usual types of caveats apply to the warranty—if you've misused the phone, dropped it into water, and so on, the warranty gets voided.

For more details about your warranty, read the warranty guide that came with your phone.

Where to Go for Help

IF YOU'RE LOOKING FOR more information or help, there are plenty of places to go:

- **Samsung's official Samsung Galaxy S5 support.** This web page has plenty of helpful information, tutorials, tips and tricks, and a searchable database of help. It's well worth the visit. Head to *www.samsung.com/us/support/* and search for Samsung Galaxy S5.

- **Google's Android forum.** If you've got questions about Android, the Galaxy S5's operating system, this forum might help. Keep in mind, though, that Samsung has customized Android for the Galaxy S5, so what you read here may or may not apply. Still, it's a good place to try. Go to *https://support. google.com/android/*.

- **AndroidForums.com.** Here's another very useful forum where Galaxy S5 fans congregate, which covers many Android phones. The one for Galaxy S5 is *http://androidforums.com/samsung-galaxy-s5/*.

- **Android Guys.** If you're interested in news and rumors about Android in general, this site is an excellent place to start. It's not specific to the Galaxy S5, but if you're an Android fan, it's worth checking out—*www.androidguys. com*.

Index

Symbols

3G/4G
  icon, 10
  networks, 183–184

A

About device setting, 391
accelerometer, 9
accented characters, 45–46
Accessibility setting, 379
accessories for Galaxy S5, 407–409
Accessories settings, 387
accounts
  Accounts setting, 382–383
  Add Account, 22, 175, 229
  company email, 335–337
  Gmail, 228–229, 236
  Google, 21–22, 231
  Google Checkout, 292
  Google Docs, 344
  IMAP email, 246–248
  OneDrive (Microsoft), 340
  POP3 email, 246–248
  Samsung, 22
  setting up email, 245–248
Add Account, 22, 175, 229
Address Bar (browser), 208–209
Agenda view (calendars), 164
Air browse
  gesture, 36
  setting, 381
Airplane mode, 6, 11, 198, 368
airport codes (Google Maps), 152
Air view
  gesture, 37
  setting, 381
alarm icon, 11
albums
  music, 100
  photo, 116–120
Aldiko Book Reader app, 309–310
ambient light sensor, 9
Android
  Android forum (Google), 416
  AndroidForums.com, 416
  Android Guys, 416
  download libraries, 294
  File Transfer tool, 323
  Freeware site, 294
  updating, 26
  version, 393, 405
Applications settings, 393–398
appointments (events)
  accepting invitations to, 170–171
  creating, 165–170
  editing/rescheduling/deleting, 170

apps
  adding to Home screen, 32
  Aldiko Book Reader, 309–310
  App screen, 24–25
  Apps icon, 23
  Candy Crush Saga, 310–311
  downloading
    with bar code scanners, 296–297
    and installing, 286–288
    from Web, 294
  Duolingo, 315
  Endomondo Sports Tracker,
    306–307
  Evernote, 308–309
  Facebook. See Facebook
  Google+, 271–274, 275
  Google Goggles, 311–312
  Google Play Newsstand, 308–309
  Google Play Store. See Google Play
    Store
  icons (Home screen), 22–23
  Instagram, 313
  managing/sharing/uninstalling,
    298–301
  multitasking and, 284–285
  My Files, 321–325
  My Magazine, 350–352
  overview, 283–284
  putting on Home screen/panes,
    300–301
  security concerns, 293
  S Health, 303–307
  Snapchat, 314–315
  troubleshooting, 302
  TuneIn Radio, 307–308
  updating, 297–298
  viewing recently run, 285–286
  Vine, 312–313
  WhatsApp Messenger, 312
archived Hangouts, 278–279
archiving messages (Gmail), 236
artists (music), 100–101
attachments
  in emails, 251–253
  in Gmail, 233–234
audio
  adding to text messages, 59–60
  formats, 101
Auto adjust screen tone setting, 375
auto-enhance feature (photos), 125
Automatic date and time setting, 386
Automatic restore setting, 383
Automatic time zone setting, 386
automatic updating (apps), 298
Auto mode (cameras), 133–134
auto-suggestions (keyboard), 43–44

B

baby monitor feature, 379
Back key, 14
Backslash key, 337
Backup and User settings, 382–384
bar code scanning
  app, 287
  downloading apps with, 296–297
barometer, 9
batteries
  changing/charging, 17–19
  icon, 12
  usage setting, 387

beaming files, 328–329

Beauty face mode (cameras), 134

Blocking mode setting, 380

Bluetooth

　connection icon, 11

　earpieces, 91–93

　listening to music via, 107

　setting, 366

Bookmarks list (browser), 202

　adding, 210–211

　History list, 214–215

　managing, 211–214

　overview, 209–210

book reader app, 309–310

boosting download speed (WiFi), 190

brightness, screen (setting), 221, 374

browser, Web. *See* web browser (Galaxy S5)

businesses, finding with Google Maps, 152–154

C

cache, cleaning out, 225

calendar apps

　events (appointments)

　　accepting invitations to, 170–171

　　creating, 165–170

　　editing/rescheduling/deleting, 170

　　notifications of acceptance, 170

　geolocation and, 172

　Google calendar on Web, 176–177

　Google vs. Samsung, 163

　multiple calendars, 172–174

　options/settings for, 174–176

　overview, 161–162

settings (Samsung Calendar), 394

synchronizing with Outlook, 177–178

views, 162–164

caller ID, 91

call forwarding, 90

Call settings, 395

call waiting, 89–90

cameras

　Camera button (Gallery app), 119

　Camera (PTP) checkbox, 320, 323

　Dual Shot feature, 133

　onscreen controls, 131–133

　overview, 20

　preset shooting modes, 133–135

　taking still photos, 129–131

Candy Crush Saga app, 310–311

car kits, Bluetooth, 93

cases, water-resistant, 20–21

cell signal icon, 10

cellular triangulation, 150

charging Galaxy S5, 16, 19

chats

　with ChatON, 280–281

　with Hangouts, 274–276

Check In icon (Facebook), 263

Chrome browser, 205

Clear button, 10

clipboard, 49

cloud-based music player app, 99

color-coding events, 169

Commuting card (Google Now), 355

Companion-Link for Google, 178

company email accounts setup, 335–337

compass button (Google Maps), 149–150

computers, connecting Galaxy S5 to, 319–320

conference calling, 86–88

Connect and Share settings, 371–372

Contacts app

    adding contacts, 78–80

    adding email senders to, 253–254

    Contacts icon, 23

    editing contacts, 80–81

    Favorites list, 83–84

    finding contact with Google Maps, 152–154

    grouping contacts, 81–82

    making phone calls from, 70–71, 75–77

    options and settings, 82–83, 395

    overview, 77–78

cookies (browser), 224

copying

    photos to clipboard, 124

    text, 51–53

    text from websites, 221–222

Credential storage setting, 391

cropping photos, 30

customizing Home screen/panes

    adding apps/folders, 32

    adding/deleting panes, 34–35

    adding widgets/wallpaper, 28–33

    deleting/moving items, 33

    overview, 27

D

Data usage setting, 369

Date/Time settings, 386–387

Day view (calendars), 164

default applications settings, 394

Default Messaging App setting, 370

deleting

    bookmarks, 211–212

    events (calendars), 170

    Gmail messages, 237

    items from Home screen, 33

    music, 331

    panes, 34–35

    personal data (browser), 225

    photos, 119

Desktop view (browsing), 220

Details button (multiple photos), 127

devices

    Device administrators settings, 390

    Device name setting, 393

    music, 102

Dialing screen, 71–72

dictionary, 43–44

Direct call

    gesture, 37

    setting, 381

directions (Google Maps), 155–157

Display settings, 374–375

DLNA (Digital Living Network Alliance) standard, 110–112

Dock area, 23

double-tap gesture, 36, 206

downloading

    apps, 286–288, 291–293

    apps from Web, 294

    apps with bar code scanners, 296–297

    boosting download speed, 190, 366

Download mode (cameras), 134
icon, 11
dragging gesture, 35
Drama mode (cameras), 135
Dropbox, 333
Dual Shot feature (cameras), 133
Duolingo app, 315

E

Easy Mode (Home screen), 27, 379
ebook reader. *See* Aldiko Book Reader
    app
editing
    bookmarks, 212–213
    contacts, 80–81
    events (calendars), 170
    History list (bookmarks), 215
    Mobile Office files, 340–343
    photos, 124–125
    text messages/email with Voice
        Search, 361
email
    adding senders to Contacts list,
        253–254
    attachments in, 251–253
    company accounts setup, 335
    creating/sending, 255–256
    editing with Voice Search, 361
    Gmail. *See* Gmail
    managing, 254–256
    message icon, 11
    Outlook accounts, 248
    overview, 227–228
    pictures in, 251–253
    reading, 248–251
    sending with Voice Search, 362

settings, 395, 412–413
setting up accounts, 245–248
Web-based mail programs, 257
Emergency mode, 6
emoticons, 50, 61
Encrypt device/SD card settings, 389
Endomondo Sports Tracker app,
    306–307
events (appointments), 165–170
Evernote app, 308–309

F

Facebook
    adding photos, 262–263
    adding widgets to Home screen,
        266–267
    basics, 259–262
    checking in, 262–263
    friends, finding/interacting with,
        264
    Instagram and, 313–314
    navigating, 263
    notifications, 266
    posting status updates, 262–263
    viewing friend's walls/info, 265
faces, tagging in photos, 122–123
Factory data reset setting, 384
Favorites
    list of frequently called contacts, 70,
        83–84
    playlists (music), 106, 107
    websites. *See* bookmarks (browser)
files
    browsing with My Files app, 321–325
    sharing
        via Dropbox, 333

via Google Docs, 344–346

by NFC/beaming, 328–329

via Group Play, 331–333

transferring

  to/from Macs, 323

  to/from PCs, 321–323

  via USB cable, 16

viewing/editing Mobile Office, 340–343

finding

  businesses with Google Maps, 152–154

  current locations, 150–151

fingerprint reader, 375–376

fingerprint sensor, 9

flicking

  gesture, 36

  photos, 122

Flights card (Google Now), 356

Flipboard app, 351

folders

  adding to Home screen, 32

  for computer/Galaxy S5 data transfers, 321

  music, 102

  My Best (bookmarks), 211

foreign languages (keyboard), 46

formatting SD cards, 20

forwarding mail (Gmail), 235

Foursquare app, 281

frozen phone fix, 412

G

Galaxy S5

  accessories for, 407–409

Airplane mode, 198

charging, 16, 19

checking storage space on, 330–331

connecting to computers, 17, 319–320

gestures on, 34–36

getting online with. *See* online access

new features in, xvi

overview, xv–xvi

resetting, 414–415

searching, 63–66

service plans, 403–404

setting up with company email accounts, 335–337

upgrading software on, 404–405

using as universal remote, 137–139

Gallery app

  photo basics, 115–120

  video basics, 127–129

  viewing pictures, 120–122

Gallery settings, 395

geolocation, 172

gestures

  on Galaxy S5, 34–36

  gesture sensor, 9

  non-touch, 36–37

Gmail

  attachments in, 233–234

  handling graphics in, 232

  managing incoming mail in, 236–239

  organization of, 235–236

  reading mail in, 229–232

  replying/forwarding in, 235

  searching, 244–245

sender information, 234–235

setting up, 228–229

using outgoing mail server, 413

working with labels in, 242–244

writing messages in, 240–242

Google

accounts, 21–22, 162, 175, 231, 382

Apps Sync for Microsoft Outlook, 177

Checkout accounts, 292

Drive app, 344–346

Earth layer, 147–148

Goggles app, 311–312

Play Music app, 111–112

Play Newsstand app, 308–309

Google+, 271–274

Google Calendar

Microsoft Exchange ActiveSync and, 178–179

vs. Samsung, 163

synchronizing with Outlook, 177

syncing

with Galaxy S5, 166

iCal with, 178

with Samsung Calendar, 173

on Web, 176–177

Google Docs, 344–346

Google Maps

browsing, 142–143

changing views, 143–145

compass button, 149–150

finding businesses/contacts, 152–154

getting directions, 155–157

Google Earth layer, 147–148

highway traffic, 145–146

overview, 141–142

searching maps, 151–153

self-location and, 150–151

Street View, 148–149

variety of layers, 149

Google Now, 14, 352–356

Google Play Store

browsing by category, 289

downloading/installing apps, 291–293

getting app details, 290–291

overview, 286, 288–289

searching for apps, 289–290

Google Tasks, 176

GPS

Google Maps and, 146, 150

icon, 11

turn-by-turn navigation and, 158

graphics in Gmail, 232

grouping contacts, 81–82

Group Play sharing feature, 331–333

groups of email messages (Gmail), 239

gyroscope, 9

H

Hall sensor, 10

Hangouts, Google

basics, 274–277

Chats label and, 236

responding to invitations, 279

retrieving archived, 278–279

videochats with, 277–279

HDMI (High-Definition Multimedia Interface) capability, 16

headset jack, 8–9

health app (S Health), 303–307

heart rate

measurement (S Health app), 305–306

sensor, 10

Help

resources, 415–416

setting, 391

highway traffic (Google Maps), 145–146

History list (browser), 214–215

Home key, 14

Home screen

adding bookmark shortcuts to, 213

adding Facebook widgets to, 266–267

adding widgets to, 28, 31–32

App screen, 24–25

customizing. See customizing Home screen/panes

Notification and Quick Settings panel, 24

overview, 22–24

panes, 25–26

putting apps on, 300–301

settings, 32

Standard/Easy modes, 27

wallpaper, changing, 28–31

HootSuite app, 281

horizontal orientation (videos), 128

Hotmail, 257

Hotspots. See Mobile Hotspots

I

images, saving online, 217–218

IMAP email accounts, 246–248

Incognito mode (browsing), 219

input methods, setting, 385–386

insertion point, moving (text), 44–45

Instagram app, 281, 313–314

installing apps, 286–288, 291–293

Internet

icon, 23

settings, 396

invitations to events, 170–172

J

jacks

headset, 8–9

multipurpose, 15–17

K

keyboard

Samsung. See Samsung keyboard

settings, 385–386

Kindle app, 310

KitKat (Android), 26

L

labels (Gmail)

basics, 235–238

organizing with, 242–244

in Web-based email, 230

Language setting, 384

language tutor app, 315

Last Transit Home card (Google Now), 356

layers (Google Maps), 143–145, 149

Legal information setting, 392

LinkedIn app, 281

links, tapping (browser), 215–216

Location setting, 369

Lock screen, 7, 375–376

Logs list, calling from, 70, 72–75

Lookout Security software, 293, 295

Loop button (music), 105

M

Macs, transferring files to/from, 323

magnetometer, 9

Maps app. See Google Maps

marking messages (Gmail), 238

memory management, 300

Menu buttons, 15

Menu key (browser), 203

messages (Gmail)

marking, 238

messaging icon, 23

settings, 397

text. See text messages

writing, 240–243

microphone, 17, 48–51

MicroSD cards, 19–20

Microsoft Exchange ActiveSync, 178–179, 336

Microsoft Office Mobile for Android, 339–343

micro USB port, 15

Missed call icon, 11

Mobile Hotspots

basics, 192–193

icon, 11

setting, 367–368

setting up, 193–195

Mobile Networks settings, 370

Model number (Samsung), 393

Month view (calendars), 164

Motion settings, 381

Movies card (Google Now), 356

moving

insertion point (text), 44–45

items on Home screen, 33

multiple calendars, 172–174

multiple email messages (Gmail), 239

multiple photos, managing, 126–127

multipurpose jack, 15–17

Multi window feature, 38–39, 376–377

music

audio formats, 101

buying/downloading, 98

creating playlists, 107–109

deleting, 331

extra features, 107–108

folder on Galaxy S5, 322

Google Play Music app, 111–112

playing, 102–106

playing on other devices, 110–112

via streaming and FM radio, 109

using Music app, 98–102

using phone while playing, 109

voice searches and, 66

mute/pause

gesture, 37

setting, 381

muting email (Gmail), 238

My Best folder (bookmarks), 211

My Files app, 321–325

My Magazine app
  icon, 23
  turning on/off, 32
  using, 350–352

N

navigating. *See also* Google Maps
  Facebook, 263
  turn-by-turn, 157–159
  web pages, 204–206
Nearby Devices setting, 371–372
Nearby Events card (Google Now),
  355–356
Network Connection settings, 366–371
Network notification checkbox (WiFi),
  189
Networks setting, 369
Next Appointment card (Google Now),
  356
Next/Previous controls (music), 104
NFC (Near Field Communications)
  technology, 328–329, 371
NOOK app, 310
notifications
  of event acceptance, 170
  of events, 168
  Facebook, 266
  Notification area (Home screen), 22
  Notification/Quick Settings panel,
    10, 24, 377
  Twitter, 271

O

Office Mobile for Android (Microsoft),
  339–343
OneDrive accounts (Microsoft), 340
One-handed operation setting, 378

online access
  3G/4G networks, 183–184
  connecting via WiFi. *See* WiFi
onscreen controls (cameras), 131–133
Outlook, Microsoft
  email accounts, 248
  synchronizing calendars with,
    177–178
over the air updates (OTAs), 63

P

palm swipe gesture (screenshots), 381
Pandora, 109, 190
panes
  adding/deleting, 34–35
  customizing. *See* customizing Home
    screen/panes
  overview, 25–26
  pane indicator, 23
  putting apps on, 300–301
panning photos (Gallery app), 120–121
Panorama mode (cameras), 134
passwords
  for invisible networks, 190
  making visible (setting), 390
  for Mobile HotSpots, 194
  for WiFi networks, 187
Pause button (video camera), 136
pause/play button (music), 104
PCs, transferring files to/from, 321–323
pedometer (S Health app), 305–306
Personalization settings, 378–381
phishing attacks (Gmail), 239
phone calls
  answering, 84–86

Bluetooth earpieces, 91–93

caller ID, 91

call forwarding, 90

call waiting, 89–90

conference calling, 86–88

Favorites list, 83–84

ignoring, 86

methods for making, 69–71

using Contacts list for, 75–77

using Dialing screen, 71–72

using Logs list for, 72–75

voicemail, 88–89

while playing music, 109

Phone icon, 23

phone numbers (Galaxy S5), 404

photos

adding to text messages, 59–60

cropping to fit screen, 30

in emails, 251–253

Menu button options, 123–126

still, 129–131

tagging faces in, 122–123

uploading to Facebook, 262–263

viewing with Gallery app, 115–120

working with multiple, 126–127

Picasa photo service (Google), 116

pitch and spread gesture, 36

playlists (music)

adding songs to, 107

creating, 107–109

definition of, 98–99

Favorites, 106

Play Music app (Google), 98, 111

Pointer speed setting, 386

points of interest (Google Maps), 152

Polaris Office app, 343–344

POP3 email accounts, 246–248

pop-up blockers (browser), 222–223

posting to Facebook, 262–263

Power/Lock button, 5–7

Power saving

mode, 19, 388

settings, 387–388

Previous/Next controls (music), 104

Printing setting, 372

Priority Inbox (Gmail), 244

privacy

browser settings, 224–225

events, 169

Internet settings, 396

Private mode setting, 381

Proximity sensor, 9

punctuation marks (keyboard), 46–47

Q

QR codes, 287–288

Quick Connect feature, 329–330

Quick settings, 24, 365–366

R

radio stations app, 307–308

RAM memory, 300

reading emails, 248–251

Read notifications aloud setting, 385

Recent Apps key, 13–14

reminders (events), 168–169

repair/warranty (Galaxy S5), 415

repetition feature (events), 168

replying to mail (Gmail), 235

Report spam button (Gmail), 238–239

reports, security (setting), 391

resetting Galaxy S5, 383–384, 414–415

resolution, screen, 8

rich tone (HDR) mode (cameras), 132

ringer

    turning off, 6, 85

    volume, 17

ringtones

    changing, 373

    setting songs as, 107

Roaming icon, 10–11

rotating photos (Gallery app), 121–122

S

Safety assistance setting, 387

Samsung

    accounts, 22, 175

    Smart TV, 137

Samsung Calendar

    vs. Google, 163

    settings, 394

    syncing with Google Calendar, 173

Samsung keyboard

    accented/special characters, 45–46

    auto-suggestions and dictionary,
        43–44

    moving insertion point, 44–45

    overview, 42–43

    punctuation marks, 46–47

    swiping text, 47–48

satellite view (Google Maps), 145

saving

    emails, 250

    online images, 217–218

web pages, 203, 219

screens

    brightness of, 221, 374

    locking/unlocking, 7

    mirroring, 137, 372

    overview, 8–10

    screenshots, 381

    settings, 374–376

SD cards

    formatting, 389

    icon, 12

    moving apps to, 299

    troubleshooting, 413–414

searching

    Address Bar for (browser), 208

    calendars, 174

    friends on Facebook, 265

    Galaxy S5, 63–66

    Gmail, 244–245

    Google Play Store, 289–290

    maps, 151–153

    text on web pages, 219

    Voice Search feature. *See* Voice
        Search feature

security

    in downloading apps, 293

    online, 222–225

    settings, 295, 389, 391

    WPA2 PSK security, 194

Seesmic app, 281

Select date format setting, 387

selective focus (cameras), 132

Select time zone setting, 387

sending emails, 255–256

sensors, built-in (screen), 8–9

service plans (Galaxy S5), 403–404

Set As setting (photos), 126

Set date/Set time settings, 386

settings

    Applications, 393–398

    Connect and Share, 371–372

    correcting email, 412–413

    Home screen, 32

    Motion, 381

    Network Connection, 366–371

    Personalization, 378–381

    Quick, 365–366

    Sound and Display, 372–378

    System, 384–393

    User and Backup, 382–384

    VPN, 338

sharing

    apps, 298–301

    files

        via Dropbox, 333

        via Google Docs, 344–346

        via Group Play, 331–333

        by NFC/beaming, 328–329

    Share button (Gallery app), 118

    web pages, 219

S Health app, 303–307

shopping for accessories, 408–409

shortcuts to apps, 33

Shot and more mode (cameras), 134

Show me as option (events), 169

Shuffle button (music), 105–106

signatures, adding to emails, 242–243, 255

SIM cards, 18–19, 390

sizing keyboard, 50

sliders, song, 104

slideshows, 124, 127

sliding gesture, 35

Smart alert setting, 381

Smart Network Switch (WiFi), 187

Smart Remote icon (Apps screen), 138–139

Smart scroll icon, 12

Smart Stay setting (screens), 374

Smart TVs, 137

Snapchat app, 281, 314–315

social networking apps, 281

software, updating, 392, 411

song lists, 104

Sound and Display settings, 372–378

spam (email), 238–239

special characters, 45–46

speech-to-text function, 357

sports tracking app, 306–307

Spotify, 109

squares, music, 102

SSIDs (Service Set Identifiers), 190

Standard Mode (Home screen), 27

starred messages (Gmail), 235

Status Bar (Home screen), 10–12, 22

Status setting (phone), 392

still photos, 129–131

storage

    checking space on Galaxy S5, 330–331

    settings, 388–389, 391

Street View (Google Maps), 148–149

Studio app, 127

S Voice app setting, 398–399

swiping text, 47–48

System settings, 384–393

T

tagging faces in photos, 122–123

tapping gesture, 35

tapping links (browser), 215–216

task killer apps, 285

Task Manager (apps), 300–301

Teletypewriter mode, 11

terrain view (Google Maps), 144

tethering (Mobile HotSpots)

 definition of, 192

 setting, 367–368

 setting up/using, 195–196

text

 copying from websites, 221–222

 copying/pasting, 51–53

 finding on web pages, 219

 swiping, 47–48

 text-to-speech, 385

text messages

 adding pictures/audio/video, 59–60

 editing with Voice Search, 361

 overview, 53–54

 receiving, 54–57

 sending, 56–59

 tips and tricks, 60–63

time

 icon, 11

 settings, 386

timeout, screen (setting), 374

Toolbox button, 378

touch and hold gesture, 35

Touch key light duration setting, 375

tracks (music), 99–101

Traffic layer (Google Maps), 145

transferring files to/from computers, 321–324

troubleshooting

 apps, 302

 email settings, 412–413

 frozen phone, 412

 resetting Galaxy S5, 414–415

 SD cards, 413–414

 warranty/repair, 415

TTY symbol, 11

TuneIn Radio app, 307–308

turn-by-turn navigation, 157–159

TVs

 playing videos on, 136–137

 Smart, 137

Twitter

 acting on tweets, 270–271

 basics, 267–270

 notifications, 271

U

uninstalling apps, 298–301

universal remote feature, 137–139

Unknown sources setting, 390

unlocking screens, 7

Upcoming Event icon, 11

updating

 apps, 297–298

 software, 392, 411

upgrading software, 404–405

USB Connection icon, 12

USB port, 15

Use 24-hour format setting, 387
User and Backup settings, 382–384

V

Verify apps setting, 391
Vibrate icon, 11
videochats
    via ChatON, 280–281
    via Hangouts, 274, 277–279
videos
    adding to text messages, 59–60
    playing on TVs, 136–137
    shooting, 135–136
    viewing with Gallery app, 115–120, 127–129
viewing
    calendars, 162–164
    Desktop view (browsing), 220
    downloaded images, 218
    friend's walls/into (Facebook), 265
    Google Maps, 143–145
    photos, 120–122
    recently run apps, 285–286
    videos in Gallery app, 127–129
Vine app, 281, 312–313
Virtual Private Network (VPN), 12, 337–339, 370
Virtual tour mode (cameras), 134
visual voicemail, 88–89
voicemail, 11, 88–89
Voice Search feature
    basics, 65–66
    editing text messages/email with, 361
    overview, 357–358
    sending email with, 362

settings, 385
using commands, 358–362
volume
    button (music), 105–106
    overall sound, 373
    phone ringer, 17

W

wallpaper
    adding to Home screen, 28–31
    setting, 375
warranty/repair (Galaxy S5), 415
water-resistant cases, 20–21
Weather card (Google Now), 356
Web
    changing service plans on, 404
    copying text from, 53
    downloading apps from, 294–296
    Google calendar on, 176–177
    searching, 64
    Web-based mail programs, 257
web browser (Galaxy S5)
    Address Bar, 208–209
    basic navigation/windows management, 204
    bookmarks. See Bookmarks list (browser)
    Chrome browser vs., 205
    controls, 201–203
    Menu key options, 218–221
    navigating web pages, 204–206
    online privacy/security, 222
    saving online images, 217–218
    selecting/copying text online, 221–222

tapping links, 215–216

web pages designed for, 206–207

websites for downloading

Android download libraries, 294

Android File Transfer tool, 323

Companion-Link for Google, 178

Dropbox for Android, 333

Google Apps Sync for Microsoft Outlook, 177

Lookout Security software, 293

music streaming/FM Radio apps, 109

websites for further information

DLNA standard, 110

Facebook, 261

Gmail accounts, 228

Google+, 271

Google Calendar, 169

Google Calendar on Web, 176

Google Checkout accounts, 292

Google Docs, 344

Google Maps, 141

HDTV HDMI adapter, 136

Help resources, 415–416

Priority Inbox, 244

Samsung help, 17

shopping for accessories, 408–409

syncing iCal with Google Calendar, 178

Twitter, 267

Web browsing speed, 210

Wi-Fi Direct, 196

Week view (calendars), 164

WhatsApp app, 281

WhatsApp Messenger app, 312

widgets

adding to Home screen, 28, 31–32

Facebook, 266–267

on Home screen, 23

moving/deleting, 33

WiFi

avoiding data plan limits with, 188

boosting download speed, 190

connecting to for-pay networks, 189

connecting to invisible networks, 190

connection settings, 187

disconnecting/reconnecting, 188

Mobile HotSpots. *See* Mobile Hotspots

overview, 184–185

settings, 366

turning on/connecting to, 185–188

WiFi Calling, 196–197, 370–371

WiFi Direct, configuring, 196

WiFi positioning (Google Maps), 150

WPS (WiFi Protected Setup) feature, 191–192

WPA2 PSK security, 194

WPS (WiFi Protected Setup) feature, 191–192

Y

Yahoo Mail, 257

Z

Zagat services, 154

zooming

    Google Maps, 142

    onscreen zoom feature (camera),
        130

    photos (Gallery app), 120

    web pages, 205

Galaxy S5

THE MISSING CD

There's no
CD with this book;
you just saved $5.00.

Instead, every single Web address, practice file, and piece of downloadable software mentioned in this book is available at *missingmanuals.com* (click the Missing CD icon). There you'll find a tidy list of links, organized by chapter.

Don't miss a thing!
Sign up for the free Missing Manual email announcement list at missingmanuals.com. We'll let you know when we release new titles, make free sample chapters available, and update the features and articles on the Missing Manual website.